D1191912

FAILING OUR VETERANS

Failing Our Veterans

The G.I. Bill and the Vietnam Generation

Mark Boulton

NEW YORK UNIVERSITY PRESS
New York and London

NEW YORK UNIVERSITY PRESS
New York and London
www.nyupress.org

© 2014 by New York University
All rights reserved

References to Internet websites (URLs) were accurate at the time of writing.
Neither the author nor New York University Press is responsible for URLs that
may have expired or changed since the manuscript was prepared.

ISBN: 978-0-8147-2487-3

For Library of Congress Cataloging-in-Publication data, please contact the
Library of Congress.

New York University Press books are printed on acid-free paper,
and their binding materials are chosen for strength and durability.
We strive to use environmentally responsible suppliers and materials
to the greatest extent possible in publishing our books.

Manufactured in the United States of America

10 9 8 7 6 5 4 3 2 1

Also available as an ebook

For Mark Jefferies for opening the door, and for Phil Melling for inspiring me to walk through it. But above all to Huw: It is always easier to walk in someone else's footsteps.

CONTENTS

Acknowledgments   ix

Introduction: "A Chance for Learning"   1

1. For the Wounded and the Worthy: Veterans' Benefits from   19
   the Early Republic to the Vietnam Era

2. The Clash of the Texans: The Making of the 1966 Cold War   53
   G.I. Bill

3. A Peacetime Bill for the Warrior: Shortchanging the   95
   Vietnam Vets

4. Mr. President (Have Pity on the Fighting Man): Nixon's   119
   Right Turn for America, Wrong Result for the Veterans

5. On the Streets and in the Schools: The Veterans   155
   Come Home

6. Denouement: Ford's War on Inflation and Teague's   177
   Last Stand

   Conclusion: "A Chance for Learning" Missed   207

Notes   217

Bibliography   251

Index   263

About the Author   273

ACKNOWLEDGMENTS

I could never hope to express anything more than a fraction of the gratitude that is owed to the people who have helped me complete this project. It is humbling to reflect back on the wonderful support I have received from friends, family, and colleagues since its inception. I am forever indebted to several individuals for having a life-changing impact on my intellectual development. Mark Jefferies was the first teacher to encourage me to take my education seriously. Without his enthusiasm in the classroom and encouragement of my writing, I cannot help but think that my life would have taken a very different course. At the University of Wales, Swansea, Phil Melling's American Studies courses challenged me in ways that made me keen to pursue a life of the mind. I was deeply saddened to hear of his passing, but his legacy surely lives on through the generations of students he inspired. Andy Wiest's terrific Vietnam War class at the University of Southern Mississippi first sparked my interest in that conflict, and his superlative books continue to shape my understanding of the war. Kurt Piehler has provided incalculable help, advice, and friendship over the years. Kurt helped me conceive of this project, and his knowledge, willingness to read chapters quickly, and insightful comments improved greatly the quality of the final manuscript. Moreover, Kurt's eagerness in helping me find conference and publishing opportunities has been enormously beneficial to my professional development. I could not have asked any more from a mentor, and I am proud to be among a growing number of scholars who are heavily indebted to his selfless support.

There are too many to name individually, but the driving force behind the book has been the veterans who, whether through formal interviews or in casual conversations, have always been generous with their time. I cannot thank them enough for sharing their experiences. Talking to them even decades after the guns have fallen silent makes one realize instantly that their wars never end. In adding to the discourse on the veteran experience, I hope that on some level this book makes the reader reflect not only on what war does to the men and women we send off to fight in our name but also on what obligations we owe them for doing so.

Archival workers continue to provide the shoulders on which so many scholars stand. I am particularly grateful for the research assistance provided by the staff at the following locations: the Lyndon B. Johnson Presidential Library in Austin, Texas; the Gerald R. Ford Presidential Library in Ann Arbor, Michigan; the Carl Albert Congressional Research Center in Norman, Oklahoma; the Cushing Memorial Library and Archives at Texas A&M University in College Station; the Dolph Briscoe Center for American History at the University of Texas in Austin; the Richard Nixon Presidential Library in Yorba Linda, California; the University of Tennessee Center for the Study of War and Society in Knoxville; and the Wisconsin Veterans' Museum and the Wisconsin Historical Society in Madison. The Lyndon Johnson and Gerald Ford Libraries both provided valuable funding for research trips, as did the Carl Albert Center. I have also been fortunate to receive generous support from the University of Tennessee History Department, the University of Alabama History Department, the University of Wisconsin–Whitewater College of Letters and Sciences, and the administration at Westminster College, Fulton, Missouri.

Along the way, I have been privileged to have spent time with some extraordinary friends and colleagues. At the University of Tennessee, Mike Taylor, Julie Sass, Heinrich Staruk, Ben Shannon, Catie McDonald, and all of the colorful crew down in the grad student offices made getting a PhD far more fun than it had any right to be. After putting up with me for two years at the University of Tennessee Center for the Study of War and Society, Cynthia Tinker has probably earned a break from me, but she's not going to get it. I left the University of Alabama with many fond memories, but more importantly with the lasting friendships of John Beeler, Merrily Harris, Court Carney, Charity Rakestraw-Carney, Rob Riser, Andrew Huebner, and Lisa Dorr, among many others. I will forever be grateful to Rich Megraw for making me his copilot on board the "Liberty Belle" B-17 and for his many great nights of hospitality. Rebecca Shrum was a fantastic colleague at the University of Whitewater–Wisconsin, helping me negotiate both the tenure process and the seasonal brews at Dexter's. Rod Wilson, Emma Kuby, Brian Bockelman, Amber Moulton, Jim Jaffe, Tony Gulig, and James Levy were among the many who helped me survive the Madison winters. Others who have shared advice, support, and the encouragement needed to help keep this ship afloat include Lucy McCobb, Lisa Davis, Kristan Stoddart, Steve Ortiz, and Sam Goodfellow.

I could not have asked for a better publishing experience than the one provided by NYU Press. NYU has a long tradition of publishing outstanding books on veterans' issues, so I was thrilled when Debbie Gershenowitz accepted my work into the fold. Debbie's early advice and encouragement for the project was instrumental in my making the final push for publication. Clara Platter has been just terrific in continuing Debbie's work and in pushing the project on to greater heights and her advice and patience have been invaluable. Constance Grady has been extremely helpful in providing swift responses to my many queries and in keeping me on track, while Alexia Traganas has worked wonders in helping me refine the final product. I would also like to thank Emily Wright for her excellent copyediting.

Everything I have achieved in life has been done with the full and unconditional support of my family. My parents, Hillary and Norman Boulton, never questioned the many daft things I have decided to do with my life, and they were always there in whatever capacity I needed. My brother Huw has had a greater impact on my life than he will ever know. Whether it is my questionable music tastes or my interests in aviation and astronomy, so much of what I have done has been in his shadow. But most importantly he has influenced the way I see the world through our many "TB" sessions at the Glancynon or the White Rose: Long may that continue. The *hiraeth* that I regularly feel being so far from home has been eased by the wonderful support I have received from Bob and Mary Brown and the whole extended Brown/Froeschner clan. I am forever appreciative of their willingness to accept a Welsh bloke from the valleys so openly into their Missouri family. All of which brings me to the person I need to thank most of all—my lovely wife Cinnamon Brown. Every day she inspires me as a teacher and a scholar, but more importantly as someone who embraces life fully and always greets the world with a smile. Having such a loving and understanding partner makes everything possible. Despite what Tom Waits said, a bird and a whale can make it!

Introduction

A Chance for Learning

Those who are guarding freedom for all of us around the world, should come home to classrooms, not to unemployment lines and checks.
—Senator Ralph W. Yarborough, May 6, 1965

"This is a historic day," proclaimed Lieutenant Colonel Bui Tin. "This is the first time in more than 100 years that there are no foreign soldiers in our country. Tonight we celebrate." Tin, acting as a representative of the Communist forces of the Democratic Republic of Vietnam, watched as the last American combat soldiers to leave his country boarded a C-130 transport plane at Tan Son Nhut airbase. For Tin, March 29, 1973, marked a culminating point in a lifelong struggle against foreign influence in Vietnam. Having joined the communist-nationalist movement in 1945, his nearly thirty years of fighting had brought victory against both French and American forces. This was a very special day indeed. Smiling, he told one American serviceman, "Our best wishes for your return," and expressed an earnest hope that the soldier might one day come back to Vietnam as a tourist. The soldiers looked back with a mixture of bemusement and scorn; some cursed, some spat in Tin's direction. To the last soldier in line, Master Sergeant Max Beilke, Tin handed a portrait of Ho Chi Minh on a postcard and a bamboo scroll adorned with a painting of a Vietnamese pagoda. Tin informed the assembled journalists that the pagoda represented Vietnamese resilience as, despite its close proximity to Hanoi's presidential palace, "the B-52s have never been able to destroy it."[1] Beilke looked at the scroll, proffered a half-hearted acknowledgment, and boarded the plane. Moments later, amidst a cloud of red dust, the roaring engines of the C-130 lifted the soldiers off the ground. America's combat mission in Vietnam was over, an ignominious end to a tortured crusade.[2]

One year later, Richard Nixon, by then embroiled in the ongoing Watergate investigations, sought desperately to find a positive footnote to America's Vietnam experience. His attempts to elevate the significance of returning U.S. prisoners of war had barely masked the country's malaise over the impending failure of America's mission to keep South Vietnam afloat. In an attempt to provide the nation with one upbeat moment of commemoration, Nixon decreed that March 29, 1974—exactly one year after Max Beilke's departure—would be a national Vietnam Veterans Day. In his presidential decree, Nixon encouraged Americans to provide "enthusiastic support to appropriate ceremonies and observances throughout the Nation." For answering the call to serve, he wrote, the veterans "deserve the profound gratitude of their countrymen," and he declared it "highly appropriate for us to acknowledge the debt we owe to those veterans who served in the Armed Forces during the conflict in Southeast Asia."[3] On the day itself, Nixon spoke at the National War College at Fort McNair. To a small crowd of injured and disabled veterans and other assembled dignitaries—including the South Vietnamese ambassador—Nixon declared that Vietnam veterans could sleep soundly at night, safe in the knowledge that they had fought in a war "honorably taken and honorably ended." But all of Nixon's smiles, all of his positive pronouncements, and all of the buoyant cadences mustered up by the military bands at the event failed to engender the desired celebratory atmosphere. The day's activities ended under darkened skies, with rain forcing the cancellation of a proposed military fly-past.

To Vietnam veteran and author Tim O' Brien, Nixon's overtures of gratitude toward the nation's returning servicemen and women smacked of tokenism, the speeches nothing more than fantasy "testaments to what should have been, not what was." The event at Fort McNair, like the whole Vietnam Veterans Day enterprise, rang hollow. No amount of parades, celebrations, or displays of pro-veteran paraphernalia across the nation could compensate for what O'Brien saw as a pattern of government neglect of the very real and tangible needs of returning veterans. Indeed, O'Brien noted that there were few actual veterans to be found in the ceremonies held in their name. Instead of listening to Nixon's sanguine remarks, many had chosen to spend their special day on Capitol Hill listening to ongoing Senate hearings—the outcome of which would have a more direct bearing on their lives than a series of platitudes. Describing the scenes throughout the week of the hearings, O'Brien wrote, "The veterans come to the hearing room like the remnants of a lost battalion, arriving in small groups, keeping mostly to themselves. They troop in wearing old jungle fatigues and bush hats, olive-drab jackets and canvas steel-toed combat boots. They come with a message: no more speeches, no more high rhetoric." Frequently, the veterans broke the silence and decorum of the occasion to register protests to the self-serving words of lawmakers and Veterans Administration officials who had come to defend their record on veterans' issues. "You can't eat bumper stickers, can you?" yelled one veteran. When the gathering adjourned with little accomplished—only the promise of future meetings in April—another veteran cried out, "April? . . . We don't want more *hearings*, goddammit." The message the veterans carried with them was a simple one: they wanted "good jobs, a useful place in society, fair treatment from the government, dignity. Mostly, though, they want a future."[4]

By 1974, the image of the neglected and troubled Vietnam veteran was certainly nothing new: The national press had been full of stories of veterans coming home isolated, ignored, shunned by their peers, and with a slew of unaddressed physical and psychological problems. In both the academic discourse and popular culture representations, such issues tended to define the image of Vietnam veterans for decades following the end of the war. But the Senate hearings at the time of Nixon's planned celebrations were to address an aspect of the veterans' homecoming story that has garnered almost no attention, scholarly or otherwise. The hearings were held to examine the possibility of a new G.I. Bill, and the veterans were there to fight for increased education benefits. They were protesting what they considered to be a violation of an unwritten contract between the government and themselves. They had taken time out of civilian life to defend the nation's interests, much like the World War II and Korean War veterans, but many Vietnam veterans discovered that the government was not providing them with the same post-service rewards enjoyed by their predecessors. They were not chasing an unearned entitlement or a bonus, just what they considered to be a much-needed readjustment benefit to help them catch up with their nonveteran peers who had attended school or pursued careers while the veterans had been in uniform. "A future," declared one veteran, "means education and training. We missed it in the war, and now we want it. No handouts, no welfare. None of that. And no more speeches. That doesn't give us a future; it gives us a pain in the ass. We'll help ourselves, *but we need a chance for learning.*"[5]

*   *   *

The G.I. Bill holds a special place in America's national consciousness. The original 1944 Servicemen's Readjustment Act, or G.I. Bill of Rights, offered returning World War II veterans an unprecedented slew of benefits for educational and vocational advancement, as well as home and business loans to improve their post-service lives. The bill evokes positive images of the nation's best and brightest heading off to college and then returning home to obtain the skills and the knowledge needed to help fuel America's postwar economic boom. Few other federal laws of the twentieth century have attracted such unqualified and universal praise for their redeeming effects on society. Politicians have frequently cited the bill's contribution to easing the nation's postwar social and economic pressures while hailing its transformative effects on the lives of those who prospered under its beneficence. On the twentieth anniversary of its signing, Lyndon Johnson praised the G.I. Bill for "increas[ing] the strength of our Nation by enlarging the opportunities of our people." According to Johnson, the bill had created "600,000 engineers and scientists, 360,000 school teachers, and 700,000 business and executive personnel." Scholars have heaped equal amounts of praise on the bill. One historian describes it as "the most sweeping piece of social legislation in American history." Another scholar has suggested that the G.I. Bill ranks alongside the Northwest Ordinance and the Homestead Act as the most significant act ever passed by the government in the promotion of democracy and social equality, while another concludes, "I feel I cannot overstate the value and meaning of the G.I. Bill. Its sweep was so vast, its impact so particular, that only one conclusion seems self-evident: The bill made a reality of Jefferson's concept of creating independent yeomen." Veterans also remember fondly the unexpected bounty that greeted them after their separation from service. Bob Dole, who used his benefits to attend law school before establishing a distinguished record as a representative and senator for Kansas, recalls, "Were it not for this program, veterans might have found themselves unemployed, standing in a bread line. . . . The GI Bill changed America, it may have changed the world."[6]

Such adulation establishes the G.I. Bill as the capstone of the sacred "Good War/Greatest Generation" narrative of World War II. In the popular image of the war, Americans united for one monumental and heroic effort to fight back the dark forces of Nazi Germany and Imperial Japan. Then, after a hard-fought victory, the warriors returned home to a grateful nation and joyous parades. As just reward for their effort, the government bestowed on them perhaps the greatest riches ever provided a mass mobilized army in the form of the G.I. Bill. The G.I. Bill then allowed World War II veterans to better their lives and created a new generation of leaders and innovators, propelling the nation to even greater heights in the postwar years.

In reality, many, if not most, World War II veterans faced some form of difficulty readjusting to civilian life. Moreover, not all veterans benefited equally from the readjustment benefits on offer.[7] However, the longstanding and somewhat simplistic narrative of the G.I. Bill undoubtedly contains much truth. The G.I. Bill did have an enormous impact on the lives of veterans, on higher education, and on the economy. Out of 15.6 million eligible World War II veterans, 7.8 million used their benefits for education and training. Over 2.2 million veterans attended schools at the college level; the remainder received vocational or farm training. Over 4.3 million obtained low-interest home loans and approximately 200,000 received farm or business loans. These provisions helped forestall a widely feared economic depression, expanded the home-owning middle class, and helped democratize higher education in the United States.[8]

Recent historiography has revealed the impact of the G.I. Bill on the development of American politics and on the meanings of U.S. citizenship.[9] There exists, however, a dearth of historical analysis on the social and political impact of veterans' benefits beyond the 1944 bill. By either ignoring or diminishing the story of Cold War veterans' benefits, scholars have left a strong impression that the original 1944 G.I.

Bill marked the end point in the turbulent history of veterans' politics. The assumption persists that the drama that accompanied the debates over veterans' entitlements at the end of the nineteenth century, or the fury of the 1930s Bonus Marches, was somehow erased by the stroke of Franklin Roosevelt's pen at the end of World War II and that everything thereafter was merely a case of working out the details. In truth, legislation such as the Vietnam-era G.I. Bills represented anything but a postscript to the history of veterans' politics. The Vietnam-era G.I. Bills had a transformative effect on post-1945 politics and society as well as a profound impact on both the meaning of United States citizenship and on the lives of millions of veterans and their dependents.

The federal government passed several major education and training G.I. Bills for veterans during the Vietnam era: the Veterans' Readjustment Benefits Act of 1966, or Cold War G.I. Bill, with subsequent increases in 1967, 1969, and 1970; the Veterans' Readjustment Act of 1972; and the Vietnam Era Veterans' Readjustment Assistance Act of 1974. Although there were other contested aspects of the bills, the provision of education benefits was by far the most controversial issue, becoming front-page news and a fiercely debated topic in Washington. For veterans, the education benefits were among the most coveted of the programs offered to aid their readjustment. While other battles over medical care and counseling—which have been widely analyzed elsewhere—may have been more immediately significant to some veterans, for most veterans the education benefits offered the most immediate avenue to personal advancement after service. Moreover, these benefits also served as a barometer for Vietnam veterans to gauge the nation's appreciation for their service.

Most veterans wanted some form of recognition for their sacrifices. The American public had given Vietnam veterans a lukewarm reception at best, but the veterans would have expected that the government would step up and provide the same material reward for service that they had provided for World War II and Korean War veterans. As the veterans' protests at the VA Senate hearings in 1974 indicated, most just wanted what they considered to be a fair reimbursement for their time away from civilian life. Many of the Vietnam generation would have grown up hearing stories of their World War II predecessors and the open arms with which those veterans were greeted by the public and government alike. Education benefits had become synonymous with the positive reception afforded those veterans. Comparable benefits would have allowed Vietnam veterans to feel that their sacrifices were similarly valued. Thus, the fight for education benefits became a symbolic as well as a practical one for the veterans. While many states enacted programs to augment the federal benefits, it was in Washington, DC, that the legislative debates that would have the biggest impact on veterans' lives took place. It is these federal battles over the Vietnam-era G.I. Bills that provide the focus of this study.[10]

In continuing the story of veterans' politics beyond the 1944 G.I. Bill, this book does far more than just "fill the gap" in the knowledge of Cold War veterans' politics—even though that gap is more than sufficient to demand attention. This book challenges the understanding of several themes vital to our conception of post-1945 U.S. history. First, and most broadly, the book provides a deeper understanding of the impact of the Cold War—and the Vietnam War particularly—on domestic society and politics. Payment of veterans' benefits contributed enormously to the growth of the federal government during the 1960s and beyond. This expansion of federal power occurred as a result of America's constant state of alertness against the potential threat of Communist expansion and the resulting need for a large draft army.[11] Over ten million veterans received Vietnam-era G.I. Bill benefits. Consequently, the cost of the Vietnam-era G.I. Bills soared to over 2.5 times the cost of the 1944 G.I. Bill and was one of the most significant sources of federal funding to higher education from the 1960s through to the bills' cessation in the 1980s.[12] Further, the benefits expanded college enrollments and affected the lives of millions of veterans and their families.

Second, analysis of veteran policymaking offers a new methodological approach to understanding the two dominant strains of postwar American political ideology—liberalism and conservatism. Studies on Great Society liberalism or on the emergence of the postwar conservative movement and its ascendency in the 1970s and 1980s invariably omit any mention of the politics of veterans' benefits. Yet, few issues forced lawmakers—from presidents on down—to define and defend their political ideologies so clearly. In politics, irrespective of party affiliation, state, or district, everyone wants to be seen as a friend of the veteran. Lawmakers from both ends of the spectrum ran the very real risk of raising their constituents' ire by opposing veterans' benefits; no one wanted to be vulnerable to the charge of betraying the nation's warriors in a time of conflict. The battles over veterans' benefits were neither a footnote nor merely a reflection of broader political trends. Rather, they necessitated the development of sophisticated ideological arguments that helped define conservative and liberal conceptions of the nature of government and the appropriate allocation of federal resources.

Third, the postwar debates on federal benefits forced lawmakers into a reevaluation of the meaning of citizenship in Cold War America. During the 1950s and 1960s, questions over the scope of federal compensation for military service reemerged—questions that had been present since the founding of the republic. The 1944 G.I. Bill had not swept aside such concerns and a diverse cast of politicians once more queried the effects of offering liberal post-service benefits on the nation's military and on the national character. The outcome of these debates redefined both the nature of military service and the reciprocal obligations between the individual and the state central to determining the nature of Cold War U.S. citizenship.

Finally, this is the first study to incorporate the G.I. Bill into the Vietnam veteran homecoming narrative. The later G.I. Bills should play a central role in our conception of Vietnam veterans' post-service lives in the same way the earlier G.I. Bill does for World War II veterans. Neglect of this story has left an incomplete understanding of how Vietnam veterans reintegrated into society and the mechanisms that were available to ease their transition back to civilian life. Taking the story of the G.I. Bills beyond the World War II generation allows for a more thorough appreciation of the veteran experience in America.

The main focus of this book is on the legislative history behind the Vietnam-era G.I. Bills. The individual bills and the main politicians involved in their passage are explored in detail so that a comprehensive picture emerges of how the veterans ended up with legislation that failed to fulfill many of their needs. The impact of education benefits on the lives of veterans is discussed only broadly to assess the social effects of the bill, but any understanding of the G.I. Bill and the Vietnam generation must begin with an analysis of the decisions made in Washington, DC. This focus necessitates a "top down" political history approach. Unlike the 1944 G.I. Bill, in which the American Legion played a central role in securing its passage, the Vietnam-era G.I. Bills were predominantly conceived and molded by lawmakers on Capitol Hill and in the White House. Despite some sporadic and sometimes dramatic outbursts of protest, Vietnam veterans tended not to organize in any unified and coherent way to lobby the government. The older established veterans' organizations, in particular the American Legion and the Veterans of Foreign Wars, tended to have the interests of World War II veterans at heart and were often slow to throw the full weight of their lobbying machines behind the Vietnam generation's cause. Because of this relative vacuum, the Vietnam-era bills tended to gain their form and function from the initiatives of individual politicians such as Ralph Yarborough (D-TX) in the Senate and Olin Teague (D-TX) in the House. Thereafter, the bills had to negotiate a tortuous path through successive obstructionist White House administrations influenced by fiscally conservative budget agencies and a less-than-munificent Veterans Administration. The debates between the Congress and the White House determined how much veterans would receive and ultimately dictated the success or failure of the programs for the veterans.

The political compromises made at the highest levels of government set the stage for the problems faced by Vietnam veterans when it came time to claim what they thought was owed to them. Overall, the benefits offered by the Vietnam-era bills were lower than those offered by the 1944 G.I. Bill, not only in terms of dollar amounts but also in terms of the quality of education they provided. One of the main reasons for these shortcomings was that the Vietnam-era G.I. Bills were not geared toward just combat veterans; instead, they covered the much larger number of Cold War veterans enlisted to meet America's global security obligations. Remarkably, the politicians involved in crafting the legislation made no meaningful distinction between Cold War veterans serving in a combat "hot spot" such as Vietnam and those veterans serving in relatively peaceful conditions at home or abroad. Because these new bills covered so many veterans who may never have faced hostile conditions or served in a time of declared war, the provision of liberal veterans' benefits fell victim to the crosscurrents of several mid-twentieth-century political ideologies.

Attacks from politicians on both the Left and the Right greatly compromised the generosity and ultimate effectiveness of the Vietnam-era bills. With so much federal funding expended on improving American society under Lyndon Johnson's Great Society, one might suspect that liberals in the 1960s would have had no hesitation in providing much-needed benefits to returning veterans. However, Johnson's hopes of minimizing the domestic impact of the Vietnam War led him to oppose sweeping legislation on the scale of the 1944 bill. Further, because the proposed Vietnam-era bills covered noncombat veterans in addition to combat veterans, the Johnson administration fought to keep benefits low, believing that most Cold War veterans were less deserving of government assistance than more impoverished sectors of society. A key component of Johnson's liberalism was his desire to provide opportunities for those with the greatest need, and Johnson did not consider veterans to be among the ranks of the needy. From the political Right, the objections of fiscal conservatives also limited the generosity of the bills. Veterans' benefits invariably constitute a significant drain on federal resources, and the scale and cost of the Vietnam-era legislation raised the ire of those politicians seeking to reign in government spending. This conservative opposition came to the fore particularly during the Nixon and Ford administrations, as both presidents brought a more parsimonious sensibility to the White House. A third ideological issue arose to further compromise the effectiveness of the bills—one that sought to define the nature of American citizenship. Some politicians raised questions over whether veterans who did not serve during a time of declared war had earned the right to lay claim on the nation's coffers. These opponents of liberal benefits argued that veterans who had never faced any real economic or physical hardship as a result of service were performing nothing more than a long-accepted obligation of citizenship. At the heart of this argument stood a desire to preserve a dimension of the American character whereby citizens would willingly sacrifice their time and bodies for the national defense and neither demand nor expect benefits in return.

In the final reckoning, this combination of political challenges resulted in education benefits for Vietnam-era veterans that fell well short of the generosity of those afforded World War II veterans. The politicians responsible for compromising the bills' effectiveness were not acting out of malice or callousness toward the veterans, as most were adhering to ideological and political philosophies that had surfaced frequently in the long history of debates over veterans' benefits. But the confluence of these philosophies greatly damaged the post-service opportunities for the Vietnam generation. The Vietnam-era bills provided neither the full tuition coverage nor the generous monthly stipend offered by the original G.I. Bill. As a result, many veterans could not afford to go to school. Those who did often suffered the burden of having to take jobs or supplementing their income through loans. Many more had to compromise the quality of their education by choosing lower-cost institutions to make their benefit checks stretch further. Particularly hard hit were underprivileged veterans—including a high percentage of minorities—who did not have recourse to additional funds. Students from wealthier families might have found their G.I. Bill checks to be a nice addition to their income, but unlike the World War II generation, Vietnam-era veterans relying solely on the checks to cover their education costs frequently struggled to make ends meet. When it came time to pay their tuition bills, few of them would have appreciated the economic and civic lessons being doled out in Washington in lieu of additional funds. The bills were not without merit, and many veterans might well have considered the amounts offered to be a reasonable reward for their service. But for many others, the benefits just did not go far enough. They did provide a significant injection of federal money into higher education, and did at least provide some funds for veterans. But they did not provide the same positive stories associated with the original bill, nor did they provide the benefits that many veterans thought they had earned. In that way, the G.I. Bill, and the lawmakers charged with taking care of the returning soldiers, failed many veterans of the Vietnam generation.

The sense of frustration was understandably more acute among veterans who had served in harm's way in Vietnam. Although most Vietnam veterans never faced direct combat, and the risks were not spread evenly across branches or type of service, the same had been true for World War II and Korean War recipients of the G.I. Bill. Veterans of those conflicts were generally granted the same benefits across the board irrespective of the level of risk they faced. Vietnam veterans understandably believed that by serving in any capacity in a theater of war they had earned the right to benefits commensurate to those offered World War II and Korean War veterans. The government's failure to provide such rewards exacerbated the sense of betrayal and resentment that many veterans felt toward their country when they returned home.

Perhaps the one redeeming element to this story is that G.I. Bill usage rates and the veterans' academic performance for those who did make it through school challenge any lingering images of Vietnam veterans as social misfits. Despite significant economic obstacles created by the low level of benefits, many Vietnam veterans seemed determined to improve their lives by returning to school. Indeed, as evidenced by their participation rates, Vietnam-era veterans proved far more interested in higher education than the much-vaunted "Greatest Generation" of World War II veterans. Although VA figures tended not to distinguish between Vietnam veterans and Vietnam-era veterans, the VA estimates that over 76 percent of eligible veterans claimed at least some form of education benefits under their G.I. Bill, with more than half of this total using their benefits for a college-level education. Thus, Vietnam-era veterans used their education benefits at a considerably higher rate than either World War II veterans (51 percent) or Korean War veterans (43 percent).[13] Moreover, 60 percent of Vietnam-era veterans who claimed these benefits did so for higher education as opposed to training compared with 51 percent of Korean veterans and 30 percent of World War II veterans.[14] One major reason for this discrepancy is that higher education had become a much more integral part of life in the 1960s and 1970s than it had been in 1945. Even so, the fact that so many Vietnam-era and Vietnam veterans used their G.I. Bill benefits for education testifies to their desire to improve their lives after service.

Similarly, despite the hostility toward the war on many of the nation's campuses, most veterans returned to school with relatively little difficulty. Many of them remained silent about their service and rarely faced confrontations with other students. Academic journals—fueled by society's broader stereotypes of maladjusted veterans—warned educators of potential trouble from the Vietnam generation. However, as was true for the World War II generation, most veterans proved to be more dedicated and academically adept students than many of their nonveteran peers. The lack of academic attention to the Vietnam-era bills means that this vital aspect of their homecoming experience has been subsumed beneath more sensational stories of homelessness, suicide rates, drug abuse, and psychological disorders. Contrary to the standard narrative, Vietnam veterans in the mid-1970s would be far more likely to be found in colleges or universities than in jails, homeless shelters, or drug rehabilitation clinics. The Vietnam veteran's thirst for education and desire for self-improvement suggest a greater commonality in the character of Vietnam and War II veterans than is often acknowledged. The government may not have upheld its end of the unwritten bargain with the Vietnam generation, but the veterans themselves were determined to make use of what opportunities they had.

* * *

This book is organized chronologically, as the main politicians involved built upon and modified the ideas and legislation created by their predecessors. The opening chapter, "For the Wounded and the Worthy: Veterans' Benefits from the Early Republic to the Vietnam Era," provides historical background on the federal debates over veterans' benefits up to the early 1960s. The chapter reveals that, for ideological and economic reasons, the provision of veterans' benefits has been a contested issue in American politics from the Revolutionary War onward. Consequently, the status of the veteran in American society has been an equivocal one, subject to the whims of changing political philosophies. Politicians from Thomas Jefferson through Franklin Roosevelt, for example, had argued that military service should be a natural obligation of citizenship and not a basis for ongoing federal benefits, whereas fiscal and small-government conservatives, such as Calvin Coolidge in the 1920s claimed that the cost of benefits placed an unnecessary financial burden on the government. The passage of the 1944 G.I. Bill seemed to have broken with this pattern by establishing a widely agreed upon model for providing benefits to future generations of veterans.

In the aftermath of World War II, however, retrenchment began from the high generosity of the World War II G.I. Bill as the same economic and ideological issues that preceded its passage returned to the fore. Because America continued to draft citizens to meet its national security needs in the shadow of the Communist threat, the Eisenhower administration called on Omar Bradley to convene a commission to review what obligations the state owed to its veterans. With the exception of Korean War veterans who received a slightly less generous G.I.

Bill than their World War II predecessors, the Bradley Commission determined that "peacetime" Cold War veterans—those drafted but not serving in a combat zone or in a time of declared war—should not be given their own G.I. Bill. The commission believed that citizens should be expected to perform military service when called upon and should not expect compensation after service. The philosophy informing this view was that most drafted veterans were not subjected to undue hardships while in uniform. They were earning a wage and learning new skills but were seldom in harm's way. Even veterans' groups such as the American Legion and the Veterans of Foreign Wars agreed with the commission's position, as they did not want their core constituents—the World War II veterans—to have to share the benefits they had earned by staring down the barrel of an enemy rifle. Again, this was something of a false dichotomy as many veterans covered under the World War II G.I. Bill never faced direct fire, but it was a dichotomy that dominated the political discussions.

Chapter 2, "The Clash of the Texans: The Making of the 1966 Cold War G.I. Bill," details the contested passage of the first of the Vietnam-era G.I. Bills, the Veterans' Readjustment Benefits Act of 1966. The chapter reveals how Senator Ralph Yarborough, a Texas Democrat, dissented from the Bradley Report and pushed for a new G.I. Bill that would compensate *all* citizens called upon for military service. From the late 1950s onward, he attempted repeatedly to pass a Cold War G.I. Bill. Each time his efforts were voted down in the Senate, as few other politicians shared his view. However, the situation in Vietnam soon changed lawmakers' opinions. Yarborough used the escalation of hostilities in Vietnam to push for his version of a G.I. Bill that gave the same benefits to all Cold War veterans, whether they were slugging through a jungle in Southeast Asia or driving a truck in Georgia. He faced significant opposition in his quest from fellow Texan Democrat Olin Teague in the House. Teague, one of the most influential figures in veterans' affairs in Washington, believed that any benefits that were not absolutely necessary were a waste of taxpayers' money, and he took a lot of convincing before accepting the need to assist Cold War veterans. In addition, Lyndon Johnson, as he attempted to construct his Great Society, believed that federal spending should be directed more to those citizens in greatest need. Johnson considered universal education programs, such as the

Higher Education Act of 1965, a more worthy source of federal spending. He stated, "It doesn't seem to me that you ought to have to go into uniform and go to boot camp, and spend 2 or 3 years in the service in order for your Government to have an interest in your education."[15] For Johnson, simply being a veteran was insufficient to lay claim on federal funds when there were many other Americans living in impoverished conditions. After much hand wringing, Johnson signed the bill into law, but not before he and Teague had both worked to reduce the levels of benefits offered.

The passage of the 1966 G.I. Bill was significant in numerous ways: In the long run, the bill helped redefine the meaning of democratic citizenship in the United States. Civilians would no longer enter the military without some expectation of future reward even if they served in peacetime. Thereafter, and down to the present day, some citizens could enter military service for the benefits on offer, possibly asking a little less what they could do for their country and expecting a little more what their country would do for them. More immediately, the bill had a negative impact on the first group of returning Vietnam veterans, who soon discovered that their G.I. Bill fell far short of their expectations and needs. They were combat veterans, but they were covered by what amounted to a peacetime G.I. Bill.

The third chapter, "A Peacetime Bill for the Warrior: Shortchanging the Vietnam Vets," illustrates some of the consequences of the political wrangling in Washington on the veterans' educational opportunities. This chapter explores the difficulties faced by many of the first veterans as they returned home to use their education benefits. The failure to distinguish between the different levels of sacrifice and the different readjustment requirements of Vietnam veterans and Cold War veterans was among the biggest flaws of the Vietnam-era G.I. Bills. Because the 1966 bill did not specifically target the needs and expectations of returning combat veterans, the benefits were not as generous as the 1944 G.I. Bill had been for World War II or even Korean War veterans. Consequently, Vietnam combat veterans discovered that their G.I. Bill did not afford them the same quality of education enjoyed by their predecessors. The result was a bitter legacy of resentment and hostility among many combat veterans who believed that the government had neglected their needs. The 1966 bill also contained an unintended race and class bias as economically disadvantaged veterans, especially minorities, suffered disproportionately from the government's parsimony because they could not afford the additional funds needed to fully cover their education. Despite the publication of numerous Veterans Administration and private reports highlighting the bill's problems, the government was slow to make any significant adjustments to the amount of benefits offered. A change in administrations and a new shift in political ideology did little to change the situation.

Having suffered from ideological opposition from the Left, veterans' benefits now became subject to attacks from the conservative Right. Chapter 4, "Mr. President (Have Pity on the Fighting Man): Nixon's Right Turn for America, Wrong Result for the Veterans," reveals that just as the plight of veterans came to the fore of public consciousness, the American political landscape shifted toward a new fiscal conservatism under Richard Nixon. The sheer expenditure and scale of the 1966 bill expanded greatly the size and scope of the federal government and had already attracted opposition from fiscal conservatives. Nixon, despite his public praise for veterans, proved more concerned with curbing government spending than with rewarding returning soldiers and sought numerous ways to thwart congressional attempts to pass a more generous G.I. Bill. Consequently, when a revised G.I. Bill finally did pass into law in 1972, it failed to address the main problems created by its predecessor.

Chapter 5, "On the Streets and in the Schools: The Veterans Come Home," highlights the role of veterans in the G.I. Bill legislative story, with a particular emphasis on the difficulties faced by Vietnam veterans in organizing as a coherent lobbying force. Many Vietnam veterans came back with such mixed feelings about their service that they were often reluctant to join veterans' organizations. Those national organizations that did come to the fore, such as Vietnam Veterans Against the War, tended to be more concerned with ending the conflict than with agitating for higher benefits, particularly during the crucial early years in which the bills were being formed. The chapter then addresses the experience of returning veterans on campuses across America. With college campuses being the focus of so much antiwar sentiment in the 1960s and early 1970s, some veterans were wary of the reception they would receive. Consequently, many were reluctant to reveal their veteran status. However, for the most part and with considerable variation depending on time and location, most veterans did not face overt hostility from their fellow students. Many did experience some discomfort at the antiwar atmosphere on some campuses, but few were targeted for hostility. Once on campus, they proved to be some of the more gifted students of their generation, a fact that is often overlooked in the popular image of Vietnam veterans.

The sixth and final chapter, "Denouement: Ford's War on Inflation and Teague's Last Stand," traces the conclusion of the Vietnam-era G.I. Bill saga. After years of complaints from the veteran community, Congress seemed on the verge of passing a generous G.I. Bill for Vietnam veterans in August 1974, but Gerald Ford negotiated several behind-closed-door deals to make sure that the bill never reached his desk. When a less expensive version of the bill finally passed both houses, Ford, just weeks into his presidency, became the first president to veto an increase in veterans' education benefits. The backlash in the veteran community and on Capitol Hill was considerable, leading Congress to override his veto by overwhelming margins in both houses. The 1974 bill did provide a much-needed boost in benefits, but for most veterans it had come far too late. Many had already struggled through college, had dropped out, or had families and careers to consider by the time the increases came into effect. The chapter concludes with a discussion of the final rounds of debates over funding levels at the end of the 1970s and reveals the continued influence of Olin Teague on limiting the benefits offered.

* * *

Had the government committed enough money to giving the veterans a full education from the outset, the veterans' benefits could have again had the same regenerative impact on society that the World War II G.I. Bill achieved. Most importantly, had the later G.I. Bills provided the same generous recompense for service enjoyed by World War II and Korean War servicemen and women, the Vietnam generation of veterans might have enjoyed a far easier transition back to civilian life. For many veterans, the "chance for learning" they demanded as they marched on Capitol Hill on a gloomy day in the spring of 1974 never materialized. On that day, the Senate hearings, wrote Tim O'Brien, ended with "rage and frustration and ambiguity."[16] As with the experience of Max Beilke clutching the bamboo scroll as he and his fellow warriors passed into history as the last combat soldiers to depart Vietnam, as with the image of rain falling on Nixon's head as he tried to raise spirits at the Honor Vietnam Veterans celebration at Fort McNair, the story of the Vietnam-era G.I. Bills provides little solace to America's Vietnam experience. The following study provides the first substantive analysis of that story.

1

For the Wounded and the Worthy

Veterans' Benefits from the Early Republic to the Vietnam Era

Though undying gratitude is the meed of everyone who
served, it is not to be said that a material bestowal is an obligation to those who emerged from the great conflict not only
unharmed, but physically, mentally and spiritually richer for
the great experience.
—President Warren Harding, September 19, 1922

No person, because he wore a uniform, must thereafter be
placed in a special class of beneficiaries over and above all
other citizens. The fact of wearing a uniform does not mean
that he can demand and receive from his Government a
benefit which no other citizen receives.
—President Franklin D. Roosevelt, October 2, 1933

Military service in time of war or peace is an obligation of
citizenship and should not be considered inherently a basis
of future Government benefits.
—Bradley Report, April 1956

The fractious political debates that would cause the problems associated with the Vietnam-era G.I. Bills had long antecedents in American
history. Since the very founding of the nation, several areas of contention have dictated the scope and generosity of benefits offered to veterans. The first was simply the economic expediency of offering benefits.
Depending on the scale and length of the military engagement, veterans' benefits have at times constituted an enormous drain on the federal budget. Fiscal conservatives often succeeded in reigning in federal

spending, even at times of greatest veteran need. The second point of contention was the potentially degenerative effects on citizenship of offering rewards for military service. From the Revolutionary War down through the era of the All Volunteer Force, lawmakers have questioned whether offering liberal benefits makes citizens more likely to enlist for personal advancement rather than for patriotic reasons. The third factor influencing the scope and nature of veterans' benefits was the notion that the rewards on offer should be proportional to the level of sacrifice. Thus, disabled veterans and dependents of the war dead tended to receive the highest priority in the allocation of funds, whereas those veterans who had served for the shortest time or in the least hazardous environments received proportionally less consideration. A fourth factor determining the nature of benefits was the government's motivation for passing them. At different times, veterans' benefits have been used as a simple reward for service, an inducement to enlist, a readjustment tool to ease the transition back to civilian life, a medium for veterans to make up educational or vocational time lost from civilian life, or a means to stimulate the economy. A final factor affecting legislation has been the lobbying power of the veteran community. The Grand Army of the Republic, for example, exerted an enormous influence on the benefits offered Civil War veterans, while the American Legion and Veterans of Foreign Wars repeatedly pressured Congress for greater benefits throughout the twentieth century. Although Vietnam veterans, many fresh out of the jungle, probably cared little and knew even less about this long history of veterans' benefits in the United States, the G.I. Bills that would have a direct bearing on their own lives were directly influenced by the debates over veterans' legislation that had waged for nearly two centuries.

The precedent of offering compensation for the hazards of military service was long established before the first shots were fired at Lexington and Concord. Taking their cue from English legal precedent, several colonies passed laws promising benefits to veterans injured in the line of service. Virginia passed the first such law in 1624, the Plymouth colony followed in 1636, and by 1777 all colonies with the exception of Connecticut pledged to care for their disabled veterans.[1] Such payments for veterans injured defending the common interest proved to be one of least controversial areas in all future discussions over veteran funding.

The idea that the rest of society should compensate any citizen whose life goals and means of earning a living might have been compromised while in uniform has historically enjoyed wide acceptance. By offering assistance to injured veterans, the government ensured that the burden of military service could be distributed in some small measure more equally across society. Although a slight hike in taxes hardly equates to the loss of a limb or other injury, the idea of disability compensation recognized that wartime hardships should not be limited to the few.

In August 1776, just weeks after cleaving from the British Empire, the Continental Congress made the first steps toward codifying the fledgling government's obligation to veterans when it passed legislation providing for half-pay for life for disabled veterans. In a more contentious measure, lawmakers also extended the colonial tradition of offering land grants to soldiers who agreed to enlist for the duration of the war, although in part these land grants represented an attempt to induce mercenaries to defect from the British. In 1780, Congress codified the principle of providing assistance for veterans' dependents when it pledged to give half-pay for seven years to the widows and orphans of Revolutionary War officers, while all veterans were to receive mustering-out pay. The provision of benefits to nondisabled Revolutionary War veterans raised early questions over which veterans were most worthy of compensation for service.

Thomas Jefferson stated his apprehensions about the potentially corrosive effect on the nation's moral character of offering pensions and payments to nondisabled veterans.[2] For Jefferson and his followers, it was the virtuous citizen-soldiers performing their civic duty who had fought and won the Revolution. Jefferson's ideal was of the upstanding republican citizen who would put down his hammer or plow when the nation was threatened and pick up the musket. The soldiers of Jefferson's republic would not require rewards for service. Instead, they would be performing their natural obligation of citizenship. For Jefferson, American citizens could enjoy the freedom from fear of standing armies and the potential higher taxes needed to sustain them if they answered their nation's call in times of peril. He, like many after him, believed that all Americans should be expected to perform military service without the expectation of reward or recompense. Those who were able to return to their fields and their workshops without injury would do so with little more than the pride they had earned from the knowledge that they had performed their civic duty. Offering liberal benefits to able-bodied veterans threatened this ideal and raised the specter of transforming the cherished Minuteman into a Hessian mercenary.

The provision of Revolutionary War pensions gave Jefferson and his acolytes particular cause for alarm. Pensions, they suggested, constituted an unnecessary reward, and many feared that they might lead to the corrupting traditions of Old World standing armies. Moreover, some lawmakers feared that creation of special privileges for veterans would set them apart from the rest of society and thus undermine the democratic intent of the Revolution. At the core of revolutionary ideology stood the repudiation of class-based elitism associated with the Old World.[3] The creation of a distinct and privileged group of veterans might foreshadow the formation of the kind of stratified society rejected in principle in 1776. In 1818, when Congress debated the passage of a Revolutionary War Pensions Act, North Carolina senator Nathaniel Macon warned that offering such benefits to those not injured in service was "repugnant to the principles of our Government, and at war with good sense and public justice."[4] For Macon, the government owed no debt to citizens who had fallen on hard times if their hardship was not related to service. Ultimately, the military exigencies of the War of 1812, combined with widespread press reporting of veterans' hardships, overrode such objections, and in 1818 Revolutionary War veterans became the first recipients of a large-scale federal pension program in the United States. Early in the program, eligibility extended only to veterans demonstrating need, but in 1832, all veterans received pensions regardless of financial condition. Despite the enactment of such legislation, Jefferson's vision of citizenship echoed long into the twentieth century, and presidents and politicians continued to question whether rewarding citizens for defending their nation undermined the democratic promise of America. As benefits grew more elaborate and generous, the questioning grew correspondingly louder.

The precedents established by the Revolutionary War eventually extended to the wars of the nineteenth century. Veterans of both the War of 1812 and the Mexican-American War received land grants while disabled veterans received compensation. The issue of pensions was resolved less quickly. Not until 1871 did veterans of the War of 1812 receive pensions. Mexican-American War veterans had to wait until 1887. Union veterans of the Civil War received benefits similar to those awarded their predecessors, but the benefits became more generous and eligibility requirements more liberal. Under the General Pension Act of 1862, disabled Union soldiers received disability compensation at a rate determined by their rank and the degree of their disability. The act also provided ongoing benefits for widows and orphans of soldiers killed in action. Instead of outright land grants, the government gave veterans preferential treatment under the Homestead Act of 1862 by allowing them to count a period equal to the duration of their service toward the length of time required for them to own the land. For the first time, veterans also received preferential treatment when applying for federal employment. Injured and disabled veterans received medical care through the National Home for Disabled Volunteer Soldiers.[5]

Factors other than outright need contributed to the expansion of Civil War benefits. The lobbying efforts of pension lawyers greatly influenced the passage of the Arrears Act of 1879 that allowed Civil War veterans to claim benefits retroactively for service-related injuries. The Republican Party, keen to expand the spoils base of its patronage network, and the Grand Army of the Republic, the powerful Union veterans' organization, helped push through the Dependent Pensions Act of 1890, which decreed that veterans could claim disability benefits even if their injury did not occur while they were in service. In effect, the provisions of the 1890 act established a permanent pension system for aging veterans who could claim some form of ailment.[6] Because of the numbers of veterans and the more liberal benefits they received, the costs to government skyrocketed by the end of the nineteenth century. By one estimate, veterans' pensions alone accounted for a staggering 43 percent of all government expenditures by 1893.[7]

The provision of liberal benefits to veterans while much of the country struggled to adjust to the economic pressures of industrialization set veterans apart as a special class in the United States. As Theda Skocpol notes in *Protecting Soldiers and Mothers: The Political Origins of Social Policy in the United States*, veterans avoided the stigma attached to government handouts because society deemed that they had *earned* their benefits through military service. Many Western countries responded to the growing pains of industrialization by offering benefits to those most negatively affected. The United States followed a different path, eschewing nationwide federal relief to their most needy. But veterans had now solidified their privileged position in society, establishing, in Skocpol's words, "a moral ordering of claims on the federal government's largesse."[8] Nineteenth-century benefits legislation was retroactive and few citizens would have enlisted in anticipation of future pensions. No one was going off to war to get rich, but lawmakers were clearly setting the precedent that the government was becoming increasingly responsible for the post-service financial status of the nation's veterans. The first major pension law of the twentieth century continued this trend, as the Sherwood Act of 1912 provided pensions to all veterans irrespective of their physical or financial health. The adoption of such an expensive obligation raised questions of just how much veterans should continue to be compensated for service. These questions intensified after the government called upon nearly five million of its citizens to serve in World War I.

The cost and inefficiency—including allegations of fraud—of the nineteenth-century benefits system prompted a change in the philosophy and distribution of benefits during World War I. The 1914 War Risk Insurance Act offered merchant seamen at risk from submarine attacks low-cost insurance to compensate them or their families in the event of death or disability. Following the recommendations of Woodrow Wilson's 1917 Council of National Defense, the government extended this provision to all of the nation's soldiers, hoping this measure would preclude the need for costly pensions at some later date. The government, for the first time, also offered benefits for vocational training—including funds for tuition, school fees, and a living stipend—for disabled veterans. Over 128,000 disabled veterans received training under this provision. The motive behind offering education benefits was that veterans would be given the opportunity to catch up on the potential opportunities they would have been enjoying had they remained civilians. Nonveterans would have attended school or learned a trade, so the government attempted to give veterans the kind of advancement in life they could have received had they not entered the military. The philosophy behind this readjustment benefit would prove highly influential on future legislation. But in the aftermath of the conflict, the most contentious debates over funding centered on the issue of a proposed cash bonus for veterans.[9]

Proponents of the bonus argued that servicemen earned less in military service than they would have as civilians and should be compensated through a one-time cash payment. While civilian wages had increased due to the wartime demands for labor, the relatively low military pay of approximately thirty dollars a month had placed veterans at an economic disadvantage relative to their civilian counterparts. Spurred on by the organizational efforts of the recently formed veterans' groups the American Legion and Veterans of Foreign Wars, nearly seventy-five thousand ex-servicemen marched on the streets of New York demanding payment of a bonus. Their efforts were initially futile.

Critics of the bonus claimed that it was financially irresponsible and further suggested that it would have a degenerative effect on the national character. In the heady laissez-faire atmosphere of the early 1920s, Warren Harding and other fiscal conservatives, such as influential Treasury Secretary Andrew Mellon, warned that the creation of an entrenched system of benefits might make veterans a special-interest welfare group. Harding even took the unusual step of appearing on Capitol Hill in an attempt to dissuade the Senate from voting on a bonus bill.[10] In addition, and despite the seemingly healthy state of the nation's finances, Harding's arguments also contained warnings about the financial burden of the bonus. In his message before the Senate he warned that such a measure might "emperil the financial stability of our country."[11] Harding chose to veto the Bonus Bill when it finally did pass both houses, and in his veto message he reiterated the view that the government owed fewer obligations to able-bodied veterans. He stated, "Though undying gratitude is the meed of everyone who served, it is not to be said that a material bestowal is an obligation to those who emerged from the great conflict not only unharmed, but physically, mentally and spiritually richer for the great experience."[12] As his glowing assessment of wartime service might reveal, Harding had never served on the front lines. His arguments contained strains of Jefferson's view that military service should not be a basis for benefits if the quality of a soldier's well-being had not been overtly harmed.

Despite this setback, veterans' organizations continue to lobby hard for the bonus bill, and Congress soon had another version of it to present to Harding's successor, Calvin Coolidge. Again, the president vetoed the bonus, arguing,

Patriotism which is bought and paid for is not patriotism. . . . Service to
our country in time of war means sacrifice. It is for that reason alone that
we honor and revere it. To attempt to make a money payment out of the
earnings of the people to those who are physically well and financially
able is to abandon one of our most cherished ideals.[13]

For Coolidge, the concept of paying citizens to fight in defense of their
national interests ran counter to the cherished image of the citizen soldiers of the Revolutionary War taking up arms to fight for the common
good in the face of external threats. Although mustering-out pay had
been a regular feature of separation from service, there seemed something vulgar about doling out such a large amount of cash so long after
service. The arguments put forward by two successive presidents had
failed to resonate in Congress as both the House and Senate voted to
override Coolidge's veto, albeit by small margins.

The Adjusted Compensation Act of 1924 promised veterans a payment—estimated to be on average about a thousand dollars—to be paid
in 1945 or to be given to the veterans' beneficiaries in the event of their
death.[14] As the effects of the Great Depression began to take effect, veterans' organizations continued to push for increased benefits on two
fronts. The first was a liberalization of pensions to veterans with disabilities. Passed over the objections of Herbert Hoover, the World War
Service Disability Act of 1930 provided benefits to veterans with non-
service-related disabilities and added considerable expense to a strained
federal budget. The second major push from veterans' organizations was
for an early payment of the bonus. When Franklin Delano Roosevelt
swept into power in 1932, he took a dim view of the increasing amounts
of money flowing out of Washington and into the hands of veterans.

Although he was hardly renowned for keeping a tight rein on the
nation's finances, early in his presidency FDR fought consistently
against giving veterans a privileged status. Before he took office, the violent struggles of the Bonus March of 1932 would have left Roosevelt in
no doubt as to the need for federal relief within the veteran community
in the midst of the Great Depression. But Roosevelt, despite benefiting
politically from the event, chose not to politicize Hoover's dreadful mis-
handling of the Bonus Marchers when they were forcibly evicted from
their encampments in Washington, DC. Indeed, despite the veterans'

display of anger, he shared much of his Republican predecessors' views on the economic and ideological impact of liberal benefits. One of his first acts after entering the White House was to place a moratorium on veterans' benefits while he reevaluated the nation's finances. According to one estimate, at the time of his action veterans comprised only 1 percent of the population while claiming almost 24 percent of the federal budget.[15] Under his Economy Act of 1933, Roosevelt cut all benefits to able-bodied veterans and significantly slashed benefits for disabled veterans. Most of the discarded disabled veterans were ones who had only recently joined the ranks of the "privileged" as a result of the 1930 Disability Act.[16] In making his decision, Roosevelt listened carefully to director of the budget Lewis Douglas. Douglas, a former Arizona congressman, served in France in World War I but believed that veterans should not be given open-ended rewards if their lives had not been impaired in any significant way. Defending his actions, in October 1933, Roosevelt addressed the American Legion Convention in Chicago and argued forcefully against sweeping veteran benefits. In language familiar to opponents of veteran privilege, he claimed that "no person, because he wore a uniform, must thereafter be placed in a special class of beneficiaries over and above all other citizens. The fact of wearing a uniform does not mean that he can demand and receive from his Government a benefit which no other citizen receives."[17] Most veterans did not share his call for self-sacrifice and continued to apply political pressure on the administration. Over the next several years, many of the provisions of the Economy Act were repealed and veterans again began to swell the federal pension rolls.

Roosevelt took a similarly hard line against advocates for the early payment of the bonus. Even as he sought to establish an expansive welfare state, FDR consistently opposed direct handouts to veterans. In 1935, he vetoed Congress's attempts to allow early payment of the bonus to needy veterans. In his lengthy veto message he claimed that the benefits already offered World War I veterans had proved sufficient and argued that veterans would be better served through the general uplifting of the nation's fortunes. He claimed,

The veteran who suffers from this depression . . . can best be aided by the rehabilitation of the country as a whole. His country with honor and gratitude returned him at the end of the war to the citizenry from which he came. He became once more a member of the great civilian population. His interests became identified with its fortunes and also with its misfortunes.[18]

Roosevelt never questioned the service and sacrifice veterans had given the nation. What he did doubt was that military service should give veterans a license to perpetually call on the government in times of hardship. Nor did he oppose giving veterans some assistance. He proposed that the government should help veterans to help themselves by channeling them into New Deal programs such as the Civilian Conservation Corps (CCC). During the less well-known and less contentious Bonus March of 1933, he placated many veterans by offering them transportation and assistance in signing up for CCC projects.[19] But to Roosevelt, giving veterans a direct handout for services that should be an obligation of citizenship seemed like too much of a boondoggle. He had no problem in passing universal legislation that helped the most desperate and needy in society, including veterans, but he did not believe that veterans deserved to be singled out for privileged treatment.

The Senate upheld FDR's veto in 1935. But due to continuing lobbying efforts and stories of veteran hardship in the press—including some of veterans being driven to suicide so that their surviving dependents could claim their bonus—the political mood changed in 1936. Significantly, 1936 was also an election year, and few politicians ever want to cast themselves as foes of veterans.[20] When FDR's anticipated veto of the bonus bill reached Congress in 1936, it was comfortably overridden in both houses. Twelve years after it was promised, but nine years before it was due, the veterans got their bonus. Soon, however, the nation would be once again called upon to put unprecedented numbers of its citizens in uniform. The battles over veterans' benefits for World War II veterans would reshape America's economic and political landscape.

Given the contentious nature of the veteran question during the interwar years, Washington started planning early for the potentially tumultuous return of the more than fifteen million veterans of World War II. The specter of the Bonus March heightened fears of what might happen if the economy could not absorb the returning soldiers. Early veterans' measures mirrored closely those offered World War I veterans.

The Selective Training and Service Act of 1940 provided an early palliative by guaranteeing that veterans could return to their jobs after service, while the National Life Insurance Act of 1940 offered servicemen and women both life and disability insurance. Dependents of soldiers received allotments under the Servicemen's Dependents Allowance Act of 1942. Finally, the Mustering Out Pay Act of 1944 offered some immediate relief to discharged soldiers in the form of small direct handouts.[21] But given the sheer numbers of veterans involved in the war effort and the precarious nature of the economy, a clear need existed for a more comprehensive benefits package.

Although many politicians tried to resurrect the idea of a bonus, most prescriptions for compensating veterans emphasized training and education.[22] With Roosevelt's consent, an informal committee was assembled within the National Resources Planning Board (NRPB) to conduct numerous studies into the potential problems facing returning veterans. Influenced by programs such as the World War I vocational program for disabled veterans, a Wisconsin state educational program set up for World War I veterans, and a similar Canadian law passed in 1941 for their World War II vets, the committee heavily favored education benefits as the most practical and least controversial way of resolving the veteran question. In June 1942, the committee's final report proposed that education and training be at the heart of any postwar benefits. The committee's motivations stemmed less from a desire to reward and remunerate veterans and more from a desire to avoid postwar social and economic breakdown. The report warned that as many as nine million unemployed veterans could reenter society. The "greatest danger" that the proposals sought to avoid, according to committee member and VA administrator Brigadier General Frank T. Hines, "was that of having idle veterans drifting aimlessly about the country in search of non-existent jobs."[23] The NRPB's work was then taken forward by Roosevelt's Armed Forces Committee on Post-War Educational Opportunities for Service Personnel.

Formed in November 1942 and headed by Brigadier General Frederick G. Osborn, the committee advocated education benefits as a means to help veterans reintegrate back into society. The Osborn Committee's recommendations, like those offered by the NRPB, found favor in the White House. Roosevelt retained his opposition to the idea of adjusted compensation or direct handouts for veterans, but he could throw his support behind a program designed to let veterans help themselves after service. One scholar has suggested that Roosevelt, ever the pragmatist, accepted the need for liberal benefits out of an appreciation of the scale of demobilization faced by society and with a view to currying favor with voters in the upcoming presidential election.[24] In his July 28, 1943, Fireside Chat he called on Congress to "do its duty" to prevent veterans returning to "a breadline or on the corner selling apples."[25] In a message to Congress in October 1943, Roosevelt restated the principle that veterans should be compensated for time lost from civilian life when he noted, "Every day that the war continues interrupts the schooling and training of more men and women, and deprives them of the education and skills which they would otherwise acquire for use in later life."[26] He urged Congress to begin the process of drafting legislation to make his goal a reality. Congress responded wholeheartedly. Before the end of the war, over six hundred separate bills entered Congress promising veterans everything from medical coverage to furlough pay. The most extensive proposals heavily favored education benefits.[27]

Few of the bills gathered much momentum until the American Legion intervened. The Legion was formed as a veteran advocacy group in 1919, comprised mainly of World War I veterans. Its members knew better than most the needs of the returning soldier, and they seemed motivated more by a genuine concern for the servicemen than by a desire to resuscitate the postwar economy. At its national convention in September 1943, the Legion approved the formation of a special committee to draft its own comprehensive veterans' bill. Heading the committee was former Illinois governor John Stelle, but it was committee member Harry Colmery, a World War I veteran and former Legion national commander, who scrawled the outline of what would become the Legion's bill on hotel stationery in Room 570 of Washington DC's Mayflower Hotel. Following a series of meetings in DC throughout the winter of 1943–44 with concerned representatives from education, labor, and the military, Colmery and the committee proposed an omnibus bill that incorporated the suggestions of the NRPB and Osborn committees, in addition to sections of the other bills circulating in Congress. The new legislation promised to include provisions for such benefits as unemployment insurance, funding for higher education, employment training, and home loans.[28] After the bill was drafted, the Legion's public relations director, Jack Cejnar, gave the legislation the pithy title of "G.I. Bill of Rights."[29]

What the Legion lacked in originality in crafting the bill, they more than compensated for in the weight of political pressure they could bring to bear on securing its passage. After the bill's introduction in Congress by Mississippi representative John Rankin in January 1944, the Legion conducted an intensive lobbying media campaign to gain public and political support that included securing promotional spots in newspapers, on the radio, and in movie theaters. William Randolph Hearst threw the considerable weight of his newspaper conglomerate behind the Legion's cause. In a letter to the *New York Journal American*, he called on the nation's politicians to "think less about their own personal 'place in history' and think more about the men whose heroism and self sacrifice make the place possible."[30] Hearst later wrote, "Republics are proverbially ungrateful. . . . It fights its wars with children . . . and when it has mutilated them or blinded them, refuses to care for them adequately or even to try properly to rehabilitate them and make their lives more endurable and useful."[31]

There were some opponents of the bill. Some educators feared that an influx of veterans might dilute the quality of the nation's college students. Harvard University President James B. Conant feared that the provision of benefits to all veterans irrespective of aptitude or need might bring "the least capable among the war generation . . . flooding the facilities for advanced education." Similarly, the University of Chicago's Robert M. Hutchins feared the bill would turn colleges and universities into little more than dumping grounds for veterans with whom society did not want to deal.[32] The Disabled American Veterans opposed widespread benefits for fear that the more pressing needs of disabled veterans might be ignored to accommodate the financial burden of the new measures. But most Americans agreed that something had to be done to aid their returning warriors. The Roosevelt administration initially favored a proposal by Utah senator Elbert D. Thomas that provided even more liberal education benefits than the Legion's bill, but the basic tenets of both bills were similar enough to make compromise relatively easy to achieve. Despite his initial sponsoring of the bill in the House, John Rankin began to question some of the provisions added by the Senate. He questioned which agency should administer the benefits, whether the legislation compromised states' rights, and whether the emphasis on education benefits was prejudicial to southern and western veterans who might normally have little interest in higher education.[33] Prejudice also lay at the heart of Rankin's other objections as he bristled at the thought that the equal provisions—particularly unemployment benefits—for all races might result in "50,000 negroes . . . unemployed for a year" in Mississippi.[34]

Such protestations notwithstanding, the G.I. Bill enjoyed a relatively smooth passage through Congress, especially for such an all-encompassing piece of legislation. On June 22, 1944, President Roosevelt signed the Servicemen's Readjustment Act into law. In private, the bill had been born largely out of a desire to preserve postwar order. But in public, Roosevelt prudently emphasized the more sanguine justification of rewarding the nation's defenders of freedom. In his signing remarks he claimed that the bill "gives emphatic notice to the men and women in our armed forces that the American people do not intend to let them down." He cast the bill as an act of gratitude for those veterans who "have been compelled to make greater economic sacrifice and every other kind of sacrifice than the rest of us, and are entitled to definite action to help take care of their special problems."[35]

Although it built upon many of the examples of previous veterans' legislation, the scope of the new G.I. Bill was unprecedented. Returning veterans had the option of claiming unemployment insurance for the first fifty-two weeks after discharge at a rate of twenty dollars a month. Over nine million out of approximately 15.4 million eligible veterans joined what became known as the "52-20 Club." Unemployment insurance offered veterans a welcome respite before deciding what to do next with their lives. On average, veterans claimed this benefit for only 19.7 weeks before finding employment or entering education or training programs. In addition, over 4.3 million veterans took advantage of the low-rate home loans. The bill also offered loans to start businesses or to invest in farming. However, the education benefits were the most well-known and, among veterans, the most appreciated aspect of the G.I. Bill.[36]

Before World War II, a college education tended to be the preserve of wealthier and generally white Americans. But because the bill did not in

President Franklin D. Roosevelt signs the "G.I. Bill of Rights" into law on June 22, 1944. *Courtesy of the Franklin D. Roosevelt Presidential Library.*

principle discriminate on the basis of race, class, or gender, Americans from all walks of life entered school, many becoming the first in their family to do so. Although some colleges, according to their rules and customs, remained closed to women and minorities, higher education became far more democratized as a result. Once a veteran had chosen the school he or she wished to attend, the veteran received up to five hundred dollars a year for tuition and—for single veterans—monthly living expenses of fifty dollars (this amount increased to sixty-five dollars in 1946 and seventy-five dollars in 1948). Veterans claiming dependents received a proportionally higher payment. The generous tuition payment allowed veterans to attend even the most elite colleges. *Time* magazine rhetorically asked veterans, "Why go to Podunk College when the Government will send you to Yale?"[37] In effect, the government had given World War II veterans a full ride for their higher education. Wherever the school, and whatever the cost, the government would pick up the tab. This was the new standard the government had set in its treatment of veterans. To claim benefits, a veteran had to have served at least ninety days and have left the service with an "other than dishonorable discharge." In return, the veteran received benefits for one full year plus a period equal to the time of his or her service, up to a total of forty-eight months. By the program's end on July 25, 1956, approximately 2.2 million veterans had used their benefits for higher education. A further 3.5 million attended other institutions of learning such as vocational schools, and about 1.4 million received on-the-job training.[38]

The genius of the 1944 G.I. Bill was its ability to reward veterans generously while managing to avoid most of the complaints leveled against previous benefits packages. Compared with previous and future debates over veteran benefits, the debates over the 1944 bill were remarkably muted. By placing training and education at the center of the veterans' readjustment needs instead of a simple cash bonus or an open-ended commitment to a future pension, legislators were able to avoid widespread accusations of turning veterans into a privileged social class. Opponents of a welfare state, including William Randolph Hearst, could support the concept of giving veterans an opportunity to better themselves rather than giving them a handout. Although in practical terms, the G.I. Bill did create, in the words of historian Jennifer Keene, "the most privileged generation in American history," at the time it was a politically acceptable and widely lauded answer to the veteran question.[39]

When the soldiers entered service, they would have had no idea of the generous bounty they were destined to receive. They would have known even less of the economic justification for their G.I. Bill benefits. Roosevelt sold the G.I. Bill as a "thank you" to the nation's veterans, a well-earned recognition for a job well done, and downplayed the economic motivation. The G.I. Bill seemed, therefore, to set a precedent that the government would take care of its veterans' "special problems" and not "let them down" after service. The original Servicemen's Readjustment Act of 1944 had also laid the broad conceptual framework for the G.I. Bills that were to follow during the Cold War and beyond. The idea that veterans should be offered educational and vocational benefits as recompense for military service ultimately became a central feature of the benefits packages offered to post–World War II veterans. But the provision of later G.I. Bills was far from automatic, and there were significant differences between the World War II bill and the later bills.

In the immediate aftermath of World War II, the 1944 G.I. Bill garnered almost universal praise for its redemptive effects on veterans' lives and on the economy. However, in order to better assess the bill's successes and failures, both the VA and the General Accounting Office conducted inquiries into the efficacy of the legislation. In addition, several congressional committees held formal hearings on the bill.[40] One report, in particular, undertaken by the House Select Committee to Conduct a Study and Investigation of the Educational, Training and Loan Guarantee Programs of World War II Veterans, was destined to have the biggest impact on later versions of the G.I. Bill. This investigation also marked the emergence of Representative Olin Teague (D-TX) as one of the most influential figures in veterans' affairs of the mid-twentieth century.

Known widely as "Tiger" Teague—a legacy of his hard-hitting high school football days—Teague had endured a tough upbringing. During the 1930s, not long after Teague had started college in Texas, his family was forced to sell their family farm as droughts hit Oklahoma. His father then suffered a heart attack, leaving Teague with no means of support other than what he could earn through his own endeavors. Having to work eight-hour days to finish up his degree instilled in him a steely sense of individualism and an antipathy for anyone who did not earn his or her way in life.[41] He enlisted in the army in 1940, and after going ashore at Normandy in June of 1944 as commanding officer of the 1st Battalion, 314th Infantry Regiment, 79th Infantry Division, went on to see some of the most vicious fighting of the Allied drive into Nazi Germany. Out of the nearly fifteen hundred soldiers in his combat unit, over two hundred were killed and a further five hundred wounded. Teague lost most of his left foot to enemy gunfire, forcing him to undergo extensive treatment and rehabilitation. The wound left him with an artificial foot and the need to wear a heavy orthopedic shoe for the rest of his life. By the time of his discharge from the army in November 1946, he had attained the rank of colonel and had become one of the most decorated U.S. soldiers of the Second World War. His awards included three Silver Stars, three Bronze Stars, and three Purple Hearts, while his outfit was awarded the Presidential Unit Citation. In his many citations, he was praised frequently for his sense of self-sacrifice and willingness to undertake perilous missions in the face of intense enemy fire.[42]

Olin E. "Tiger" Teague (center) in uniform shortly before he was injured in the fight against Nazi Germany. *Courtesy of the Cushing Memorial Library and Archives, Texas A&M University.*

In August 1946, Teague entered Congress as the Democratic representative for the Sixth Congressional District in Texas. When asked why he entered public service, Teague once commented, "I landed on Utah Beach and saw hundreds of bodies stacked up. I started thinking about what causes hell like that, and I decided it was government. I decided I wanted to do something about it."[43] The self-reliance and work ethic he had learned in college and the sense of sacrifice he had exhibited while in uniform engendered a strong antipathy for anyone expecting something for nothing from the government. Teague's political philosophy was that every citizen ought to set aside selfish material interests if they were detrimental to the common good. In announcing his candidacy he vowed to fight against those "people who put their own welfare ahead of the welfare of our country."[44] He opposed much of Harry Truman's Fair Deal for its continuation of FDR's social programs, stating, "It is time for our government to stop doling out money. Money given to people who have not earned it and do not deserve it, tend[s] to make parasites out of people."[45] From day one in office, he wholly embraced the conservative ideals of the southern wing of the Democratic Party, which included an adherence to states' rights and to limited federal government. These were the values Teague carried with him when influential fellow Texas Democrat Sam Rayburn suggested that Teague serve on the House Veterans' Affairs Committee.

Early on in his tenure on the Veterans' Affairs Committee, he made it quite clear that he was not going to add his voice to the chorus of cries for more liberal benefits emanating from the veteran community. His ideals on fiscal restraint soon placed him in opposition to the more powerful veterans' organizations whose raison d'être seemed, to Teague, to be to squeeze every cent out of the government for their members. In 1952, he wrote one of his constituents,

> Unfortunately . . . our country has gone too far down the road where everyone and every group is looking for something for nothing; and everyone wants economy until it touches them personally. The veteran group is fast becoming the largest single segment of our population, and have [sic] long been one of the strongest pressure groups the country has had. But just because they represent that patriotic portion of our society, I can see no just cause for disrupting our entire national economy by wrapping up the entire budget and tie [sic] it with a ribbon and pass it over to them.[46]

So that he could push legislation that would assist the neediest veterans while not bankrupting the government, Teague formulated his own hierarchy of the most deserving. At the apex were disabled veterans and the orphans and widows of veterans killed in service. To these groups, he stated, "I will support any increase to our widows and children of deceased veterans, as I think we owe them more than we do the returned able-bodied veteran."[47] For those veterans who suffered no such hardship he commented, "in spite of the interest in veterans I have, I am not one who believes they should have the world with a fence around it."[48] Teague soon put these ideas into practice when he incurred the wrath of both the American Legion and the chair of the House Veterans' Affairs Committee, John Rankin, by opposing legislation that would have given a pension to all veterans of both world wars. When challenged on his opposition by American Legion lobbyist General John Thomas Taylor, Teague replied, "as long as I am in Congress I can assure you that I will do what I think is right for all people, not for any small group."[49] This philosophy set the pattern for Teague's approach to veteran benefits: he would throw his support wholeheartedly behind legislation for veterans that he deemed to be in desperate need or who had suffered disproportionately as a result of their service, but he would not support blanket legislation for veterans just because they wore a uniform. Even on the original G.I. Bill, his was one of the few voices in Congress expressing concern about the costs and the value of the program.

Teague's skepticism over the bill was partly personal, but mostly philosophical. Personally, he had received little benefit from the program, having completed his education and being married with children before the start of the war. "For people in my age group," he wrote, "it did practically nothing."[50] More significant was Teague's desire to cut government spending and save taxpayers' money, combined with a fervent belief that veterans should serve their country as a matter of civic duty and not as a means to personal economic gain. When one Korean War veteran wrote Teague inquiring about the possibility of a new G.I. Bill, stating, "I have faithfully served my country; but will my country faithfully serve me[?]" the congressman replied, "The duty to bear arms in defense of this country is a constitutional obligation which one acquires just as soon as he is born. . . . [A]ny [G.I. Bill] legislation so enacted will be a gift of a thankful country for the service rendered by you men."[51] Writing to another veteran, he reiterated that "one of the foremost duties of citizenship in this great country of ours is the duty to take up arms in defense of our country, and nowhere in the Constitution does it state that those who do will be recompensed for it in the form of a G.I. Bill."[52] Teague's fear was that the 1944 bill had set a precedent that every citizen taking up arms would now feel entitled to similar rewards after service. The degrading effects on both the national character and the economy that, he feared, could result from such expectations led him to confess, "I am not so sure that we have done a wrong thing by originating the principle of a G.I. Bill."[53]

Some of Teague's worst fears of the profligacy of the 1944 bill were realized when he headed a congressional investigation into the program over an eighteen-month period from 1950 to 1952. Teague's committee heard testimony from VA officials, educators, veterans, and other parties affected by the G.I. Bill and soon uncovered what he described as "scandalous waste on the part of the government, on the part of participating schools and on the part of individual veterans."[54] The expansion of government programs frequently brings out opportunistic miscreants seeking to get rich on the federal dime; because the G.I. Bill guaranteed a fixed tuition of up to five hundred dollars to accredited institutions, some colleges had begun to raise their tuition rates accordingly, seeking to maximize their return from the flood of newly affluent veterans swelling their rolls. In what Teague described as acts of "outright sin," further stories emerged of fly-by-night schools offering specious courses in order to attract veterans and cash in on the benefits windfall.[55] Teague's committee also uncovered stories of veterans undertaking frivolous and unnecessary vocational courses in order to claim benefits. In Philadelphia, he related incidents of "a swarm of cab drivers . . . enrolled in night schools, but [who] never showed up. They hacked all day and rested at night, drawing Government checks monthly for subsistence."[56] Even some states' employees were complicit in turning a blind eye to abuses because doing so brought more federal money into their localities. Teague told one disabled veteran that such fraud prevented Congress from passing more generous benefits for those in greatest need. "I doubt you can comprehend," he told the veteran,

> the skullduggery that takes place and how some men will do everything to get something for nothing. . . . The whole GI Bill . . . was wonderful in intent . . . but there are so many damned crooked people who abuse the program that it makes it so difficult to get legislation through Congress for people who sincerely need it and deserve it.[57]

Stung by these revelations, Teague emerged from the investigation more determined than ever to make sure that every federal dollar for veterans' benefits was accounted for and, above all, necessary.

By the time Teague's committee handed its report to Congress in February 1952, the Cold War had already turned hot in Korea, and discussions had already begun over the possibility of resurrecting the G.I. Bill for a new cadre of veterans. Teague was determined that if such a

bill were going to be passed, he was going to have a major say in its ges-
tation. Despite his reservations over the 1944 bill, he accepted that

> [t]he boys who entered the Armed Forces prior to World War II did not
> do so with the idea that they were getting a G.I. Bill in return. However,
> a grateful nation enacted such a bill, and put it in the statute books. It
> has set a precedent, and for that reason it is only right, at this time, that
> something be done for the veterans of the Korean conflict.[58]

His concern for the fighting man was deep seated and sincere. Wanting
to witness conditions in Korea first-hand, he made an unscheduled and
unannounced trip in January 1952, spending fifteen days on the front
lines talking to American soldiers. But equally sincere was his devotion
to making sure that the mistakes of the first G.I. Bill were not repeated.

At the outbreak of the war, legislators were reluctant to extend benefits to participants of an undeclared war. But as Korea devolved into a
very real war in all but name, the calls for benefits comparable to those
offered World War II veterans grew louder. By March of 1952, lawmakers had tabled thirty-three separate bills to provide G.I. Bill benefits to
Korean War veterans.[59] The three bills given greatest consideration in
the House Veterans' Affairs Committee differed in the amounts they
offered and in the way the benefits were to be administered. One proposed a simple extension of the same benefits offered under the original
1944 bill. Korean War veterans would receive the same annual 500-dol-
lar tuition payment in addition to a 75-dollar-a-month stipend for living
expenses. The American Legion, so instrumental in the passage of the
original act and eager to see its handiwork continued, understandably
favored this option. A second bill, tabled by John Rankin, proposed that
the government would pay only half of a veteran's tuition costs up to a
total of three hundred dollars. Rankin proposed a five-dollar increase
in the monthly living stipend to offset the reduction in tuition benefits.
The third proposal departed most radically from the original bill and
proved to be the most contentious.

On the basis of his findings as head of the House investigation into the
1944 bill, Teague proposed a new G.I. Bill containing one controversial
position that he would stick to throughout his involvement in the education benefits debates in the coming decades. Teague believed that the best

way to curb the kind of fraudulent incidents uncovered by his investigation would be to make any future payment of education benefits *directly* to the veterans themselves and not to the schools. The veterans would then have the discretion to spend their benefits at the institution of their choosing. Teague believed that if veterans were given the money directly, they would be less likely to go to a school with high tuition because they would be left with less money on which to live and pay expenses. In theory, this measure would eliminate the incentive for institutions to raise their tuition rates while still giving veterans full discretion to choose their course of study. He incorporated this view into his own proposed Korean G.I. Bill, H.R.6425. Teague suggested that a fixed monthly sum of $110—more if a veteran claimed dependents—paid directly to the veteran should cover adequately all of the veteran's educational needs.

Teague's bill attracted immediate criticism. The American Legion expressed concerns that under either Rankin's or Teague's bills, the failure to pay tuition costs in full might discourage veterans from entering higher education.[60] The *New York Times* questioned whether the veterans might be forced to avoid courses that required higher out-of-pocket expenses for books or materials if they were forced to cover all of their expenses out of a fixed monthly sum.[61] Representatives of some colleges with higher tuition rates understandably feared that the rewards reaped under the original bill would be lowered substantially as veterans might favor more inexpensive options. Officials at private colleges, in particular, feared that the bill would drive veterans into low-cost public schools. Teague remained unmoved by their pleas. When the president of Baylor University raised concerns over Teague's bill, the congressman wrote him,

> This bill is written in an attempt to restore some lost educational opportunities to those service men and women whose educational or vocational ambitions have been interrupted or impeded by reason of active service in the Armed Forces, and secondly, the bill is written for the benefit of those taxpayers who will pay for this education for the veterans. . . . I believe you are just asking for Federal aid to education and that is not the purpose of this bill.[62]

Teague's arguments won out, and the version of the bill that finally emerged from the House Committee on Veterans' Affairs at the end of

May 1952 retained the central contested feature—that money for tuition should be paid directly to the veteran.

The bill survived an eleventh-hour attempt by Illinois Republican representative William Springer to add a direct tuition payment amendment, and on June 5, the House voted by an overwhelming 361–1 to pass Teague's legislation into law. The only dissenting vote came from Maryland Republican James Devereux, a brigadier general who had spent almost all of World War II as a prisoner of war, and whose token objection was to the Rules Committee's decision to forbid amendments and limit debate on the bill to only forty minutes on the House floor. The Senate passed the bill by voice vote on June 28, and on July 16, President Truman signed Public Law 82-550, the Veterans' Readjustment Assistance Act of 1952.[63]

The Korean G.I. Bill did not reach the generous heights of the 1944 bill. In part, the reason for this more conservative approach to benefits was a perception among some lawmakers that the first G.I. Bill had been overly generous.[64] Moreover, in congressional hearings on veterans' benefits, some educators admitted that the economic need for a G.I. Bill following Korea would be far less than it had been after World War II. The expanding postwar economy seemed to offer more opportunities for veterans to reintegrate without the need for additional government assistance. A spokesman for the Association of Land-Grant Colleges and Universities admitted that the "situation [was] entirely different from . . . the end of World War II."[65] In its final form, the Korean G.I. Bill offered benefits to veterans who served from June 27, 1950, until the official declaration of the end of the conflict (this date would come on January 31, 1955). The 1952 bill provided education benefits of $110 per month for a veteran with no dependents. This sum increased to $135 for one dependent, $160 for two or more. Benefits could be claimed for a period equal to 1.5 times the veteran's service up to a maximum of thirty-six months. As Teague had sought, veterans had to pay for all of their tuition costs, books, supplies, and living expenses out of their monthly stipend. Korean veterans also received similar home loan benefits to those offered World War II veterans. The provision for unemployment insurance remained, but Korean veterans had less time than their "52-20" predecessors to form a "club," receiving twenty-six dollars a month for only twenty-six weeks. Though certainly a leaner piece of legislation, the 1952 bill still proved an effective readjustment tool and was a similar expression of gratitude to its illustrious predecessor. Although attending more expensive private institutions might be more of a strain, the final bill still covered the majority of a veteran's education costs and still offered him or her a wide choice of places to pursue an education.

Veterans had received benefits in an inconsistent manner for centuries until the World War II G.I. Bill, but with the passage of similarly sweeping legislation for Korean veterans, the government created a heightened expectation among future generations of veterans of what the nation owed them for their sacrifice during a time of war. In many respects, the 1944 and 1952 G.I. Bills challenged notions of U.S. citizenship. While that was not their intent, they had begun to establish a precedent that liberal education benefits would be given to those who wore a uniform during times of war. Certainly some Vietnam veterans, when it came their turn to answer the nation's call, would have had some expectations of similar recompense for their service. But even though the Korean G.I. Bill helped create a blueprint for later G.I. Bills, the passage of benefits for Vietnam veterans was by no means automatic. Indeed, from the mid-1950s onward, the debate over what kinds of veterans were most worthy of benefits gained renewed impetus in the government. In particular, questions arose over whether benefits should continue to be offered to veterans who suffered no perceptible physical or economic harm from their military service. Few lawmakers denied that disabled veterans should receive recompense for their sacrifice. To that end, the government continued to extend disability benefits throughout the 1950s, with Olin Teague usually at the forefront of such measures. But the continued provision of more general benefits to all servicemen and women received far greater scrutiny.

When elected in 1952, Dwight Eisenhower brought a more fiscally conservative sensibility to the White House than his immediate predecessors. With two world wars and the ongoing Cold War draft having created millions of veterans, he grew increasingly concerned about the rising costs of ongoing benefits. By Eisenhower's own estimation, 40 percent of adult males were veterans by the mid-1950s, and some lawmakers feared that veterans and their families could soon make up half of the entire population.[66] So, when Congress passed a veterans' pension bill in the election year of 1954—against Teague's strong objections but under heavy lobbying pressure from veterans' organizations—Eisenhower took action. On January 14, 1955, he issued Executive Order 10588 creating a special Commission on Veterans' Pensions to "carry out a comprehensive study of the laws and policies pertaining to pension, compensation, and related non-medical benefits for our veterans and their dependents."[67] In a later letter of clarification, Eisenhower wrote of the need "for a constructive reappraisal of the standards under which such benefits should be provided." Noting the exponential growth of the veteran population and the growth of more universal welfare programs, Eisenhower noted, "It is our duty to arrange our affairs so that future generations will inherit an economic and social structure which is fundamentally sound and in which obligations, including those owed to veterans and their survivors, are distributed equitably and not as an unwelcome burden."[68] As an old soldier, Eisenhower was clearly not aiming to cheat the veterans out of their dues; rather, his proposed commission represented part of his broader economic agenda to reassess federal spending in an attempt to reduce the government's outlay and eliminate costly or unnecessary programs.

Eisenhower also had strong ideological reasons to reexamine veterans' benefits. Cut from a similar conservative cloth as Olin Teague, Eisenhower objected to what he saw as the government's pandering to special-interest groups under FDR's New Deal and Truman's Fair Deal. Eisenhower thought that Truman had given too many concessions to farmers, unions, and racial liberals. Decrying overt government interference in the economy, Eisenhower noted, "a paternalistic government . . . can gradually destroy, by suffocation in the immediate advantage of subsidy, the will of a people to maintain a high degree of individual responsibility."[69] He believed that such groups should set aside their selfish interests for the sake of the common good, aiming for what one biographer describes as a "corporate commonwealth . . . a harmonious society free of class conflict, selfish acquisitiveness and divisive party politics."[70] He accepted that he could not entirely roll back the New Deal and Fair Deal and once commented, "[s]hould any party attempt to abolish social security and eliminate labor laws and farm subsidies, you would not hear of that party again."[71] Indeed, Eisenhower added over ten million Americans to Social Security rolls and increased spending on public housing programs.[72] But as with Teague, his unease with the growing role of the government in American life reflected the concerns of many postwar conservatives.

Following nearly two decades of expanding federal power that had seen the construction of a welfare state and unprecedented government intervention in the economy, conservative politicians and intellectuals began to challenge what they saw as an assault on traditional values of hard work and individuality.[73] Their fears were naturally heightened by the ample evidence of the threat of state control provided by America's Cold War Communist foes. For conservatives, the more benefits the government provided its citizens, the more likely it became that those individuals would lose their sense of initiative, their drive, and their civic virtue. Barry Goldwater, in his 1960 manifesto *The Conscience of a Conservative*, declared that "one of the evils of Welfarism" was that "it transforms the individual from a dignified, industrious, self-reliant spiritual being into a dependent animal creature without his knowing it."[74] Moreover, the more citizens became beholden to the government for their livelihood, the more discretion the government would have in controlling their lives. For many on the Right, therefore, the expanding welfare state threatened the nation's moral character and could ultimately destroy individual freedom.

Eisenhower hoped that his commission could develop a new guiding philosophy that would incorporate these conservative values and make veterans' benefits more equitable for all of society. At no point was the principle of providing veteran benefits in question, but he did not want the government to keep writing checks if the costs were detrimental to the nation's economic health and were not absolutely necessary for a veteran's readjustment. To head the commission, Eisenhower appointed Omar N. Bradley. The two had formed a close bond in the planning and implementation of the D-Day invasion of Normandy. Following Bradley's success in leading the First Army through northern France, he had enjoyed an illustrious postwar career. He served as the head of the Veterans Administration from 1945 through 1948 and guided the agency through its difficult task of helping over fifteen million World War II veterans reintegrate back into society. Bradley went on to serve as army chief of staff in 1948, then became the first chairman of the Joint Chiefs of Staff in 1949, and attained the rank of five-star general in 1950.[75] For more than a year, the Bradley Commission—as it became commonly known—gathered demographic data on the nation's veterans, interviewed public officials concerned with veterans' benefits, and sent out thousands of questionnaires to veterans to gauge their readjustment needs. Their final report became one of the most important documents on veterans' benefits to emerge in the mid-twentieth century.[76] Its conclusions influenced public policy for the next decade and had a direct bearing on the later debates surrounding the Vietnam-era G.I. Bills.

Initially slated to submit its findings on November 1, 1955, the Bradley Commission delayed giving its report to the White House until April 23, 1956. Noting that previous benefits had accrued in a somewhat ad hoc fashion, the commission "endeavored to develop a philosophy and guiding principles, on the basis of which our national obligations to veterans can be discharged generously."[77] The commission determined that benefits should continue to be used as a means of "equalizing significant sacrifices that result directly from wartime military service."[78] To that end, the commission lauded the efforts of the previous G.I. Bills as the "best way to meet the Government's obligation to nondisabled war veterans" by offering "constructive assistance when it is most needed."[79] The G.I. Bill, the report concluded, "as a whole has fully discharged the Government's obligation to nondisabled veterans and has provided benefits that in many cases more than balanced any handicaps resulting from military service."[80]

But the commission also noted that the "rehabilitation of disabled veterans and their reintegration into useful economic and social life should be our primary objective."[81] With that in mind, the commission recommended some controversial measures to reduce the government's commitment to veterans who suffered no significant hardship as a result of service. Echoing the familiar refrain of generations of politicians, the commission stated, "Military service in time of war or peace is an obligation of citizenship and should not be considered inherently a basis of future Government benefits." While recognizing that any type of military service required some sacrifice on the part of individuals, the commission found that finite readjustment benefits such as the G.I. Bill provided sufficient compensation but that ongoing benefits such as pensions constituted a "special privilege."[82] Moreover, the commission argued that the establishment of a comprehensive Social Security system in the United States precluded the need for generous veterans' pensions.

The commission also called for restrictions on the eligibility of veterans for future readjustment benefits. Specifically, it warned against providing a full slate of benefits for veterans serving during conditions that it considered peacetime. The definition of peacetime for the committee members included those veterans who had not served during a time of national conflict such as World War II or Korea. As long as the Cold War remained cold, veterans did not warrant a warm reception from the government. The commission proposed that "the Government's postservice obligation to peacetime ex-servicemen should be limited to compensation and assistance for such significant disabilities as may arise directly out of military service."[83] Cold War veterans should continue to receive medical care and employment assistance, but, the commission argued, "military service does not involve sufficient interruption to the educational progress of servicemen to warrant a continuation of a special educational program for them."[84] In the short term, the two most significant findings of the Bradley Report were that military pensions should not be automatic and should be tied directly to a veteran's financial need and that noncombat Cold War veterans had not suffered sufficient hardship to warrant liberal benefits packages such as a G.I. Bill.

The Bradley Commission had fulfilled Eisenhower's brief to reexamine veterans' benefits in the context of the nation's changing demographic and economic situation. Its proposals sought to establish a realistic framework in which to craft future benefit packages. It agreed with the long-established traditions of providing medical care to veterans and enacting measures to compensate them for time lost from civilian life. But the commission also realized that given the sheer number of veterans in the nation and the growth of general welfare programs, there ought to be limits to the government's obligation. In practical terms this meant a reevaluation of the tradition of offering ongoing pensions and a new philosophy of grading entitlements according to how much a veteran had actually suffered from military service and how much his or her life had been disrupted.

Any attempt to interfere with veterans' benefits invariably raises the ire of the veterans' organizations. The Veterans of Foreign Wars and

Omar Bradley (right) presenting the Bradley Report to Dwight D. Eisenhower (center) on March 31, 1956. *Courtesy of the Dwight D. Eisenhower Presidential Library.*

the American Legion quite openly made it their primary objective to ensure that veterans retained their hard-earned but privileged status. The VFW did not even wait for the publication of the Bradley Report before denouncing it. Following their annual national encampment at the end of August 1955, the VFW adopted a resolution that castigated the government for failing to enact increases in "hospital facilities and in compensation and pension benefits for veterans." The VFW then claimed that the Bradley Commission had been convened "with the obvious purpose of finding ways and means to reduce veteran benefits."[85] One *VFW Magazine* article gave forty-two pointed statements on "What's Wrong with the Bradley Report." Again, the author, Omar Ketchum, framed his critique by offering a definition of citizenship that called for the continued privileging of veteran status. Ketchum claimed that "military service is extraordinary service which transcends the normal duties of citizenship and, consequently, entitles veterans with honorable service to special consideration."[86] In July 1956, the Legion was even more vitriolic in its condemnation, passing a resolution that denounced the Bradley Report as "an abortive monstrosity."[87]

Some veteran organizations took a more level-headed view of the report. In a 1957 letter to the *New York Times*, Kenneth Birkhead, executive director of the progressive American Veterans Committee, called for a more rational approach to veterans' benefits when Congress debated H.R.52, a measure that would have given the same benefits to a veteran with flat feet as to a veteran with a 90-percent-service-related disability.[88] Deriding the lobbying actions of established older veterans' organizations such as the American Legion, Birkhead noted, "the bill was pressured through Congress by the old-line veterans' organizations who are more concerned with the amount of money they can get from the Government than with providing for real needs." Casting his constituents as the "thinking veterans" versus the "professional veterans," Birkhead agreed with the Bradley Commission's central contention that veterans' benefits needed to be more rationally thought out and more related to actual need. He concluded, "Understanding of these problems by thinking veterans and citizens who are not blinded by the brass of some self serving veterans' organizations can have a decisive effect in assuring that Congress will not bow again to this pressure."[89]

The report certainly resonated with Olin Teague. As a member of the VFW, he took to their magazine in support of the Bradley Report's guiding philosophy of fiscal responsibility. Already stung by the abuses under the first G.I. Bill, he cited the exploitation of veterans' medical care as further evidence of the need for greater accountability for federal dollars. He highlighted one case—which he admitted was extreme—in which a veteran with a half-million-dollar net worth spent twenty-five days in the hospital "at the taxpayer's expense" after claiming poverty under oath. Teague called on both the government and the veterans to demonstrate greater fiscal restraint so that, in the long run, they would remove "some cause for public disapproval and thereby help protect veterans' benefits." The report also echoed Teague's belief that disabled veterans ought to be given unwavering support as, for many, their benefits constituted their only source of income. He drew a sharp distinction between their sacrifice and that of able-bodied noncombat veterans who might have "rendered little real service."[90] Responding to a letter he received from one veteran, he wrote, "I certainly realize there are plenty of men who went through the hells of war who receive nothing for it, but I am not interested in helping chiselers who, just because they put on a uniform expect to wear a halo the rest of their life and expect the taxpayers to take care of them."[91]

The impact of the Bradley Report was almost immediate. Soon after its release, the House Committee on Veterans' Affairs—over Teague's objections—narrowly passed H.R.7886, a bill calling for increased pensions for World War I veterans. The American Legion lobbied hard for the bill's passage. The House eventually passed a watered-down version of the bill, but the Senate took no action before the adjournment of the 84th Congress, effectively killing the measure. Other veterans groups opposed the bill as well. The Disabled American Veterans and AMVETS organizations both denounced the measure for its emphasis on providing benefits for able-bodied veterans potentially at the expense of those with greater needs.

The commission's findings also found a receptive audience in the White House. Eisenhower expressed his disapproval of H.R.7886, and in his annual budget message to Congress in January 1958, he called for a reconsideration of "laws providing veterans benefits and services which now overlap other growing public benefit and welfare programs."[92] The following year, he recommended a needs test for determining eligibility for veterans' pensions. Further, in his 1961 budget message, Eisenhower recognized that noncombat veterans should remain a separate category in determining readjustment benefits because they "undergo fewer rigors and hazards than their combat comrades."[93] Because of the minimal disruption to their civilian lives and educational opportunities while serving in peacetime conditions, Eisenhower agreed with the commission's contention that readjustment benefits to peacetime veterans should be curtailed. At the end of his presidency, Eisenhower sought to put these principles into practice as under the aegis of the Bradley Report, and for the first time since Franklin Roosevelt's Economy Act of 1933, the White House sought to cut veterans' benefits. In April 1959, Eisenhower submitted a proposal to Congress to tie future pension payments to the economic needs of veterans. With some modification, Congress accepted the president's proposals. Under Public Law 86-211, the new pension system took into account such factors as a veteran's annual income, net worth, and spouse's income in determining eligibility and rates. By the end of the 1950s, therefore, there appeared to be a tentative consensus developing at the federal level that veterans' benefits ought to be offered to those demonstrating greatest need.

As the nation entered the 1960s, a new generation of citizens would soon be turned into warriors to fight in America's then longest and most controversial war. The debates over funding for nearly three million Vietnam veterans would resurrect questions of military obligation and the enormous costs of providing them with benefits. The administrations of Lyndon Johnson, Richard Nixon, and Gerald Ford would once more attempt to balance the problem of giving soldiers equitable rewards for service with the nation's social and economic needs. Each president would bring different economic philosophies and ideological views to the veteran question; to a varying degree, each one would attract criticism from the press, the public, and the veteran community for failing in their charge of taking care of returning soldiers. With the escalation of hostilities in Vietnam, a new and bitter chapter in the long history of veterans' benefits loomed.

2

The Clash of the Texans

The Making of the 1966 Cold War G.I. Bill

It doesn't seem to me that you ought to have to go into uniform and go to boot camp, and spend 2 or 3 years in the service in order for your Government to have an interest in your education. . . . I think we just must not rest until each child—GI or no GI, boy or girl, rich or poor—has the opportunity to get the kind of education that he needs and that his country needs for him to have in order to defend it.
—President Lyndon B. Johnson, October 25, 1964

I appeal to you to include the five million veterans of the Cold War in your plans for the Great Society. They are the only Americans denied a fair opportunity in life by their own government.
—Senator Ralph Yarborough, November 11, 1964

It is not the intention of this legislation to establish a program which completely subsidizes the cost of a veteran's education or training program, as well as his living costs. . . . It is expected that in many cases the veteran will be required to make a contribution to the cost of his own education.
—Representative Olin Teague, February 7, 1966

The debates surrounding veterans' benefits at the end of the 1950s should have had a limited impact on the passage of a G.I. Bill for Vietnam veterans. Even the Bradley Commission accepted the need for readjustment benefits for veterans who had served in a hostile environment and during a time of conflict such as the one in Korea. But the

Vietnam veteran's access to benefits became complicated by attempts in Congress at the end of the 1950s and early 1960s to pass a sweeping Cold War G.I. Bill, one that would offer benefits to *all* servicemen and women irrespective of when and where they served. Such a broad-ranging bill challenged the findings of the Bradley Commission because it promised to reward veterans who most likely had never faced fire and, in theory, would not have undergone the same rigors as veterans of World War II or Korea.

Notwithstanding his apprehensions over excessive government generosity, Teague had pushed through a bill to provide education benefits to some noncombat veterans in 1955. His bill allowed anyone entering service up to January 31, 1955—the date of the termination of the Korean G.I. Bill—to lay claim to the full benefits offered to Korean War veterans. This meant that any soldier enlisting in January 1955 would get the same reward as one who had slogged his way through Inchon or "Frozen Chosin." Teague's reasoning was that it would be "morally wrong" to deny some veterans a chance to have accrued their full benefits if they had not spent enough time in service by the January 31 termination date.[1] Not all veterans were happy with this proposal: One infantryman who had served as a machine gunner and squad leader in Korea wrote Teague that the bill "makes a mockery of the benefits given those who served when there was a fight and this includes veterans of all the wars of the United States from the War of Independence through the Korean War."[2] Teague's bill did, at least, deny benefits to anyone serving after January 1955, but new proposals in Congress soon took the idea of a G.I. Bill for noncombat veterans much further.

The main architect of a more wide-ranging Cold War G.I. Bill was Texas senator Ralph W. Yarborough, the legislator who, alongside Teague, was destined to play the most significant role in volatile debates over veterans' benefits of the 1960s. Like Teague, Yarborough was a Texas Democrat and decorated World War II veteran; but their similarities did not extend far beyond that. Their military careers and years of public service had left them with very different political views on the nature of government. After an adventurous young adulthood that had taken him from a brief stint at West Point to Weimar Germany, Yarborough earned a law degree from the University of Texas in Austin in 1927. His trial exploits caught the attention of Texas attorney general James Allred, who made Yarborough his assistant. Throughout his public career, Yarborough would always display an affinity for the oppressed or underrepresented. Under Allred's tutelage, Yarborough gained a reputation for fighting for "the little guy" against social injustice and political and economic corruption. He believed that the instruments of the state could and should be used to ensure that no citizen would be denied the opportunity to reap the rewards of their individual initiative and hard work. His endorsement of a regulatory state and his opposition to unrestrained capitalism established him as an ardent supporter of Franklin Roosevelt's New Deal. After serving as a district judge at the end of the 1930s, Yarborough found a new avenue for his civic engagement when World War II broke out. At the age of thirty-eight, Yarborough could have avoided the draft, but he still answered his nation's call. With his legal background, he was commissioned as captain in the Judge Advocacy Group. Not content with a stateside post at the Pentagon, he requested an overseas combat post and was in Europe by the end of 1944. Although his legal duties kept him far behind the tip of the spear, he witnessed firsthand the devastation of Europe as his 97th Infantry Division engaged in the final months of fighting against Nazi Germany. Yarborough's unit was heading to the Pacific when news came through of Japan's surrender. His previous experience in public service resulted in his appointment as the governing officer of Japan's Honshu Province under General Douglas MacArthur.[3]

After reestablishing his legal career upon his return to Texas in 1946, Yarborough began his move into politics. In 1952 and 1954 he challenged the incumbent Allan Shivers for the governorship of Texas, but facing the well-established, well-financed, and ethically questionable Shivers political machine, he was unsuccessful on both occasions. When Shivers declined to run for a fourth term in 1956, Yarborough tried again. This time his opponent was Texas senator Price Daniel Sr. Again, Yarborough failed. This would not be the last time that Yarborough would clash with the more conservative wing of the Texas Democrats. But in his defeats Yarborough had built up enough of a public profile that he was able to win the election for Price's vacated Senate seat in 1957. The following year, he won the state election outright to secure his first six-year term as the junior senator from Texas.

Having finally won over the imperious Democrats in Texas, Yarborough found an even more overbearing antagonist awaiting him in Washington. Senate Majority Leader Lyndon Johnson had not favored Yarborough's nomination in the Democratic primary, preferring the more conservative and less outspoken opponent Martin Dies. The senior senator from Texas then wasted no time attempting to put Yarborough in his place. He delayed Yarborough's swearing-in ceremony, claiming that all of the state election results had to be certified first. Yarborough had to secure the intervention of House Speaker Sam Rayburn before Johnson finally moved. From day one, recalled Yarborough, "Lyndon wanted you under his thumb."[4] Of their fraught relationship in the coming years, he noted that "Lyndon Johnson would give you carrots one day and then stab you in the back with a sword the next day. He was treacherous as hell."[5]

When he finally reached the national stage, Yarborough set about putting his progressive views into practice. Bringing a distinctly populist style to politics, Yarborough—his biographer, Patrick Cox, notes—adopted an almost evangelical style, complete with anti-establishment messages, "enthusiastic, hand-waving and fact filled performances."[6] His campaign slogan for his 1958 senatorial run was, "Put the Jam on the Lower Shelf, So That the Little Man Can Reach It."[7] And Yarborough remained firmly committed to the idea that the government should ensure that every American could have access to the jam. This notion lay at the heart of his liberal idealism. He shared the views of conservatives like Teague and Eisenhower that a citizen's hard work and initiative should be rewarded; he just wanted to make sure that everyone had an equal opportunity to gain those rewards. For Yarborough, an activist government represented the best solution to curbing social or economic injustice. Inevitably, this philosophy led him to become one of the most progressive southern legislators on the issue of civil rights, and in 1957 he and Johnson became the first senators from Texas to vote for a civil rights bill.[8] Thereafter, Yarborough fought hard for every major civil rights bill during his time on Capitol Hill. In his first year in office, Yarborough also sought to increase the salaries of postal workers and coauthored public works programs through the National Highway Act and the National Housing Act.[9] After accepting his first major committee appointment on the Committee on Labor and Public

After much delay, Ralph Yarborough (left) finally gets to take the U.S. Senate oath of office from Vice President Richard Nixon (right) and Senate Majority Leader Lyndon Johnson (center). Yarborough's progressive leanings would place him at odds over G.I. Bill benefits with both future presidents in the years that followed. *Courtesy of the Dolph Briscoe Center for American History, the University of Texas at Austin.*

Welfare, Yarborough made funding for education a cornerstone of his legislative agenda. He considered access to education one of the more effective ways of ensuring that everyone had a chance to improve his or her life. Consequently, he was coauthor and one of the main sponsors of the 1958 National Defense Education Act. Up until the 1944 G.I. Bill, the federal government had played a limited role in funding education, preferring instead to keep it a state and local issue.[10] The NDEA offered loans to promising students in the areas of math, science, and foreign languages. The act also provided funds for summer training for science teachers and the production of textbooks by eminent scientists, all with the goal of revitalizing the nation's scientific and technological base in the wake of the Soviet launch of Sputnik in October 1957.[11] Buoyed by his success in promoting education legislation, Yarborough introduced the Veterans' Education Act of 1958, a new G.I. Bill for Cold

War veterans who had served since the expiration of the Korean War bill on January 31, 1955.

The new legislation would address two burning issues for the neophyte senator: first, it would provide a further influx of public funds for higher education. As with the NDEA, Yarborough tied this need in with the nation's defense requirements, suggesting that highly skilled workers were essential to maintaining the nation's dynamism. Indeed, he saw his bill as the perfect program to augment the NDEA, arguing in a press release that "[t]here is a proven need that a much higher percentage of all Americans be professionally trained. . . . [T]his act would help to supplement programs emphasizing scientific and engineering training."[12] When he introduced his new G.I. Bill to the Senate, he explained the second main reason for its conception. With characteristic rhetorical flourish, he invoked an image of the nation's abandoned service personnel brought home from far-flung places to a life spent forever catching up with their civilian peers. He asked his fellow senators to

> [p]icture the young soldier returning home with his honorable discharge. He left home a boy and came home a man, and therein lies the trouble. He's not generally sufficiently trained or educated to earn a living in a man's world. Conditions at home have changed. Younger brothers and sisters require the family income for day-to-day living. He cannot or will not call on his folks to support him—to spend their meager family savings on his education. . . . The direct result of this military cycle is that interrupted education is not resumed. The young veteran returns not to higher schooling, but to a lifetime of unskilled and semi-skilled work.[13]

In the plight of the struggling veteran, Yarborough had found another worthy cause and another perceived injustice that could be corrected through federal intervention. As with most beneficiaries of his legislative accomplishments, the veterans represented a group that had been disadvantaged through no fault of their own. In a letter to the *New York Times* promoting his bill, he claimed that because so many potential draftees could obtain college and marital deferments, "only about 45 percent of our young men must bear the burden of military service" and should, therefore, receive compensation for their lost opportunities. "The cold war G.I. Bill," he continued, "corrects this injustice by helping these young veterans continue their education after its substantial interruption."[14]

Yarborough's legislation reflected the diminished threat its noncombat beneficiaries would have faced by giving them less generous benefits than those offered either Korean War or World War II veterans. After undergoing some modifications in committee, the final bill presented to the Senate on July 21, 1959, proposed to give veterans a monthly living stipend of $110 for higher education. By Yarborough's own estimation, the bill was "not as generous with Cold War veterans as the Korean Conflict law was. . . . The payment of $110 per month now will buy only as much as $78 would buy in 1952. In addition," he added, "the average college tuition rate in America has gone up 71% since 1952."[15] The bill also offered no mustering-out pay, no business loans, and recipients had to have served at least six months instead of the three required under the previous bills.

When the legislation, now titled S.1138, reached the floor of the Senate, Yarborough resurrected the argument that the burden of military service should be more evenly shared among all citizens. He argued that as a result of the latent "threat of war" created by the Cold War, "it becomes a matter of great national concern when some individuals have to carry a grossly disproportionate share of the burden of citizenship."[16] He immediately attempted to head off his opponents' cries that veterans' benefits had become mere handouts by noting that the G.I. Bill, with its provision of training benefits, was "typically American" because of its "emphasis on self-help [and] individual initiative."[17] The loudest voice of opposition came from Samuel James Ervin, Democratic senator from North Carolina, who emphasized the considerable costs of the measure. Claiming to speak on "behalf of a group of Americans who are sometime[s] forgotten, namely the American taxpayers," Ervin warned of the dangers of creating "the greatest debt ever thrust upon posterity by any generation."[18] Despite its obvious costs, the bill passed the Senate by a vote of fifty-seven to thirty-one with forty-eight Democrats and only nine Republicans supporting it.

Outside of the Senate, few others shared Yarborough's enthusiasm for a new round of veterans' measures. Veterans' organizations offered only lukewarm support. The VFW supported the bill, but the American Legion opposed it, reluctant to share its hard-fought-for rewards with those who had never faced fire. More importantly, Yarborough's arguments failed to convince many in the House and, in particular, failed to sway perhaps the most influential voice in veterans' affairs in DC: Olin Teague.

In 1955, Teague had become chairman of the House Veterans' Affairs Committee, a position he would hold for the next seventeen years, and he soon earned the title of "Mr. Veteran" on the Hill. From the mid-1950s onward, nearly all important veterans' legislation required Teague's approval for passage. There emerged an informal agreement between the Senate Finance Committee and Teague's Veterans' Affairs Committee whereby, according to a Brookings Institution study, "All consequential veterans' benefits legislation would first be acted upon in the House. Then the Finance Committee would move bills that Teague endorsed and drop bills he opposed."[19] Such was the sway Teague now held over veterans' affairs that Yarborough was left with no doubt that his fellow Texan would hold the emperor's thumb over his legislation.

During hearings on the Bradley Report in the House, Teague stated that "I can never get away from the fact that those who stay under combat conditions are entitled to more than those who do not."[20] He remained deeply conflicted over the costs and consequences of Yarborough's bill, commenting in 1960 that "I have had no problem before the Veterans' Affairs Committee which has troubled me as much as the 'Peacetime G.I. Bill.'" He could support the idea of peacetime benefits in principle, but held reservations over the idea of generous handouts, adding, "it is most difficult for me to tell a young man that we draft and send all over the world that he is not just as much a 'veteran' as some man who served in the United States back in the war years. On the other hand I am not sure that it is right to guarantee every young man an education who goes into military service for the rest of time."[21] Teague stalled on making a final decision on Yarborough's bill, delaying hearings in his committee until January 1960. He did float an alternative Cold War G.I. Bill for the committee's consideration, but this move was largely a symbolic gesture to insert his views into the discussion. At no point did he give any indication that he intended to fully support either measure. Instead, he repeatedly cited the likelihood of a presidential veto as the reason for his inertia, stating that "it may be a dis-service to attempt to pass a bill when you know in advance that the President is going to oppose it."[22]

Olin E. Teague chaired the House Committee on Veterans' Affairs from 1955 to 1972. During this time, he became the most influential law-maker on Capitol Hill in veterans' legislation. Teague's fiscal conserva-tism would have a profound impact on the Vietnam-era G.I. Bills. *Cour-tesy of the Cushing Memorial Library and Archives, Texas A&M University.*

The concept of a Cold War G.I. Bill had, indeed, received a cool recep-tion in the White House. Eisenhower relied heavily on the conclusions of the Bradley Report in framing his opposition. In his budget message to Congress in January 1960, he suggested that the lack of hazards faced by most Cold War veterans, in addition to the wages and skills they received in service, was reason enough not to offer them extensive ben-efits. "Those who serve in peacetime undergo fewer rigors and hazards than their usual comrades," he noted. "Such benefits are not justified because they are not supported by the conditions of military service."[23] Eisenhower was not entirely opposed to funneling federal dollars into higher education where he saw a need, as he had proven in signing the 1958 National Defense Education Act. But the G.I. Bill was a step too far for Eisenhower in terms of its impact on the budget and its challenge to the notion of military service being a natural civic duty. In the face of such opposition, and given Teague's own concerns, Yarborough's bill never even made it out of the House Veterans' Affairs Committee.

Given his influence in the House, Teague could have been more pro-active in lobbying for the bill's success, and Yarborough was in no doubt that his fellow Texan should have done a lot more. He blamed Teague for killing the bill and was quite vocal in expressing that view to anyone who would listen, including the press. In a May 1960 weekly radio address released for the Texas airwaves he stated, "If the House Veterans' Affairs Committee chairman does not have sufficient concern for the education of cold war veterans, then the plan will most likely die in his committee or come out too late to be passed, that is, killed by his own inaction."[24] Yarborough's criticism was particularly pointed and, given that Teague was opposed for reelection by one of Yarborough's friends, Teague's supporters charged that Yarborough's motive was to unseat his antagonist. The charges may not have been entirely unwarranted, as the attacks continued. In September, Yarborough stated that Teague's "actions against our veterans and their families in Texas and nationally are an outrage and a disgrace."[25] In response, Teague told one supporter, "I am afraid that Senator Yarborough is stupid, or at least he thinks the American people are stupid to believe that any one person has the power to kill a bill or prevent it from being voted on. Rumors around Capitol Hill are that he is close to being a mental case. Certainly his actions on this matter would seem to prove it."[26] Their relationship hardly improved thereafter. In 1962, Teague wrote President John F. Kennedy to complain that Yarborough was deliberately blocking a VA appointee in Texas "for one reason—because he was considered to be a friend of mine," adding that "Senator Yarborough is unhappy with me for opposing the so-called peacetime GI bill." He threatened to withdraw his cooperation with Kennedy's legislative agenda if Yarborough's actions continued.[27]

Yarborough refused to give up on his goal of passing a Cold War G.I. Bill. As his repeated and unsuccessful attempts at the governorship of Texas in the 1950s had revealed, he was no quitter. In January 1961, he introduced the Veterans' Readjustment Act, a bill that was almost identical to the one that had passed the Senate in 1959. His arguments in favor of the bill had not changed much either. He still sold the bill as "an act of justice" for Cold War veterans. If the emotional appeal failed, he played up the national security benefits, arguing that "the great danger

we face from Russia is not in her present armaments, but in her effi-
cient schools. We cannot ignore this chance to nullify their threat."[28] In
a press release he described the bill as "part of this nation's full frontal
attack on Communism."[29]

This time, the opposition he faced was even stronger than in 1959.
Philip Sam Hughes of the influential Bureau of the Budget (BOB) wrote
Lister Hill, then chairman of the Senate Labor and Public Welfare Committee, to argue that the conditions that peacetime veterans faced were
not harsh enough to warrant significant readjustment benefits. He also
suggested that soldiers' needs could be taken care of through "programs
open to all of our people."[30] Even the Department of Defense (DOD)
opposed the new bill. Cyrus Vance wrote Hill to explain the DOD's
position, arguing that "[p]rograms of educational and vocational assistance encourage personnel to leave military service immediately after
accruing the maximum benefits which can be gained. This results in
a serious handicap to the Armed Forces in their efforts to attract and
retain qualified personnel on a career basis." Vance claimed that nearly
50 percent of airmen left the air force to pursue further education when
covered under the Korean War G.I. Bill, whereas only 20 percent had
left for educational reasons during the years following the bill's expiration.[31] Such was the lack of momentum behind the bill, it did not even
reach the floor of the Senate until the summer of 1962. When it did,
several senators voiced their disapproval. South Carolina's Strom Thurmond read out letters from both the BOB and the DOD expressing their
reservations. Ohio Democrat Frank Lausche highlighted the lack of
support in the White House, in the VA, and in the veteran community
as sufficient reason to kill the measure. Yarborough read in vain several
letters in support of the measure, but after several hours of debate the
Senate shelved the bill without even submitting it to a vote.

When the Eighty-Eighth Congress convened in 1963, Yarborough
tried again. This time he warned his fellow senators that by failing to
pass the act, "we will be giving away the future of these patriotic young
men, we will be giving away part of the economic growth of this country, . . . and we will be giving [away] the confidence which the American people and the veterans have that the Congress of the United States
does not forget the devotion of her servicemen who have served in all
four corners of the globe."[32] There were many prominent senators who

shared Yarborough's vision. In statements before Yarborough's Veterans' Affairs Subcommittee, George McGovern said of the Cold War bill, "As one who benefitted in my own education from the World War II G.I. Bill, I feel that this measure is an act of simple justice to thousands of our young men." Hawaii's Daniel Inouye noted that the nature of the Cold War meant that "any crisis spot in the world can become a front line position almost overnight dependent on upon the machinations of the opposition." Yarborough used a similar line of argument, noting that in the wake of recent crises in Berlin, Cuba, and the Congo anyone serving in the 1960s might "have considerable assurance that a new crisis, a new outbreak of guerilla warfare, another country thwarted by communist aggression, will bring them into the middle of a hot war." These words proved to be prophetic. But for the time being, the lack of an immediate military threat resulted in the Senate once more failing to approve the bill.

The Kennedy administration had also expressed its opposition to Yarborough's bill. Kennedy had initially voted for the measure while serving in the Senate in 1959. But in one of his few public statements on veterans' benefits as president, he reiterated the Bradley Report's main contention that "[o]ur first concern in veterans' programs is that adequate benefits be provided for those disabled in the service of their country."[33] The Veterans Administration also opposed widespread benefits to what they considered peacetime veterans. VA administrator J. S. Gleason indicated that his agency favored proposals circulating on Capitol Hill to extend vocational readjustment benefits to disabled veterans, but he agreed with Kennedy that such benefits should not be offered to nondisabled Cold War veterans.[34] Gleason testified before Yarborough's committee that "service under current conditions does not present on a widespread basis the same rigors and hazards as does wartime service; . . . I do not believe these readjustment programs, education, training and loan, are needed at the present time."[35] As many veterans would soon discover to their cost, the VA tended to function as a bureaucratic rubber stamp for the executive branch and was seldom a strong advocate for the veterans in whose name it served.

Yarborough might have been forgiven for giving up at this point. Three times he had fought for a Cold War G.I. Bill, and only once had he even managed to get it passed in the Senate. Even with Kennedy, his friend and a former supporter of the bill, in the White House, its chances for passing had not improved in 1963. With Lyndon Johnson, his old antagonist, ascending to the presidency in 1964, he might have expected little change in fortune. But Yarborough and Johnson's relationship had improved, somewhat, even if the path to their new modus vivendi had been a tortured one.

Their relationship had initially soured further when Yarborough failed to back his fellow Texan's bid for the Democratic nomination for president in 1960, favoring Kennedy. Yarborough was as much attracted to Kennedy's vision for America as he was repulsed by Lyndon Johnson's politicking. Having remained an ardent supporter of Kennedy's New Frontier initiatives over the next three years, Yarborough was in the young president's motorcade when it turned onto Elm Street in Dallas on November 22, 1963. Knowing the importance of Texas's Electoral College votes, Kennedy had hoped that his trip would help bolster his support for the following year's presidential election. He had also hoped to unify the Democratic Party in the state for the forthcoming campaign. As Yarborough had found out during the 1950s, Texas Democrats were deeply divided between the conservative elements and the more progressive wing headed by Yarborough. Yarborough was two cars behind the president's limousine when the fatal shots were fired. He recalled that the "rancid smell" of gunpowder "stayed in our nostrils for minutes as we raced toward Parkland Hospital."[36] Yarborough and Johnson were united briefly in grief, but a more lasting realization developed in the wake of the tragedy that they could better achieve their political ambitions by working together. Johnson endorsed Yarborough in the Democratic primary, allowing the now senior senator to defeat his Republican challenger and Connecticut transplant, George H. W. Bush. Any amity between the two Texans only went so far. Yarborough put their accord down to the fact that Johnson was too preoccupied as president to pay him too much heed. For Yarborough, having a president who was willing to help promote his liberal agenda was more important than bearing grudges. As he rather coolly noted much later, having Johnson in the White House "was better than having a reactionary president who wouldn't sign progressive legislation."[37]

Yarborough either initiated or stood behind nearly every major piece of social legislation of Lyndon Johnson's Great Society. According to biographer Patrick Cox, "If LBJ was the grand architect in the design of the Great Society, then Yarborough earned the title of Chief Engineer."[38] Looking back on the achievements of the Great Society, Yarborough once recalled, "Johnson tried to take credit for my work. . . . My programs were eighty percent of his Great Society. . . . [Johnson] admitted that to me once."[39] Yarborough was the only senator from the former Confederate States of America to support the Civil Rights Act of 1964 and he then fought for the passage of the 1965 Voting Rights Act. He was also at the forefront of Johnson's War on Poverty, steering through the Senate the Job Corps, VISTA, Head Start, the 1966 Model Cities Act, the 1965 Housing and Urban Development Act, and the Office of Economic Opportunity. He also pushed for the landmark health care legislation that created Medicare and Medicaid. Later, in what was to prove one of his last initiatives, he introduced the Conquest of Cancer Act, which Richard Nixon would sign into law as the National Cancer Act of 1971.

Some of Yarborough's greatest legislative achievements came in the field of education. Having already secured the passage of the NDEA in 1958, he sponsored the Secondary Education and Higher Education Acts of 1965. The Higher Education Act of 1965 promised to give teeth to Yarborough's dream of universal access to education. In one dramatic stroke, the act overturned the historical reluctance of the federal government to get involved in higher education. The act gave direct scholarships to those students demonstrating financial need and offered federal insurance on student loans and subsidies for interest on the loans. Students from middle- and lower-income families could benefit from the act's work-study provisions whereby the government would cover the majority of the costs of employing students in university or community service positions. In addition, the act offered funds for universities to improve their buildings and facilities and aimed to improve the quality of the nation's teachers by establishing the Teacher Corps.[40] If Olin Teague earned the title "Mr. Veteran" in DC, Yarborough could claim the mantle of "Mr. Education."[41]

The emerging symbiotic relationship between Johnson and Yarborough did not yet encompass Yarborough's vision of a new Cold War G.I. Bill. Early on in his presidency, Johnson gave little indication of supporting the initiative. He did, however, mark the twentieth anniversary of the signing of the original G.I. Bill with a ringing endorsement of its contribution to society. "The G.I. Bill," he noted, "increased the strength of our Nation by enlarging the opportunities of our people."[42] When he made these comments, the commander-in-chief had his troops scattered throughout the globe, but there seemed no immediate reason to consider a new G.I. Bill. To be sure, the situation in South Vietnam had deteriorated rapidly since Johnson had taken over the presidency. But even in this tense Cold War hot spot, few anticipated the massive costs in both blood and treasure that would follow.

By the end of 1964, the United States had over twenty-three thousand service personnel stationed in South Vietnam, and nearly 150 men had already lost their lives. As the nation's crusade gathered momentum in Southeast Asia, Ralph Yarborough saw the opportunity to relaunch his own crusade to secure a new G.I. Bill of Rights. Despite his previous failures at getting a Cold War G.I. Bill passed, in 1964 he chose the occasion of Veterans Day to telegram Lyndon Johnson to urge the president to consider a new program of education benefits for veterans. Cleverly appealing to Johnson's burgeoning sense of social justice, he wrote, "On this Veteran's [sic] Day I appeal to you to include the five million veterans of the Cold War in your plans for the Great Society. They are the only Americans denied a fair opportunity in life by their own government."[43] Some of the so-called peacetime veterans—those who had served after the Korean War—were already making it clear to the new president that they needed such legislation. David R. Davies, a first-year Wisconsin college student and army veteran, served from October 1959 through February 1962. In July of 1964, Davies wrote Lyndon Johnson, hoping that the new president might be more receptive than his predecessors to offering assistance to noncombat veterans. Davies wrote to explain his financial struggles after leaving the service. He complained that the army had provided him no special skills and that he was forced to delay his "ultimate goal" of attending college and had to take up a series of menial jobs. Speaking up in support of a Cold War G.I. Bill, Davies wrote, "I sincerely hope that your administration will review the potential value of theis [sic] vitally needed legislation. I think it would be tragic for [a] bill of this kind to be perpetually by-passed by seemingly more important legislation."[44] The mother of another concerned veteran wrote Johnson to inform him, "Were I not employed, it would be impossible for our son to continue his education. We are not alone in this, there are many young men who having served their country, would like to go to school."[45] But it was the escalating situation in Vietnam and the prospect of a new cohort of veterans in need that was to breathe new life into Yarborough's old idea.

On January 6, 1965, Yarborough introduced yet another Cold War G.I. Bill, S.9. Patterned after the Korean War G.I. Bill and closely resembling his previous attempts at a Cold War G.I. Bill, S.9 offered educational and vocational assistance to veterans who had served between January 31, 1955, and July 1, 1967, if they had served for more than 180 days and had left the service in good standing. Benefits would be paid for a period equal to 1.5 times the length of service. The single veteran would be able to claim $110 a month for education, $135 if he or she claimed one dependent. The day after submitting the bill, Yarborough wrote Johnson to remind him, "No other group in our society has done as much for their government for so little, at so great a cost to themselves."[46]

He also took his message to the press, outlining his hope for "A Fair Deal for the Cold War Soldier" in an article for *Harper's Magazine*. In the article, Yarborough called for public support for the new bill as he urged "a great many Americans to demand it—in the name of both justice and common sense."[47] Arguing for the potential economic benefits of a new bill, Yarborough noted that the original G.I. Bill had provided the nation approximately "625,000 engineers, 375,000 teachers, 165,000 natural and physical scientists, and 220,000 workers in medicine and related fields."[48] In an argument that would resurface repeatedly in the debates over veteran funding to follow, he claimed that the extra earning potential of those trained would ensure that by 1970, the G.I. Bill would have paid for itself because of the extra taxes paid back to the government. The G.I. Bill, he concluded, represented "one of the government's few profit-making ventures."[49] Finally, he suggested that such a program could eliminate the millions of dollars paid out in unemployment compensation to veterans discharged without any easily marketable skills.

Johnson remained unmoved. An internal White House memo from December 1964 laid out the administration's five points of opposition.[50] The last three of the five points were pragmatic. Point number three made the observation that there was no massive demobilization, as had occurred after World War II, and that most veterans acquired

Ralph Yarborough explaining the merits of his G.I. Bill to a group of young sailors in 1965. *Courtesy of the Dolph Briscoe Center for American History, the University of Texas at Austin.*

some marketable skills while in service, and therefore there was less need to help veterans readjust to civilian life. Point number four noted that veterans' organizations had little interest in the new legislation as they tended to devote their efforts to securing benefits for "hot-war veterans." Point number five reiterated the Department of Defense position that a Cold War G.I. Bill might dissuade service personnel from making a career out of the military. These last three arguments added little of substance to the debates that had already taken place in the wake of the Bradley Report. But points one and two revealed a more deep-seated philosophical opposition to a new G.I. Bill in the Johnson administration.

The first objection raised in the White House memo was that "[a]n expansive program only for ex-servicemen undercuts the strategy of persuading the Congress to ensure full educational advantages for all."[51] The cost of a new G.I. Bill threatened the administration's plans for universal education programs such as those pending in the Higher Education Act. Johnson's attempts to transform America into a Great Society contained numerous prescriptions to aid those citizens still marginalized because of such factors as race, lack of education, or endemic poverty. Through corrective federal legislation, Johnson hoped to refocus the nation's resources to help those citizens he considered most greatly in need. In this goal, he shared a common political ideology with Yarborough. But unlike his fellow Texan, Johnson did not consider the average Cold War veteran's needs to be that great.

Heavily influenced by the social programs of the New Deal, Johnson wanted his Great Society to provide every citizen a more equitable share of the nation's considerable wealth. Like Yarborough, he saw education as an integral way of achieving this goal. According to biographer Irving Bernstein, Johnson believed that education "offered equality of opportunity, a level playing field, to young people who lived in poverty, to blacks, to Mexican-Americans, and to women, an appealing concept to a democratic populist."[52] With federal investment directed at the sectors of society that needed most assistance, education could give every American the opportunity to better his or her life, irrespective of social condition. In a speech delivered at the dedication of Florida Atlantic University at Boca Raton in October 1964, Johnson outlined his vision for the future of higher education in America when he called for "a new future of full equity in educational opportunity for all Americans." He added, "advanced education is no longer a luxury just to be enjoyed by the child of the banker, or by the children of fortunate families. . . . [I]t is a necessity for every American boy. . . . To deny it to the children of poverty not only denies the most elementary democratic equality, it perpetuates poverty as a national weakness."[53]

The second objection outlined in the memo more clearly reflected Johnson's liberal vision as it noted, "The G.I. Bill approach is not selective—not according to need, not according to ability, not according to motivation."[54] The original G.I. Bill had turned veterans into a privileged class after World War II. But the government and the public had accepted the provision of such rewards because those veterans had faced fire. A Cold War G.I. Bill might upset Johnson's goal of creating a more equal society by unfairly rewarding those veterans whose lives had not been seriously impaired by service or who had no financial need for benefits. For Johnson, there still existed many other sectors of society that were far more deserving of federal support. As with many of his social programs, Johnson harked back to the New Deal and the same universalist approach to veterans' benefits adopted by Franklin Roosevelt. As Roosevelt had with his Economy Act of 1933, Johnson questioned whether veterans—especially noncombat veterans—should be placed on a pedestal when the needs of so many other sectors of society for government aid seemed more pressing. Later in his Boca Raton speech, Johnson highlighted the success of the original G.I. Bill, but only to illustrate the potential of providing universal education benefits. He praised "[t]he proud achievement of the GI bill," but added,

> [I]t doesn't seem to me that you ought to have to go into uniform and go to boot camp, and spend 2 or 3 years in the service in order for your Government to have an interest in your education. And yet there is not a Member of Congress today that would look back on that GI bill and say, "We made a mistake in making that great adventure and that great decision." The GI bill challenges us to [provide] programs of loans and scholarships enabling every young man and woman who has the ability to move beyond the high school level. So I think we just must not rest until each child—GI or no GI, boy or girl, rich or poor—has the opportunity to get the kind of education that he needs and that his country needs for him to have in order to defend it.[55]

As his legislative agenda soon proved, Johnson was quite prepared to throw the weight of the government behind those who needed extra assistance, but he remained unconvinced that noncombat service justified such benevolence.

One week after Yarborough submitted S.9, Johnson made no mention of veterans in his message to Congress on his vision for education in America. He reiterated his universal approach to federal education assistance as he called for "better education to millions of disadvantaged youth who need it most [and] . . . the best educational equipment and ideas and innovations within reach of all students."[56] Similarly, in response to Yarborough's Veterans Day letter to Johnson, Lee White, associate special counsel to the president, informed Yarborough that "greater assistance must be given to those potential college students who would not otherwise be able to secure higher education. . . . [O]f course, the proposed programs would not bar veterans."[57] Under legislation such as the Housing Act and Higher Education Act, veterans could claim federal assistance to help them reintegrate into society, and Johnson hoped these general benefits would suffice. Yarborough remained convinced that the veterans' sacrifice deserved more.

Johnson's questioning of veterans' privileged status also manifested itself in controversial cutbacks to other services. In his January 1965 budget message to Congress, he suggested that federal expenditure should be geared more toward "meeting fully our obligation to those who were disabled in the defense of the country and to their dependents and survivors" than to veterans claiming benefits for non–service-related care.[58] Soon thereafter, his administration considered several cost-cutting proposals for the VA. In what was sold as an attempt to modernize and streamline the organization, the proposals included the closure of eleven VA hospitals in addition to residence homes and marginal regional offices. Yarborough and Teague led a chorus of opposition on the Hill, but some of the most vociferous opposition came, not surprisingly, from the veterans' organizations. With a characteristically zealous defense of veteran privilege, VFW commander-in-chief John A. Jenkins proclaimed that he was "shocked and appalled and ashamed" at the proposals.[59] Donald Johnson, national commander of the American Legion, warned that the president's proposals were the start of a drive to subsume all veterans' care into broader Great Society programs. Excoriating what he saw as a "two-year drive to tear down the structure of programs," the legionnaire forewarned his constituents that it was the administration's intent to "depress veterans' programs below the level of the general social welfare programs of the Great Society as a preliminary to eliminating them." Equating the cuts with the Economy Act of 1933, Donald Johnson then charged his namesake in the White House with targeting "the special status and recognition historically accorded America's veterans—the bottom stone of the entire veterans' benefit program."[60] Duly antagonized by this perceived challenge to their raison d'être, both organizations began an intensive lobbying campaign against the cutbacks. Johnson was fast gaining an unwelcome reputation as an antiveteran president.

Meanwhile, as Yarborough and the White House hit an impasse over the Cold War G.I. Bill, the Veterans Administration had begun work on a compromise program. In the late fall of 1964, VA administrator John S. Gleason indicated that his agency was beginning to break with the administration and see the merits of Yarborough's proposals. On November 19, 1964, Gleason informed the White House that the proposed new benefits could, in fact, serve to enforce the ideals of the Great Society and not betray them by helping to elevate the national education level. Gleason now accepted Yarborough's argument that military service incurred sacrifice on the part of the veterans. He informed Johnson's special assistant, Bill Moyers, that Cold War benefits "would be a valuable and feasible step in achieving the Great Society" and that "if the President sponsors legislation to provide Federal assistance generally in obtaining a college education, certainly persons who served their country, many times at a sacrifice, during the present 'Cold War' period should have a first claim to benefits."[61] Gleason acknowledged that Yarborough's previous proposals had been too costly, but he believed that a scaled-down, less expensive version, based on the Korean G.I. Bill model, might serve both the veterans' needs and the social engineering goals of the administration.

Unfortunately for Yarborough and the veterans, in December 1964 Gleason resigned his post to return to private business before he could get anyone in the White House to listen to his proposals. Johnson replaced him with William Driver, an imposing, six-foot-three career VA employee and veteran of both World War II and Korea. Even though Driver credited his own success to the law degree he earned under his G.I. Bill, he proved less open to Yarborough's proposals than Gleason had become by the end of his tenure. Early in 1965, Driver presented the VA's views on S.9 and sought to establish an alternative that more closely fit the administration's more parsimonious approach. Driver informed Senator Lister Hill, chairman of the Committee on Labor and Public Welfare, that he did not agree with Yarborough that all post-Korea veterans should be eligible for benefits. He reiterated the White House position that this objection "does not depreciate in any way the need for appropriate Federal legislation to improve the availability of education in this country," and endorsed the view that generally available federal student aid programs could compensate veterans sufficiently. Driver did at least raise the possibility of extending benefits for those veterans serving "in a period of hostility, or disabled by such service." Paying benefits to those who served during times of war tended to attract little opposition among the public or in political circles, and Driver proposed that a new "hot spots" G.I. Bill could be enacted for those veterans serving in "warlike conditions" such as those developing in Vietnam or the Dominican Republic.[62]

Driver further tried to convince the perpetually obstructionist Bureau of the Budget (BOB) of the merits of such a program. He told BOB director Kermit Gordon, "The immediate situation in Viet Nam creates a climate favorable to enactment of legislation. . . . Realistically and equitably, I believe we must afford some additional recognition by way of wanted veterans' benefits to those members of our armed forces serving in such hot spots as Viet Nam."[63] Limiting benefits chronologically and geographically to areas designated by executive order as hostile would greatly reduce the cost and the political obstacles to enacting a new G.I. Bill. Similar proposals had already begun to enter Congress. On January 15, Massachusetts Republican Leverett Saltonstall introduced a bill that would have made veterans of hot spots eligible for benefits similar to those offered under previous bills.

The BOB remained unmoved by the new proposals. The bureau's Sam Hughes wrote Lee White to endorse the White House's objections to S.9 and also to repudiate the VA's compromise proposal. Hughes noted that since 1963, servicemen facing hazardous conditions had been given an additional fifty-five dollars a month in pay, an amount he deemed sufficient to preclude the need for further educational and readjustment benefits. The only thing to which the BOB would consent was an increase in disability payment and the extension of an automobile grant to veterans injured in service. Hughes cautioned the White House to "firmly hold the line" against anything more generous and to push instead for broader public programs.[64]

By the middle of 1965, the battle over S.9 heated up, with few signs of compromise. In May, Yarborough again wrote the White House to lay out his justification for S.9. This time he appealed to Johnson's political savvy. Claiming that the bill would probably pass both houses when put to a vote, Yarborough informed the president that the Republicans were positioning themselves as "the Party concerned with helping the fighting man." Support of S.9, he suggested, would allow the Democrats to regain the mantle of "friend to the GI." He also appealed to Johnson's sense of social justice, arguing that because of various deferments, the majority of draftees tended to be "poor boys who cannot finance college or marriage. . . . [T]hey are the type of boys that you and I grew up with, but they are the minority of their age group who are pushed off into service for two years or longer." He ended his letter with the usual emotive plea that "[t]hose who are guarding freedom for all of us around the world, should come home to classrooms, not to unemployment lines and checks."[65]

In June, Yarborough submitted the final report of the Committee on Labor and Public Welfare on S.9. Here Yarborough made his most thorough defense of the bill yet. Since the Bradley Commission, most opponents of a Cold War G.I. Bill argued that noncombat military service did not incur enough sacrifice on the part of veterans to warrant readjustment benefits. In his committee report Yarborough systematically laid out the reasons why Cold War veterans *did* suffer disadvantages relative to nonveterans and, therefore, deserved additional compensation. He outlined the potential threats around the globe from the Soviet Union, from China, and in Vietnam and the Dominican Republic as evidence that the definition of peacetime in the 1960s was far different from the peacetime conditions of the 1930s. The presence of the Cold War draft demanded that civilians faced significant disruptions in their lives and were denied the opportunities of the nation's "free enterprise, [and] individualistic way of life." Only the ongoing threat of war, noted Yarborough, demanded such sacrifices.[66]

Yarborough accepted the point that Cold War service did not involve comparable sacrifice to wartime service. This principle was reflected in the comparatively lesser amount of assistance offered under S.9. Under previous G.I. Bills, veterans had to serve ninety days before becoming eligible for benefits; S.9 decreed that the veterans serve 180 days. The bill also denied business loans and mustering-out pay to Cold War veterans. Moreover, S.9 offered only $110 in education benefits per month to veterans, the same amount offered Korean War veterans over a decade previously. This amount failed to take into account the rising costs of tuition and living expenses in the intervening years but perhaps more accurately reflected the lesser readjustment needs of noncombat veterans.

The committee report went on to reject calls for a benefits package that aided only those who served in hostile areas. Yarborough's reasoning was that the original G.I. Bill was not meant to be a reward for facing fire. Instead, it was designed to compensate veterans for time lost from civilian life. Military service necessitated such a sacrifice irrespective of where one served. In addition, because only a president could designate an "area of hostility," such a declaration "would be an admission of U.S. active military participation in the conflict and would be contrary to the foreign policy of the United States."[67] Eventually, the committee reported out S.9 favorably, but not unanimously. Five senators, led by New York Republican Jacob Javits, offered a minority view that favored Leverett Saltonstall's hot spots bill. Javits and his fellow dissenters remained unconvinced by Yarborough's arguments and advocated instead benefits only for those "who have been subjected to the hazards of war," adding, "it is our sincere belief that in accord with long established American tradition it is these veterans who are entitled to these benefits."[68]

By highlighting in the report the very real sacrifices made by Cold War veterans, Yarborough aimed to undercut the argument that most veterans had not been negatively impacted by military service—one of the main tenets of opposition to S.9. Combined with the economic, military, and social engineering arguments, the bill was finally developing momentum on Capitol Hill. On July 19, 1965, the Senate voted on the measure. Walter Mondale opened the debate by relating how the G.I. Bill had helped him continue his education after service in the Korean War. He reiterated Yarborough's argument that the country was not really at peace because of Cold War tensions. Next, Hiram Leong Fong (R-HI), cosponsor of S.9, praised Yarborough for having "steadfastly and tirelessly led the struggle for enactment of this vital program."[69] Fong attempted to allay many of the old fears over veterans' benefits. Praising the patriotism of those currently in uniform, he lauded the Cold War G.I.s as "the Minute Men of our times." He also reiterated that the bill was first and foremost a readjustment measure and not a bonus offered to those merely carrying out their patriotic duty. "Every American," proclaimed Fong, "owes a duty to serve his country, but we as Members of Congress know that there is a corresponding responsibility on our part to take care of them."[70]

But following the obligatory patriotic epithets from other sponsors of the bill, the debate turned more confrontational as several senators attempted to add amendments that would have changed the nature and philosophy of Yarborough's legislation. Leverett Saltonstall introduced the most contentions amendment. As his own bill, S.520, had advocated, his amendment attempted to limit eligibility for benefits to veterans of hot spots only. Strom Thurmond—with whom Yarborough had figuratively and literally fought over civil rights legislation the year before— spoke up in defense of this proposal.[71] Echoing similar sanguine notions put forward by Warren Harding in the 1920s, Thurmond noted, "It is an honor for a man to serve his country in peace or in war. I do not look upon one who serves in peacetime as having his life jeopardized to the extent that his country owes him the same kind of consideration given to veterans of World War II or the Korean conflict."[72] Yarborough, Saltonstall, and Robert F. Kennedy then engaged in a lively debate over the problems involved in placing such limitations on eligibility. Yarborough and Kennedy pressed Saltonstall on whether soldiers in areas such as the Dominican Republic or Berlin should receive benefits, or B-52 pilots flying out of Guam who might happen to crash in the South China Sea—an area technically outside of a declared hot spot. The lack of clarity in defining such areas and conditions, claimed Yarborough, pointed to "the utter unworkability of the amendment."[73] Saltonstall finally called for a voice vote on the amendment. Thirty-six senators voted for it, fifty-two against, with twelve not voting.

Two further amendments were then dismissed with far less discussion. Colorado Republican Peter Dominick had an amendment to limit benefits only to veterans of South Vietnam voted down by a vote of fifty-three to thirty-one. In retrospect, this amendment had great merit because it could have led to higher benefits for those who needed it most in the coming years, but it received little debate. Kentucky Republican John Cooper tried, as he had done in previous deliberations on Cold War G.I. Bills, to convert education benefits to loans instead of outright grants. This measure, Cooper suggested, would avoid rewarding those with no real interest in higher education. Unconvinced, the Senate voted it down by a vote of sixty-five to twenty. With the deliberations over, S.9 passed the Senate by a vote of sixty-nine to seventeen. Yarborough had done his part, but this was not the first time a Cold War G.I. Bill had left the Senate. Now the administration and the House had to reverse their earlier obstinacy if the bill was to become law. While the Senate moved forward apace, Lyndon Johnson remained largely silent on the bill, preferring instead that the VA present the administration's views on Capitol Hill. In July, Johnson dismissed the veterans' benefits issue, claiming there was already enough legislation to keep Congress busy for the remainder of the session. And as far as Vietnam was concerned, he had far graver things on his mind as the month drew to a close.

On July 28, a somber-looking Johnson gave a televised speech in which he committed a further fifty thousand soldiers to South Vietnam. Noting that "I do not find it easy to send the flower of our youth, our finest young men, into battle," he described the decision as "the most agonizing and the most painful duty of your President."[74] This increase brought U.S. numbers in South Vietnam to 125,000, and soon thereafter monthly draft calls almost doubled to thirty-five thousand a month. Though conflicted by this move, Johnson was clearly committing the United States to a much more intensive conflict than he was prepared to publicly admit. Moreover, he remained determined to limit the domestic impact of the military build-up. Consequently, he refused to mobilize the national reserves and chose instead to rely on draft call-ups to fulfill the military's manpower needs.

The desire to immunize the public from the costs and consequences of the burgeoning conflict further diminished the administration's willingness to embrace a new full-blown G.I. Bill. Endorsing such a measure would be recognition that the nation might be wading into the same treacherous waters as in World War II and Korea. But the pressure for a stronger executive position on the G.I. Bill issue was growing and was emanating from many concerned parties. William Driver informed Johnson that "a recommendation by the President is justified in principle and would be well received both by the Congress and by the public."[75] Bill Moyers, special assistant to the president, warned that the White House needed to be more proactive for fear that Yarborough's bill might "slip through unless we act."[76] Several concerned citizens also let their feelings be known to Johnson. The mother of one marine informed Johnson that her son told her of his hopes for the passage of the Cold War G.I. Bill because "[i]t would help a lot if we felt we had something to come back to and felt that somebody gives a damn about us."[77] The uncle of another Vietnam soldier wrote Johnson, "a word from you to both Sen. Ralph Yarborough, and Rep. Olin Teague would hasten this bill to a favorable conclusion."[78] Johnson still refused to take a strong stand on the veterans' benefits issue. Instead, he consented to a BOB request for an "informal and quiet working group to rack up alternatives," comprised of the agencies most affected by the bill.[79]

The informal group worked throughout the fall and gave numerous prescriptions for an administration-backed bill. The Bureau of the Budget, Veterans Administration, Department of Health, Education, and Welfare, and Department of Defense passed around various proposals, and by December, the nucleus of an administration bill was taking shape. As the VA and the administration had always wanted, the new bill would limit eligibility to veterans serving in hostile areas. One suggestion for the wording of the bill specified that benefits should be "for the purpose of providing educational opportunities to those veterans whose readjustment problems have been accentuated by hazardous duty or service in areas of special hazard, such as Vietnam."[80] In a cost-saving measure that clearly pleased the BOB, eligibility for benefits would be extended only as far back as October 1, 1963. This date would have left all of the veterans who had served between January 31, 1955, and October 1, 1963, with no claims to benefits. The Department of Health, Education, and Welfare proposed that veterans who had not served in a combat area could receive a grant for college of up to eight hundred dollars per year or a lesser training allowance to be administered under the Manpower Development and Training Act.[81] As it had under Kennedy, the Department of Defense continued to cling to the belief that education benefits would hurt personnel retention, prompting Yarborough to later complain to the *Austin American* newspaper that "I had the support of Kennedy and Johnson until they went to the presidency. Then they began to listen to [Secretary of Defense Robert] McNamara. He seemed to mesmerize them."[82] While the administration refined its plans, Olin Teague's Veterans' Affairs Committee had begun to stir in the House.

In 1960, Teague's committee had effectively killed a previous attempt at a Senate-passed G.I. Bill, and in the fall of 1965 Teague seemed in no rush to pass the newer version. In a meeting with Sam Hughes of the BOB, White House special assistant Douglass Cater, and the VA's William Driver, Teague indicated that he would take no action on any education bill other than opening committee hearings.[83] Yarborough claimed that Teague's committee "had been dragging its feet purposely."[84] In part, the committee's sluggishness was logistical. A total of 133 different House members had submitted 139 bills regarding veterans' education benefits through which Teague's committee had to sort. Many of them duplicated each other, but Teague's committee still had some forty-seven viable bills to consider, including two authored by Teague. Most offered either wide-ranging benefits similar to Yarborough's S.9, or limited benefits only to veterans of hot spots. But the delay also resulted in part from Teague's determination to stamp his authority on the final legislation. The White House was aware of Teague's ego on veterans' issues. The BOB's Charles Schultze warned, "He would like the ball himself. He would just as soon have the Administration make only general statements about this and let his committee work the bill."[85]

At the end of August, 1965, Teague's House Veterans' Affairs Committee held hearings on the numerous proposals for a new G.I. Bill, including Yarborough's. The hearings provided the setting for a thorough and revealing examination of the differing economic and ideological perspectives on veterans' benefits and, crucially, provided Yarborough a forum to make his case directly to Teague and the House. Of the many bills in front of the committee, the ones that received the most serious discussion were Yarborough's S.9 and the hot spots bills that sought to limit a new G.I. Bill only to those veterans in the direct line of fire. The VA's William Driver put forward the administration's opposition that "service under current conditions does not present on a widespread basis the rigors and hazards as does wartime service" and that an expensive G.I. Bill would undermine Johnson's goal of "making educational opportunities more readily available to everyone."[86] Driver also cited the availability of the universal education provisions of the Great Society and the NDEA as a reason not to provide widespread benefits to all veterans. Although Driver was correct in highlighting that there existed more educational opportunities for veterans in 1965 than for those in 1945 or even 1955, his, and the administration's, position sought to change the effects of the G.I. Bill in subtle, but very significant, ways. The original G.I. Bill had provided full coverage of a veteran's educational costs. The suggestion from Driver was that a new G.I. Bill did not have to provide similar coverage; rather, it would be just one part of a broad range of ways veterans could pay for school. In effect, it was an acceptance that the government did not have an obligation to guarantee the same educational opportunities that veterans of World War II enjoyed.

The star of the hearings was undoubtedly Ralph Yarborough, who provided a thorough, erudite, and compelling case for his Cold War G.I. Bill. This was his chance to convince his House counterparts of the merits of his bill, and he was not about to waste it. Teague sat and watched as Yarborough eviscerated the litany of House objections raised against S.9 in a presentation described by committee member Paul Fino (R-NY) as "very enthusiastic, very exuberant, [and] very enlightening."[87] Yarborough was very calculating in opening his comments by reminding Teague of the similarities between his S.9 and Teague's own Korean War G.I. Bill. Yarborough noted that S.9 followed the form and function of the Korean bill and that the Korean bill had rewarded noncombat veterans because anyone who entered service in January 1955 (when the Korean bill expired) could still claim benefits even if he or she left service in 1959 and had never heard a hostile shot fired. Teague remained silent. Yarborough then noted that S.9 also reflected the relatively diminished danger faced by noncombat veterans by offering less funding and by requiring 180 days of service for eligibility instead of the ninety required for the 1944 and 1952 bills (Yarborough had initially favored ninety days but was willing to compromise on this point). By Yarborough's own reckoning, veterans in 1965 would have to receive $153.68 a month instead of the $110 he was suggesting to afford the same quality of education that Korean War veterans had been able to buy with their $110. Addressing those who claimed that Cold War veterans should not receive as much as Korean veterans, he stated, "I say to those people . . . they are not getting as good a deal."[88]

Next, Yarborough addressed the question of civic obligation and military service. He affirmed that his bill was not a bonus and was not an unearned entitlement. He shared the concern that benefits should not be something citizens sought out for military service. "This bill," he stated, "is a veterans' readjustment bill, not a bonus bill." S.9 was intended to help enlisted men and women catch up for time they had lost from civilian life, not give them a significant advantage over their civilian peers. He expressed his faith that the American people would not lower themselves to such base motivations and stated, "To those who would reduce the purpose of this bill to those concepts, I can only retort that I conceive the level of patriotism in our country to be of a higher level." In words that echoed closely those of the Bradley Report, he argued that "[s]ervice to one's country should be, and presently is, based on a moral obligation to defend the principles by which we live." For Yarborough, then, a new G.I. Bill was not designed to turn veterans into a privileged class; rather it was designed to ensure that those veterans called from civilian life were not disadvantaged by service. "Everyone," he claimed, "should have 'the pursuit of happiness' without being penalized unfairly for securing the safety of the rest of us. . . . [T]hey are saving the liberties we are all enjoying."[89]

Finally, to the suggestion of limiting the bill to just Cold War hot spots, Yarborough raised several objections. The first was a practical one. If the administration was required to designate areas of peril for America's soldiers in order for them to receive benefits, the very act of this declaration might escalate diplomatic tensions. Such actions might, he suggested, cast the U.S. as an aggressor in potentially combustible situations and could prove imprudent "at a time when we are trying to reach an accord with the Communist world." Yarborough's second objection to the hot spots bills proved even more compelling. His bill, like the previous G.I. Bills, was a readjustment tool for veterans. This meant that it was designed to correct educational or vocational shortcomings incurred from time spent away from civilian life. Where and how that time was spent was irrelevant to Yarborough; a veteran's readjustment needs were not determined by the nature of his or her service. "Why must we say to our servicemen," he asked, "that you must place your body on the firing line before you are deemed worthy of being educated?"[90]

To support this position, he offered persuasive evidence that the G.I. Bills for World War II and Korea were offered to all veterans who served within the designated time frames for those conflicts and did not discriminate according to type of service. Both of those vaunted bills gave benefits to soldiers who were serving in what could be considered peacetime conditions. Using figures provided by the Department of Defense, Yarborough revealed that veterans who were eligible for the World War II G.I. Bill but who never served overseas included

25 percent of the army, 13 percent of the navy, and 29 percent of the marines. For Korea, the numbers of those servicemen who could claim benefits without serving in the combat theater were even more pronounced. Thirty-four percent of eligible army veterans did not serve overseas during the time of the Korean War, along with 61 percent of marines and 61 percent of air force personnel. Seventy-nine percent of navy servicemen and women served outside of the theater of operations. Moreover, these numbers did not take into account those who may have served in hostile areas but in support positions that incurred little risk. "These personnel," commented Yarborough, "who never saw the glimmer of the far-off shore and never heard the sound of hostile cannons rumbling in the distance received the needed educational benefits of the G.I. Bill, and rightly so."[91] The Cold War veteran, the senator concluded, was worthy of similar consideration, irrespective of wherever or whenever he or she served. The Cold War demanded that citizens continue to be drawn from civilian life. The global nature of the conflict dictated that soldiers had little control over where they served or under what conditions. To Yarborough, the very act of service was sufficient to entitle veterans to assistance when they were attempting to catch up with those who had not served.

After watching his longtime antagonist put on an impressive show in his own backyard, Teague finally spoke up. When he did, he did not address any of Yarborough's points directly and remained quite reserved in his comments. He limited himself to the vague statement that his opposition to a liberal Cold War G.I. Bill "has not changed in 10 years," and—hinting at his fiscal conservatism—that his goal was to pass a bill that "we can live with." One point upon which Yarborough and Teague agreed was that the Department of Defense's claim that a G.I. Bill would hurt retention levels made little sense. Rather than inhibiting recruitment, Teague thought that a new G.I. Bill might attract more citizens into uniform. "I think the Department of Defense," he claimed, "is as wet as a wet hen."[92] The hearings continued with several representatives who had sponsored hot spots bills continuing their objections to S.9. But these voices of opposition were diminishing. Opposition in the House had been the biggest stumbling block to Yarborough's previous attempts to pass a Cold War G.I. Bill. Now, that opposition was crumbling. Vietnam had changed everything.

When Yarborough had fought for a Cold War G.I. Bill in 1959 and again in the early 1960s, few people were convinced by his arguments. But 1965 had been a critical year in the United States' intervention in Vietnam. Operation Rolling Thunder, the sustained bombing of Communist targets in Vietnam, had begun in February. Marines had landed ashore in Da Nang in March. Johnson's call for more troops in July meant that by the year's end, there were 184,000 American troops in South Vietnam. Close to fifteen hundred had already died, with a further five thousand wounded.[93] The need for a new G.I. Bill had gained far greater urgency. When Yarborough introduced the bill on the floor for the fourth time in January 1965, Alaskan senator Ernest Greuning noted, "there is an additional reason for this legislation which did not exist in previous congresses. Entitled to such assistance are not only cold war draftees but also the participants in our undeclared war in South Vietnam."[94] Several representatives who had sponsored legislation similar to S.9 also cited the situation in Vietnam as the reason a new bill was now needed. South Dakota's E. Y. Berry noted that soldiers in Southeast Asia "are facing the same hazards as their brothers-in-arms in World War II and Korea. In the steaming jungles of Vietnam sometimes it's far worse."[95] Crucially, however, most agreed on one point that made them favor a more expansive Cold War G.I. Bill over legislation geared exclusively toward Vietnam Conflict veterans: they now saw Vietnam as only one part in the broader threat faced by America in the Cold War.

By 1965, Yarborough's colleagues were becoming convinced of his point that the deteriorating situation in Vietnam provided sufficient evidence that at any time the Cold War could erupt in hostilities and, therefore, all military personnel lived with the same constant threat of danger. For this reason, lawmakers were willing to classify those servicemen and women serving in Southeast Asia as eligible for the same benefits as all Cold War veterans. Having established this paradigm, Congress abandoned any special consideration to the distinct sacrifice of combat theater veterans in Vietnam in crafting its legislation. Because Vietnam combat veterans were now lumped in with all other veterans, their suggested level of benefits was kept low as the lawmakers sought to reduce the costs of the program. Not surprisingly, when those veterans emerged from "the steaming jungles" of their "very real war" several years later, they were left to wonder why the government now considered their sacrifice to be less than that made by their World War II and Korean War "brothers-in arms."

Vietnam also forced a major reevaluation in the attitude of veterans' organizations toward Yarborough's legislation. The American Legion had never organized in support of a Cold War G.I. Bill, holding fast to the notion that Cold War service did not generally require sufficient disruption in veterans' lives. Legion representative John Corcoran informed Teague's committee that his organization had not taken a stand on such legislation because it was "related to persons who had not had war service." He now conceded that the increasing Cold War tensions as exemplified by Vietnam "now justify and, in fact, compel the American Legion to take an active part in seeking fair treatment for present members of the Armed Forces."[96] While no declared state of war yet existed for the United States, he argued that "acts of war" were now being committed as a part of the Cold War. For the Legion, conflicts such as Vietnam represented the new reality of warfare in the nuclear age. Not entirely abandoning their conservatism, the Legion did suggest that the new G.I. Bill ought to cover only those veterans who had served since August 5, 1964—the formal start date of America's military involvement in Vietnam. That way all Vietnam veterans would be covered, but not those veterans who had served between 1955 and 1964.

Similarly, the VFW's Francis Stover informed Teague's committee that his organization believed that "military service in peacetime had changed," and in an age of prosperity "it is fair that our government should show its grateful appreciation."[97] Just weeks before the House hearings, the VFW had, at its Chicago convention, adopted a resolution supporting benefits for "all members of our Armed Forces who are serving on active duty in our protracted struggle against communism."[98] In his monthly Capitol Digest column for *VFW Magazine*, Stover noted that the resolution "recognizes while only a comparative few may face enemy fire, all are ready to serve when the need arises."[99] The bill now enjoyed the support of the two most powerful veterans' lobbying organizations. Before Teague's hearings were concluded, their stamp of approval was replicated by representatives from the education community and from organized labor. Along with the strong support in the Senate and growing support in the House, the Cold War G.I. Bill was now building significant momentum.

Yarborough kept up the pressure on all concerned. He flooded the press with regular news releases on the virtues of the bill. As the *Austin American* reported, he gave speeches to everyone who would listen, including "Democratic or veterans groups from Boston to San Diego." He was delighted to see veterans rally on behalf of the bill. Maryland veterans attended many of the hearings in DC while others across the nation undertook letter-writing campaigns. When asked if he was behind any of the mobilizing efforts, Yarborough told the Austin newspaper, "Let's say that we didn't discourage any activity on behalf of the bill."[100] His efforts were paying off.

By the end of 1965, Teague was beginning to accept the inevitability of a universal bill. Again, it was Vietnam—and, perhaps, a recognition that the prevailing winds were blowing against him on the Hill—that had led him to this realization.[101] He had come to accept that the nation did have an increasing obligation to the new round of men and women being sent to Southeast Asia. Teague remained one of the more ardent supporters of Lyndon Johnson's military escalation in Vietnam and spent many hours discussing strategy with the president and his top advisors. He believed in the virtue of America's mission and advocated using all means necessary short of nuclear weapons to bring a swift and successful conclusion to hostilities. Teague also counted General William Westmoreland as a close personal friend. In addition, in 1965 Teague had one son flying covert missions in Laos and another soon to join the State Department's Agency for International Development mission in Saigon. A visit to Vietnam in November and December of 1965, in which he briefly visited with his son, reaffirmed his first-hand knowledge of the devastating impact of war on young lives. As he wrote to one of his constituents, this was no "red carpet" tour. As he had done in the Korean War, Teague traveled to the theater of war with the intention of uncovering the reality of the conflict, warts and all. He called in favors from fellow Texans and former World War II colleagues to gain access to some of the more dangerous areas of the war zone. He noted that a new G.I. Bill was one of the most important concerns raised by the soldiers and promised them that upon his return he would pass a new G.I. Bill "out of committee in January or February."[102] But staying true to his nature, if there was to be more universal legislation, he wanted to make sure that it was not as costly as Yarborough's proposal.

To that end, Teague favored a less expensive program, one that would limit the further growth of the federal government. Teague had watched with displeasure as liberals in his own party had set about expanding the role of the government under Lyndon Johnson. He balked at education programs that offered assistance to the impoverished or to what he saw as draft-dodging college students. Indeed, Teague found much to dislike about the Great Society and the general leftward drift of his nation. He opposed civil rights legislation, for instance, because it infringed on the rights of individuals to make their own choices. Upset by the unrest on the nation's campuses, which he blamed on the growing permissiveness of society, he even introduced legislation in 1969 that would cut federal funding to any schools that did not clamp down on unruly faculty. In introducing the bill, he argued that "[t]hese disorders are ridiculous, and we're fools if we continue to support schools and faculty members who in many cases actually encourage them. There is a great deal of difference between academic freedom and the support of anarchy and the encouragement of law violators."[103] Teague also labeled antiwar protesters "a dumb bunch . . . doing exactly what Hanoi would like for them to do."[104] Unsurprisingly, he consistently opposed Johnson's main Great Society social initiatives. Favoring guns over butter, Teague told one Texan voter, "I think it is high time we were more aggressive in Viet Nam and less aggressive with the war on poverty here at home."[105] But for Teague, a new G.I. Bill was more of an earned reward, especially now that the likelihood of facing fire had become that much greater.

With Teague now converted, a Cold War G.I. Bill seemed inevitable. All that remained was to work out the scale and generosity of the new law and to convince the president of its merits. In December, the administration had shown a draft of its far less costly hot spots bill to Teague before introducing it to his committee under the designation H.R.11985. Teague claimed to be under "heavy pressure" from the BOB and the DOD to pass the scaled-down benefits package, but he now seemed dedicated to a more universal bill. Douglass Cater informed Lyndon Johnson that Teague's response to the bill was one of "grave reservations and [he] seems to be leaning towards the Korean-type version."[106] Teague's own bill, H.R.12410, reflected his preference for benefits that covered all Cold War veterans, but he shared some of the administration's concerns over the cost of Yarborough's bill. Teague's bill

Olin Teague and Lyndon Johnson pore over a map of South Vietnam. Teague was one of the more outspoken advocates of America's mission in South Vietnam, not wanting to yield an inch in the global fight against communism. Teague visited Vietnam on a number of occasions and had two sons serve in Southeast Asia. *Courtesy of the Lyndon B. Johnson Presidential Library.*

would cost approximately $327 million in its first year compared with $360 million for Yarborough's S.9. Johnson's hot spots bill would have cost only $150 million for the first year.[107] The main savings in Teague's bill over S.9 came from reducing the monthly allowance from $110 to $100 a month, and providing benefits at a rate of only one month for every month served. S.9 offered benefits for 1.5 months for every month served. The BOB pushed Johnson to continue pressuring Teague into passing out an even less costly bill. On January 29, Schultze asked the president to "[c]all representative Teague and indicate that while we continue to support Cold War G.I. benefits, the bill now being considered by the Committee is unacceptable."[108] But on February 1, Teague's Veterans' Affairs Committee unanimously approved his H.R.12410. Thereafter, the passage of the bill moved swiftly.

Despite the differences in cost between S.9 and H.R.12410, the Cold War G.I. Bill avoided going into conference. To appease Yarborough, Teague agreed to keep the senator's title S.9 on the bill if he agreed to the House's reductions in costs. Reluctantly, Yarborough consented and a final compromise version of the Veterans' Readjustment Benefits Act of 1966 went back to a vote in both houses. Teague opened proceedings in the House on February 7. He claimed that the bill had the support of the administration and all of the main veterans' groups. He proclaimed it "a bill that every Member can vote for and be happy with."[109] In an admission that would soon come to have significant bearing on the lives of veterans, Teague emphasized "that it is not the intention of this legislation to establish a program which completely subsidizes the cost of a veteran's education or training program, as well as his living costs. . . . It is expected that in many cases the veteran will be required to make a contribution to the cost of his own education."[110] Again, by refusing to promise to underwrite the full costs of a veteran's education, Teague willingly accepted that the Vietnam generation would not enjoy the same level of benefits as its predecessors. Even though the 1944 G.I. Bill never explicitly promised to pay for all of a veteran's education costs, in reality it did. The generosity of the original bill combined with the relatively low tuition costs after World War II gave veterans the option of attending almost any school of their choosing without having to contribute any of their own money. By the late 1960s, veterans who returned home expecting the same total coverage that their predecessors had enjoyed now found that the government had no intention of picking up their entire tab.

Debates on the floor of the House highlighted both the promise and the problems of the proposed new legislation. William Jennings Bryan Dorn (D-SC) stated, "This bill is necessary. It is fair and it is timely. The American people are ready for this legislation."[111] Paul Fino (R-NY) called the bill "a tribute to our veterans, not a grudging concession to national opinion."[112] But the praise was far from universal. A succession of House members rose to express their reservations over the low monthly allowance. Robert Dole (R-KS) called the bill "not completely satisfactory," while Richard Roudebush (D-IN) described the payments as "inadequate."[113] Many attacked Lyndon Johnson for pressuring the House into passing a less expensive measure. John Saylor (R-PA) called the bill "a disgrace" and fumed, "we are afraid to give these men who are out defending our lives and our country any more than $100 a month under the threat of a Presidential veto."[114] Had they been given the opportunity, Roudebush and Saylor might have sought further debate or even added amendments to the bill in order to make it more generous. But Teague made sure that could never happen.

When Teague's powers of persuasion failed to convince his fellow representatives of the merit of his bill, he employed a different tactic. Teague reported his bills out under the Suspension of the Rules parliamentary procedure. This measure was in place generally to help noncontroversial bills pass the House with little need for debate or amendment. It dictated that debates on bills would be limited to forty minutes and that no amendments could be added to the legislation. Therefore, House members could not effectively touch Teague's bill once he had put his stamp of approval on it. Representatives who considered the 1966 bill too sparing were denied the chance to offer any alternatives. Frank Horton (R-NY), who had submitted an earlier bill offering higher benefits, lamented that he could not introduce an amendment to increase the monthly allowance. Philip Burton (D-CA) spoke for many when he said, "Although I will support it, my one objection to the bill is that it does not go far enough. However, half a loaf is better than none."[115] Under the Suspension of Rules, the bills did require a two-thirds majority instead of a simple majority, but this proved no problem for Teague: he convinced his fellow legislators that any votes against his bill would delay veterans getting any kind of support. With the war escalating, no one wanted to be tarred with that brush. In the coming years of debates education benefits, Teague would use this procedure repeatedly to get his way. With only the occasional voice of objection, the House tended to yield to him quite meekly: The House passed the bill by a vote of 388 to 0.

Before the bill went forward to the White House, the Senate had to approve Teague's changes in a vote that took place on February 10. Yarborough expressed his disappointment at the "insufficient" benefits, but conceded that the reductions "are not yet seriously crippling to the goal of providing a full program of educational and other readjustment benefits."[116] Senators raised few objections to the House changes. Peter Dominick (R-CO) even called them a "welcomed improvement" and praised Teague's "fiscal prudence."[117] The amended bill passed the Senate by a vote of ninety-nine to zero. Mike Mansfield (D-MT) concluded the Senate's debate by praising Yarborough's efforts in securing its passage.

"This action today," he stated, "represents a high mark in many long and arduous battles for veterans by the senior Senator from Texas. Veterans are indeed fortunate in having an advocate of his great skill and tireless devotion."[118]

Lyndon Johnson still could have exercised his power of veto over the bill at this stage, but no president had ever blocked a veterans' education program and the political costs of doing so could have been considerable. William Driver indicated that the administration's interest in seeing a Cold War G.I. Bill pass "has been intensified since the escalation of combat activities in Vietnam."[119] And while Johnson had hoped for a reduced benefits package, he appeared to have little enthusiasm to carry the fight any further with a veto. White House staff members informed the president that, "despite its obvious disadvantages, you will want to associate yourself fully with the benefits that will flow from this bill."[120] After the House vote, the *New York Times* carried the front-page headline "President Loses." But Johnson's defeat was not total. His pressure on Teague to cut costs had resulted in a final bill that few considered generous. The signing ceremony was delayed until Teague and Driver returned from overseas, but on March 3, 1966, Johnson signed the Cold War G.I. Bill into law in a public ceremony in the East Room of the White House. Johnson, Yarborough, and Teague were joined on the day by Defense Secretary Robert McNamara, Secretary of State Dean Rusk, Vice President Hubert Humphrey, General William Westmoreland, and several representatives from veterans' organizations. In his signing remarks, Johnson stated, "Because it is for education, I am going to sign this bill, even though it provides hundreds of millions of dollars more than I thought it advisable to recommend or to ask for this year."[121] Later on in the day he quipped, "I just had my budget busted wide open this morning by my colleagues from Texas, but it was on behalf of soldiers who needed education. It couldn't be busted for a better purpose."[122]

Yarborough's crusade had reached a moderately successful conclusion. Upon accepting a pen from the signing ceremony, he commented, "I have never felt so happy as when I stood at our President's elbow as he signed that bill."[123] The 1966 Cold War G.I. Bill, Public Law 89-358, did ensure that nearly four million veterans who had had their lives interrupted by military service since the end of the Korean War could claim benefits to help them further their education or career objectives.

Standing just over the president's right shoulder, Ralph Yarborough can barely contain his glee as Lyndon Johnson signs the 1966 Cold War G.I. Bill into law on March 3, 1966. The president and fellow Texan Olin Teague (far right of the image) look a little more circumspect. *Courtesy of the Lyndon B. Johnson Presidential Library.*

In some ways, the bill was a challenge to the long-standing precedent of not offering benefits to those soldiers who had never served directly during a time of hostilities. The bill went against generations of presidents and politicians concerned with the economic effects on the nation and the moral implications for the nation's soldiers. Some opponents of the 1966 G.I. Bill continued to argue that military service was something for which every citizen should be held accountable and should be a matter of civic pride. Fears persisted that the new benefits had opened the possibility that military service could now be a viable means for economic or social advancement and not a natural obligation of living in a republic. A 1968 *New York Times* editorial called the concept of Cold War benefits for noncombatants "retrograde in its philosophy" and warned of the "creation of a permanent privileged class of veterans, a postwar mercenary class uncongenial to the national heritage . . . [that would] aggrandize and solidify the specialized status of the veteran and the concept of veteran versus citizen."[124] But, by 1966

Yarborough had successfully countered such arguments by placing the benefits in the context of the nation's perpetual Cold War preparedness and the increasing numbers of dangerous situations faced by the nation's soldiers.

Soon, however, the problems of the new G.I. Bill became apparent. The central flaw in the 1966 G.I. Bill was that it was crafted with the average Cold War veteran in mind, not the combat veteran who might have far greater readjustment needs and expectations. When Vietnam-era veterans began to come home, they were presented with a bill that might have been acceptable for veterans who had serviced B-52s in the Midwest throughout their military service but it was a bill that fell far short of what the combat veterans thought they had earned on the field of battle.

3

A Peacetime Bill for the Warrior

Shortchanging the Vietnam Vets

One of the virtues of the World War II GI Bill was that it provided scholarship money for young men from working-class and lower middle-class backgrounds who would otherwise have had little opportunity for further education. On the surface, the GI Bill enacted in 1966 seemed to do the same thing, but in reality, the level of benefits was so low that participation was greatly restricted for veterans of lower class families who lacked additional resources to draw upon for support.
—*The Nader Report*, 1973

I am a Vietnam veteran . . . with combat experience. I had to endure a great deal of suffering and all I wish now is to have a fair reimbursement from the government for my education.
—Michael W. Dubrick, April 28, 1972

We recognize the GI Bill was not designed—and given the diversity of tuition charges among schools, could not be equitably designed—to cover all of a veteran's educational costs.
—Olney B. Owen, Veterans Administration,
    November 30, 1971

Both during and immediately after the passage of the 1966 G.I. Bill, questions arose about whether the bill had gone far enough in providing adequate readjustment benefits for the new generation of veterans returning to civilian life. The government did, at least, recognize the limitations of the 1966 bill, and soon after its passage both Congress and the Johnson administration examined the option of raising the education benefits. In September 1966, Johnson created a special task force by executive order to examine veterans' benefits. William Driver chaired the task force, which also included representatives from the DOD, the BOB, and the Department of Health and Welfare. Their report, submitted on November 19, included a proposal to increase the monthly allowance to $130 for the single veteran, up from $100, with comparable increases for veterans claiming dependents. The task force also recommended that veterans should be allowed to finish their high school degrees without having to cut into the number of months for which they could claim benefits for higher education. Johnson took the recommendations to heart and sent a special message to Congress on January 31, 1967, on "America's Servicemen and Veterans." The main purpose of his proposals was to "remove the inequalities in the treatment of our Vietnam veterans" and, in keeping with the ideals of the Great Society, "to enlarge the opportunities for educationally disadvantaged veterans."[1] Johnson praised the nation's servicemen and women for "again fighting and giving their lives in the defense of freedom" and added, "It is essential that we convey to them . . . our full recognition and gratitude for their service in Vietnam and in other troubled areas of the world."[2]

He put these principles into practice by proposing the Vietnam Conflict Servicemen and Veterans' Act of 1967. The act incorporated most of the recommendations of the task force, including the thirty-dollar increase in veterans' education benefits and the provisions to help disadvantaged veterans finish their high school education without affecting their college benefits. In addition, Johnson called for disability compensation at full wartime rates for those who served after August 5, 1964, and more liberalized pensions, medical benefits, and life insurance for veterans and their dependents. Johnson had decided the time was right to reward the "defenders of freedom." "With these benefits," he hoped, "we can assure them that we do not intend to let them down in their hour of need."[3]

Sufficiently chastened by the outcry on Capitol Hill, Johnson had also reversed his earlier plans to downsize the VA, declaring in the process, "Candor compels me to admit I have seen some of the hospitals and some of the testimony . . . and they raise doubts in my mind whether we were a hundred percent right."[4] By acceding to calls to keep the threatened hospitals and care facilities open and also promising to include veterans' groups in future policy planning, he was rapidly gaining widespread approval from the veteran community. The VFW praised him for reversing his "antiveteran" trend, and offered its "appreciation for his magnanimous action on behalf of all veterans."[5] But while Johnson was rediscovering the veteran cause, Yarborough had not been idle. In fact, he had preempted Johnson's G.I. Bill proposals by introducing his own legislation to increase benefits early in 1967. Once more, Yarborough's legislation erred far more on the side of generosity than the White House hoped.

Yarborough's new bill, again titled S.9, called for similar increases in monthly allowances, but his bill was much more costly because it offered farm-training, on-the-job-training, and flight-training benefits. The previous G.I. Bills had offered these, but the VA considered them unnecessary because requests for farm and job training had declined precipitously between the 1944 and 1952 bills. Moreover, the VA decried that veterans had undertaken much of their flight training for recreational rather than vocational purposes.[6] A. W. Stratton, chief benefits director of the VA, described the White House bill as "the sounder approach" and pushed for its enactment ahead of S.9.[7] As with the administration's bill, because Yarborough still made no distinction between Cold War and Vietnam combat veterans, his proposed increases offered benefits that were considerably less generous than those given to previous combat veterans. Further muddying the waters, S.16, a bill introduced by Joseph Montoya (D-NM) on the same day as S.9, did seek to provide full wartime benefits exclusively to Vietnam veterans. These benefits would have included full wartime disability compensation rates (roughly 20 percent higher than for noncombat veterans), increased medical benefits, and a $250 burial allowance. But again, there was little consideration given in Washington to the specific needs of returning Vietnam combat veterans as opposed to the needs of Cold War veterans. After eight months of negotiation, an amalgam of the three proposals, under the title S.16, passed the House on August 17 with a 404–0 vote and the Senate on August 23 by a vote of 88–0. The new bill provided all single veterans a monthly stipend of $130 per month with proportional increases for dependents. Johnson's provision of allowing for a high school education remained, as did Yarborough's calls for training, albeit with some stricter eligibility requirements. Pilots, for example, had to have a private license before receiving benefits for a commercial license to eliminate the possibility that veterans would take to the air for recreational purposes. Similarly, farmers had to be already enrolled in an agricultural course or employed in an agricultural position that would benefit from additional training.

On August 31, Johnson held another public signing ceremony in the East Room of the White House, and S.16 became Public Law 90-77. He claimed that the new bill "gives those now in service the same veterans' benefits that have been granted to their brothers in other wars."[8] The bill received a generally enthusiastic reception around the country. Believing the administration's claims that the Vietnam veterans were now gaining treatment equal to that of their predecessors, the *Asheville Citizen* commented, "This bill gives GI's especially those of the Vietnam era, a break they should have." The *Wichita Falls Times* similarly observed, "When a young American, fresh out of high school and on the threshold of adulthood, must spend a year or two fighting for his country, he deserves more tangible rewards than praise and medals. He gets them under the terms of the new 'GI Bill' signed into law by President Johnson."[9]

But the reality remained that the benefits being offered did, in fact, fall well short of the previous iterations of the G.I. Bill. Johnson, therefore, continued to study the veteran question during his final months as president. He established further commissions to study veterans' benefits, one in 1967 and another in 1968 headed by Robert McNamara. He also examined such proposals as "VIPS" (Veterans in Public Service), which sought to place veterans in public service roles such as teachers or firefighters, and "GIVER" (G.I. Volunteer for Education and Redevelopment), which promoted the idea of training veterans to teach in deprived areas.[10] He signed his last significant veterans' education legislation on October 23, 1968. The bill incorporated one key provision offered in previous G.I. Bills (but absent in the 1966 version) by providing one and a half months of benefits for every month a veteran had served but only after he or she had served for eighteen months. The 1966 bill offered only one month of benefits per one month of service. The 1968 bill also extended education opportunities to widows of veterans for the first time. Previously, only the minor dependents of veterans killed or fully disabled could claim benefits. At the signing ceremony, one of Johnson's last before stepping down as president, he offered his thanks to Yarborough, Teague, and Driver for their work over the previous five years before signing Public Law 90-631 into law.[11]

On paper, the new benefits seemed to provide at least a decent opportunity for most Vietnam veterans to enter higher education. And perhaps for those veterans who had served in relatively peaceful conditions, the benefits were roughly commensurate with the sacrifice and service they had rendered their country. But what of the servicemen and women engaged in the battle to keep South Vietnam afloat? Their military service took place in anything but peacetime conditions. Even though, as with World War II and Korea, a majority might not have faced direct peril on a constant basis, many did.

Numerous studies of the combat experience of soldiers who served in Vietnam reveal that the nature of their wartime conditions was at least as brutalizing as it had been to veterans of either World War II or Korea. Many Vietnam veterans returned home with readjustment problems every bit as great as, if not greater than, veterans of those conflicts. Only in the years after Johnson left office did the majority of Vietnam veterans return home. Only when these veterans began to return en masse could any judgment be made on the effectiveness of their benefits as a readjustment tool. The generosity of the previous G.I. Bills had made higher education a feasible and attractive proposition allowing veterans to get their lives back on track. Because debates over the 1966 bill had become enmeshed in wider issues such as democratic obligation and universal education programs, the education benefits first available to Vietnam veterans did not provide the same kind of crutch. Although the 1967 and 1968 amendments aimed to make benefits more comparable, by 1968 Vietnam veterans were still receiving only twenty dollars more than Korean War veterans, despite the rising costs of tuition in the intervening years. Even though Yarborough only had the best of intentions at heart when he fought for a more universal Cold War G.I. Bill, the fact that Vietnam combat veterans would receive the same education benefits as other Cold War veterans compromised the effectiveness of their G.I. Bill as a readjustment tool. Those combatants who came home from Vietnam expecting the same kind of full ride to school soon discovered that for them the 1966 Veterans' Readjustment Act proved to be the wrong bill in the wrong place at the wrong time.

The problems of the bill and the frustrations of the veterans were summed up in a 1969 letter by Vietnam veteran Dennis Rainwater to Lyndon Johnson's successor, Richard Nixon. Having completed a tour of duty in Vietnam as a first lieutenant, Rainwater faced the choice of remaining in Vietnam and gaining a promotion to captain or leaving the service and claiming his hard-earned benefits. With a wife and baby awaiting him in Oklahoma, Rainwater chose the latter and returned home with the goal of continuing his education. Despite anticipating a smooth transition back into civilian life, he soon discovered that his G.I. Bill fell far short of providing him the educational opportunities he sought. In addition to taking sixteen hours of classes, Rainwater had to work a forty-hour week to support his family while in school. Rainwater asked Nixon, "at a time when you are trying to get support for your Vietnam policy, how can you expect such treatment of Veterans to go unnoticed?"[12]

Similarly, the *VFW Magazine* surveyed the dire situation for many returning veterans in 1969 and related the testimony of another midwestern veteran who revealed,

> I have no resentment toward those who went to college, or even rioted while I was in Vietnam, because, tough as it was, I wouldn't have missed the chance for anything—now that I'm back I can say that. But frankly I don't know how I can make out on what we are getting. My wife, Linda, has to work on the side as a typist and we have two small children to look after. I have a job in a gas station after classes. When I get home at night, it's all I can do to study and it's tough on Linda, too, because she has to take care of the children, fix supper and do the wash. Our parents have been swell and have helped a lot, but we can't go on sponging off them. I just don't know what I'll do if I don't make it.[13]

Another veteran interviewed for the magazine added, "I don't know how some of these guys make out at all. A lot of them have just given up and gone back home. I know I'd quit if I weren't single and didn't have parents who were able to help a lot."[14]

Clearly, the protracted legislative battles that had raged at the highest levels of government since the Bradley Report had resulted in a G.I. Bill that seemed to discriminate against combat veterans. The Cold War did not remain cold for every American soldier, and yet those veterans facing fire in global hot spots fell under the same umbrella as those who never stared down a Communist foe. By casting such a wide net and incorporating all veterans, the bill failed to provide the appropriate support to those soldiers on the front lines of America's Cold War struggle. As a consequence, by the end of the 1960s, in the tone and tenor of the veteran angst there arose a growing sense of betrayal and a perception that the government had abandoned its returning warriors.

The first rumblings of discontent over the level of education benefits had surfaced under the Johnson administration. But as millions more veterans returned to civilian life during Richard Nixon's tenure, the crescendo of criticism rose proportionally. Significantly, it was also during the Nixon years that the image of the troubled and neglected Vietnam veteran gained prominence in the news media. Newspapers and magazines began carrying stories of veterans returning with drug or psychological problems, unable to find work, and whose financial and physical readjustment needs the federal government seemed to ignore. Throughout the late 1960s and early 1970s, press reports left the overwhelming impression that Vietnam veterans were facing a difficult readjustment. The *New York Times* contained numerous stories of veteran hardship. Front-page headlines such as "The Vietnam Veteran: Silent, Perplexed, Unnoticed" and "Postwar Shock Besets Ex-G.I.'s" gave an overall impression of veteran suffering.[15] Specific stories on unemployment rates, psychological problems, violent crimes, and drug abuse added the dramatic details.[16] Other print media followed suit. The *Wall Street Journal* noted that unlike with the World War II veteran's return, "the boys are not cheering, nor the men shouting, nor the ladies turning out."[17] The *Washington Post* described Vietnam veterans as "Aliens in Their Land."[18] *Newsweek* highlighted veterans' problems in a 1971 article titled "The Vietnam Vet: 'No One Gives a Damn.'"[19] In 1974, the Senate Committee on Veterans' Affairs printed a collection of *Source Material on the Vietnam Veteran*. Chairman Vance Hartke stated that the compilation "is intended to present a representative spectrum of views concerning these veterans which have appeared in print since the Vietnam

Conflict began."[20] The overwhelming majority of press articles in the 900-page collection presented a damning view of the veterans' readjustment. Not every veteran came home to such difficulties. Those suffering from drug problems or unable to find a job remained a minority. But circumstantial evidence mounted that suggested that many veterans were facing very real readjustment difficulties. A generous G.I. Bill could have alleviated many of these problems, and many veterans wondered why it was not forthcoming.

The veterans' complaints focused almost exclusively on the parsimony of their educational allowances, and they wrote to any politician who they thought could make a difference. Ralph Yarborough, unsurprisingly, received numerous letters from veterans eager to share their tales of hardship. One Pennsylvania veteran wrote Yarborough to explain, "My tuition this year amounts to $2350 with about another $150 for books. The $155 [a month] G.I. Bill benefits which I receive do not even cover my monthly apartment rent, let alone living expenses."[21] Another veteran informed the senator that the increased benefits were "an urgent necessity," adding, "At any time in a nation's history it is not right to play politics with those who have served their country but especially when many of those who make [their] decisions are questioning their earlier judgments. The unpopularity of the war unfortunately does not help those who are most directly involved in it."[22] Veterans of one Texas community college wrote House Speaker Carl Albert to complain, "We need either increased wages or increased benefits for the services we rendered to our country. In these times of economic adjustment, we have discovered that gainful employment is extremely difficult, if not impossible to obtain."[23] Another veteran wrote Albert, "I am a Vietnam veteran . . . with combat experience. I had to endure a great deal of suffering and all I wish now is to have a fair reimbursement from the government for my education."[24] Others complained to the speaker of their "considerable difficulty meeting the cost of going to college," or that "the G.I. Bill has been a great help and has enabled us to attend college at night, [but] it is still not enough to live on with the high cost of living."[25] Joseph Mulholland, associate dean at Fordham University, wrote the New York Times to add, "The disproportionate majority of the deprived and disadvantaged, both black and white, who have fought in Indochina receive stingy handouts; they deserve . . . generous benefits."[26]

Tales of the veterans' economic struggles soon mounted in the press. The *Washington Post* carried news of a "Veterans' Rights March" in the DC area where veterans carried banners with slogans such as "We Demand Decent Living Income for GIs, Vets, and Their Families."[27] A *New York Times* article contained the testimony from one air force veteran who stated, "You want to know what I think of the benefits? I think they stink, man. For the kind of church change they pay you in the service they ought to give you enough for an education when you get out."[28] Tim O'Brien, in a 1974 article for *Penthouse*, related stories of veterans with difficulties making ends meet. One veteran had to borrow money and take a job in a textile factory that paid only two dollars an hour when he tried to use his G.I. Bill in 1969. The veteran recalled, "We ran up plenty of bills, just barely hanging in there . . . me working like a bull all the while trying to study, sweating in the factory, dashing to class."[29]

One of the main failings of the first Vietnam-era G.I. Bill resulted from the changes in the distribution of benefits enacted since the original bill of 1944. Olin Teague's discovery of widespread abuse under the original bill led him to become an outspoken advocate of paying tuition benefits directly to the veterans and not to the schools. His view prevailed in the 1952 and 1966 G.I. Bills. While paying veterans directly may have succeeded in reducing incidents of fraud, it also placed considerable restrictions on how and where veterans could pursue their education. Because Korean and Vietnam-era veterans received a fixed monthly stipend from which to pay for tuition, fees, and books, many found that attending higher-cost institutions, particularly private schools, left them with insufficient funds on which to live. The World War II veteran never had these problems. The original G.I. Bill paid enough in tuition to allow veterans to attend almost any school they wanted. Vietnam veterans did not have this guarantee. If it was Teague's intent to force a veteran to be more self-reliant and to work harder for his or her education, he was certainly getting his wish. But this ideological posturing was causing considerable hardship for many.

Rising tuition costs compounded the veterans' financial difficulties. Tuition in many schools had as much as quadrupled since World War II. Frank V. Otto, director of the New York State Division of Veterans' Affairs, used his G.I. Bill after World War II. It paid his full tuition at Columbia State and gave him sufficient money on which to live every month. Surveying the plight of the Vietnam veterans his agency served, Otto told the New York Times, "There's no way a vet can go to college on the G.I. Bill today, unless he's got some money of his own."[30] Similarly, John Reavis, assistant dean of the University of New York, pointed out, "In 1945, the returning veteran could sustain himself and his family on the G.I. Bill. Today, the cost is astronomical."[31] The authors of a study by the University of Illinois and Parkland College Veterans Association called on lawmakers "to bring benefits up to a level comparable to successful programs of the past" after pointing out that tuition at the University of Illinois had risen 307 percent between 1947 and 1970, fees 430 percent, books 433 percent, and room and board 183 percent.[32]

An additional unforeseen problem arose from the decision to make direct tuition payments to veterans and not directly to the institution of higher education: Differing tuition costs in different states meant that the monthly stipend went further in some states than in others. The monthly stipend was the same across all states. Therefore, in states with a well-developed, low-cost public school system, such as California and Arizona, Vietnam veterans used their benefits in greater numbers compared with their contemporaries in states with high tuition rates, such as Connecticut, New York, and New Jersey. Simply put, because education was cheaper, the money went further and college represented a more affordable option for some veterans than others depending on where they lived. By one New York Times estimate, California veterans received $890 million in federal benefits through 1972 compared with only $315 million in New York. Having a potentially less-educated veteran population caused concern for some northeastern politicians. Westchester representative Ogden Reid noted, "Whenever educational opportunities are less than those of other states, this puts you at an economic disadvantage." New Jersey Democrat Henry Helstoski, chairman of the House Veterans' Affairs Subcommittee on Education and Training, added, "High tuition costs and high living costs are worst in the metropolitan area. . . . You're absolutely clobbered in a 50-mile radius around New York City."[33] By 1973, only 37 percent of New York's Vietnam-era veterans had used their benefits compared with 51 percent of California's veterans.[34] Although different regions may have had dissimilar attitudes toward education, the differences here seemed to be a consequence of the varying costs of tuition. As Helstoski commented, the usage rates "do not reflect a difference in desire—the desire goes across the board."[35]

The sense of public outrage over inadequate benefits intensified throughout Nixon's time in office. Incredulous newspaper editorials helped push the issue of education benefits to the center of the wider discourse on society's neglect of the Vietnam veteran. On July 4, 1969, the *New York Times* called for an increase in education aid to veterans, describing the benefits as "clearly inadequate in terms of today's college costs."[36] The problems persisted, and in a 1972 editorial, the *Times* commented,

> Unlike the men who fought in World War II, the veterans of Vietnam have served in a war over which the country has been sharply divided. The Vietnam War, moreover, called for sacrifices only of those who were in the armed forces, while their compatriots at home have remained largely unaffected.
>
> The veterans of Vietnam ought therefore to receive financial benefits at least comparable to those afforded the veterans of World War II. Yet the educational G.I. Bill of Rights today constituted a niggardly handout, compared to the full funding of college studies which made the post–World War II G.I. Bill so significant a landmark in the expansion of educational opportunities.[37]

Peter Braestrup of the *Washington Post* attacked the government for "Abandoning Our Vietnam Veterans" by failing to enact legislation to increase benefits.[38] The *Boston Globe* cited the Vietnam veterans' "cut-rate educations" and opined that "because the war is unpopular, because the Vietnam veterans do not include the sons of the rich, the powerful and the articulate . . . nobody cares."[39] The *Oklahoma Journal* added, "it is shameful, and our chickens are sure to come home to roost in future times when we may need the services of young Americans to keep our country safe."[40]

One of the few national organizations looking out for the interests of the Vietnam veteran, the National Association of Concerned Veterans (NACV), offered further evidence of the veterans' troubles in a

1973 report on education funding. Based on a study undertaken by the Canisius College Veterans' Club of Buffalo, New York, the NACV report compared the average financial situation of veterans attending schools during the school year 1945–46 and 1971–72. Taking into account rising tuition costs, living costs, and dollar inflation, the report revealed clearly that the 1971–72 benefits placed considerable restrictions on where a Vietnam veteran could pursue an education compared with the options enjoyed by a World War II veteran. Initially, the report offered some solace for the Vietnam veteran. It found that if they used their benefits to attend a public institution at the in-state tuition rate, then the veterans fared rather well. In fact, the 1971–72 benefits paid veterans 10.6 percent *more* than the 1945–46 benefits, even taking the increase in costs into account. But if a veteran chose to attend a private institution, even at the in-state rate, the World War II veteran received 77 percent more than the Vietnam-era veteran. According to the report, the average tuition costs of private education had risen from $769 in 1945–46 to $1,957 in 1971–72 after adjustment for inflation. This made private schools prohibitively expensive for most of the Vietnam-era veterans unless they had some additional funds. Similarly, if a veteran had to go out of state to pursue an education, his or her G.I. Bill became precipitously less beneficial. A World War II veteran paying out-of-state tuition and expenses at a public institution received 36.7 percent more in benefits than the Vietnam-era veteran. For an out-of-state student attending a private institution, the World War II G.I. Bill paid veterans 79.6 percent more than the Vietnam veteran received. The report concluded,

> In 1945, the veteran, due to the provisions of the G.I. Bill, had freedom of choice as to which institution of higher education he wished to attend. The main factor allowing him this freedom of choice was the tuition allowance. As our study has revealed, the average tuition cost for all types of educational institutions, both public and private, fell below the $500.00 ceiling of annual tuition allowance. We believe that each Vietnam Era Veteran should be granted the same degree of choice today that his father had in 1945.[41]

On the education benefits issue, the major veterans' organizations added their voices to the growing outcry. VFW commander-in-chief

Richard Homan noted that "inadequate subsistence payments are dis-
couraging thousands of Vietnam veterans from entering college" and,
having studied the problems facing veterans, concluded that "a situation like this is unfortunate for the country and for the young men who
have been fighting our fight in Vietnam and manning the barricades of
freedom in the four corners of the world."[42] Similarly, American Legion
national commander J. Milton Patrick commented, "It was cruel, I think,
to write a G.I. Bill to help Vietnam veterans get the education that the
WW2 and Korean veterans got, and then set the benefit 'so low that it is
no benefit to the more needy Vietnam vets.'" "Can we not," he added, "in
fairness ask for *enough to go to school*?"[43]

Ralph Nader, the prominent consumer rights activist, offered further
evidence of the veterans' difficulties when he commissioned an extensive investigation into the Vietnam veterans' experience. Published in
1973 as *The Discarded Army: Veterans after Vietnam; the Nader Report
on Vietnam Veterans and the Veterans Administration*—the *Nader
Report*, as it was more commonly named—studied the federal response
to the problems faced by Vietnam veterans with particular emphasis on
the role of the Veterans Administration. The report noted that of all the
federal programs and benefits offered, "none has been more prized by
returning soldiers than the education benefits under the G.I. Bill," but it
confirmed that "the major complaint of Vietnam veterans . . . has been
that the current level of benefits has lagged behind those available after
World War II."[44] The report also corroborated one of the other main
criticisms against the bill, namely, that low payments placed considerable restrictions on the type and location of schools most could afford.
Noting that 49 percent of veterans had used their benefits in California,
where they could make use of a highly developed system of low-cost
public schools, compared with just 29 percent in Pennsylvania, which
had a proportionally higher number of expensive private institutions,
the report concluded that "[v]eterans from states that lack extensive
systems of public higher education have much less opportunity to use
the G.I. Bill."[45] In addition, the report revealed that "[w]hile World War
II veterans were slightly more likely to attend private colleges than the
general population, Korean and Vietnam-era veterans have been more
likely to attend public institutions."[46] The report conceded that this factor resulted in part from the failure of the later G.I. Bills to pay direct

tuition and also from the proliferation of public schools since the end of World War II.

One of the more scathing criticisms of Vietnam-era education benefits contained in the report was that the low levels of payments discriminated against the underprivileged and, in particular, disadvantaged minorities. Veterans relying solely on G.I. Bill benefits and with no recourse to alternative funds had far more limited educational opportunities than middle-class or affluent veterans. The *Nader Report* concluded,

> One of the virtues of the World War II GI Bill was that it provided scholarship money for young men from working-class and lower middle-class backgrounds who would otherwise have had little opportunity for further education. On the surface, the GI Bill enacted in 1966 seemed to do the same thing, but in reality, the level of benefits was so low that participation was greatly restricted for veterans of lower class families who lacked additional resources to draw upon for support.[47]

African American veterans, in particular, faced additional problems beyond those experienced by many of their white counterparts after leaving the service.[48] At the end of the 1960s and in the early 1970s, unemployment remained endemic to young black males. According to one estimate, almost 30 percent of black male veterans between the ages of twenty and twenty-four were out of work compared to less than 6 percent of white veterans of the same age group.[49] Almost 90 percent of African American Vietnam veterans came from working-class or underprivileged families. Moreover, the median incomes of African American families remained considerably lower than those of their white counterparts throughout the Vietnam era and beyond. As a consequence, for most African American veterans, going to college on the G.I. Bill was simply not an option.[50]

Stories increased in the press of black veterans struggling to make ends meet. In 1968, the *New York Times* reported on one former "tunnel rat" who, three months after leaving the army, could not find employment and "doesn't have much to show for his year under fire. He's living back home with his mother, brother and sister on a dreary, littered street in a battered four-story red brick tenement house."[51] Another such story detailed the post-service experience of African American veteran Sergeant Dwight H. Johnson, a Congressional Medal of Honor recipient who was shot and killed while committing an armed robbery at a grocery store.[52]

A more generous G.I. Bill might have provided an avenue to economic advancement for black veterans, and no doubt it did help some attain an education or vocational training. But, as Tim O'Brien noted, "For Black Vietnam veterans, many of whom think they fought a racist war, the modern GI Bill is another piece of the white man's tokenism."[53] At a benefits protest march in Washington, DC, in May 1973, one black veteran with two children interviewed for the *Washington Post* remarked, "It's been rough. I do odd jobs and things. . . . Ever since I've been out, it's been a hard time for me." Another, noting that his benefits failed to cover his living expenses, stated, "It's really a problem. . . . All the food expenditures, gas and so forth are going up."[54] A veterans' counselor at a New York community college observed,

> The average white, middle class vet, with a high school degree and some tolerance for bureaucracy can get what he wants out of the V.A. . . . For the middle-class vet who can get support from his parents or who has a wife who can support him, . . . the benefits are a boon, a nice supplement. But they won't finance an education.[55]

In April 1971, New York veterans formed the United Black Veterans of America seeking greater benefits for minority veterans. One member commented,

> As blacks and minority-group members, we feel we aren't getting a fair share of opportunities even though we have given so much of ourselves in the service of America. . . . [W]hen we came out we discovered [America] did not seem to recognize our role in fighting for her, as is evidenced by the lack of fair and equal opportunities for black veterans.[56]

Many black veterans benefited from public service organizations such as the Urban League's Veterans' Affairs Program and from college veterans' clubs.[57] But such programs offered mere palliatives to the deeper-seated problem of an inadequate G.I. Bill.

Some African Americans faced a further complication. The military had five types of service discharge at the end of the Vietnam War. Over 90 percent of veterans received honorable discharges, making them eligible for the full slate of benefits. A dishonorable discharge precluded a veteran from receiving any benefits. Other classifications required a review by the Veterans Administration to determine eligibility. As is well documented, by the end of the Vietnam War, morale declined as the military effort wore down. Incidents of indiscipline increased as no soldier wanted to be the last one killed in a crusade that had long since expired. For African Americans, the problem seemed particularly acute. Racial tension, though not pervasive, became an increasing feature of military life in Vietnam. Mirroring the fractured nature of late-1960s American society, a combination of lingering white racism and growing militancy among African Americans contributed to occasional incidents of racial violence in Vietnam. A race riot broke out at the Long Binh stockade in 1968. At Cam Rahn Bay, outrage spread among black servicemen when white soldiers raised a Confederate flag to mark the assassination of Dr. Martin Luther King Jr.[58] As one veteran recalled, "There was a whole change of attitude. Even among those, like me who were *committed* to the war. You began to wonder, 'What am I really fighting for?' After Dr. King's death there was a greater sense of being black."[59] When one white veteran responded to continuing media coverage of the death of Dr. King with a racial slur, one black veteran recalled, "we commenced to give him a lesson in when to use that word and when not to use that word. A physical lesson."[60]

Occasionally, large-scale incidents grabbed the attention of the media. In October 1972, the front page of the *New York Times* carried a report of an incident onboard the *U.S.S. Kitty Hawk* where forty-six sailors suffered injuries resulting from a racial confrontation. Black sailors reportedly lashed out against their menial jobs and what they considered endemic discrimination in the navy.[61] Compounding the problem for black soldiers, statistically more whites were likely to report incidents of racial assaults than black soldiers. One House Committee on Armed Services report revealed that penalties for African American soldiers found guilty of misconduct tended to be harsher where the punishment was left to the discretion of white officers.[62] Morocco Coleman, himself a victim of a trumped-up criminal charge during his tour of duty, wrote Lyndon Johnson and *Ebony Magazine* to complain of "the disproportionate numbers of black GIs that were being court-martialed and rail roaded off to prison in Vietnam."[63]

The result of this combination of increased racial tension and, in the words of author James Westheider, a "command structure [that] was overwhelmingly white, often racist, and usually apathetic to blacks concerns" was that black soldiers received a disproportionate number of bad conduct or dishonorable discharges.[64] Consequently, many found that they could not obtain desperately needed benefits when they left the service. Given the lack of economic opportunities open to them in the 1960s, many African Americans had entered military service for economic advancement.[65] As one veteran recalled, "There weren't many opportunities for blacks in private industry then. As a graduate of West Point, I was an officer and a gentleman by act of Congress. Where else could a black go and get that label just like that?"[66] Mainly because of the low level of benefits, nationally only 25 percent of African American veterans had used their education benefits by 1973, compared to 46 percent of white veterans.[67] By 1980, a nationwide Veterans Administration survey indicated that the completion rates for African American veterans claiming college-level benefits stood at only 36.4 percent, compared with 60.2 percent of white veterans. Additionally, the survey found that African Americans expressed a lower overall rate of satisfaction with their veterans' benefits.[68] Although many African American veterans might have anticipated using military service as a springboard to obtaining a college education, they soon discovered that the government was unwilling to cover the costs. Consequently, many of them were forced to abandon their goals; the Vietnam-era G.I. Bills never became the readjustment tool that they had hoped for and—in many cases—needed.

Frustrated by the government response to their problems, veterans directed much of their ire toward the Veterans Administration. Much of the media criticism of the VA at the start of the 1970s centered on the medical treatment of wounded Vietnam veterans. With advances in medical technology and the advent of medevac helicopters, Vietnam soldiers survived many injuries that would have proved fatal on the battlefields of World War II and Korea. As a consequence, the number of severely injured veterans increased proportionally, and VA hospitals sometimes struggled to cope with the influx of new patients. Again, the press quickly picked up on stories of veteran neglect. The *New York Times* opined, "Ironically, while the demands of war are endless for the youth called upon to risk their necks and limbs there, the wounded are not assured of receiving the utmost in medical care once back in the United States."[69] Further headlines such as "Crippled Veterans Find Hospitals Crowded and Attitudes at Home Ambiguous" and "Ex-G.I. Says Neglect Cost Him an Eye" reflected a growing perception that the VA was failing those veterans in greatest need.[70] Exacerbating the problem, the *Nader Report* claimed that the VA allocated a majority of its thinly stretched resources to the chronic medical problems of its older veterans, often to the detriment of the wounded Vietnam veteran. *Life* magazine, in one of the more notorious stories on the mistreatment of veterans, published a series of images from the Bronx veterans' hospital in May 1970. The pictorial showed veterans in various states of neglect, including images of wheelchair-bound veterans left sitting under running showers for hours at a time. Further charges arose in the press and in the veteran community that the VA failed to offer the necessary support to veterans plagued by drug addictions picked up in Vietnam. The VA did eventually open up drug centers around the country to aid addicted veterans, but the perception grew that these efforts never went far enough.

Veterans and educators also criticized the VA for its inefficient distribution of education benefit checks. Many veterans complained of tardy payments or bureaucratic intransigence in the application process. Tim O'Brien slated the VA for "[l]ate checks, delayed checks. Unanswered telephones. Slothful, insensitive VA offices. Computers that stop payment on benefit checks if each item on complicated application forms isn't properly completed."[71] Joseph Mulholland, assistant dean of the Liberal Arts College at Fordham University, described veterans' benefits as "inadequate [and] . . . often delayed for months," and described the VA's bureaucracy as "all but impenetrable."[72] Most galling for the veterans was the VA's continued role as little more than a mouthpiece for the White House's financial retrenchment. The *New York Times* accused the VA of "[t]aking its cues from an Administration whose idea of economy is billions for war with cutbacks at home, . . . [while failing] to ask for the funding necessary to make a dent in the problems veterans encounter."[73] Chief culprit was Donald Johnson, Nixon's choice to succeed William Driver as head of the VA.

Johnson cut an imposing figure, standing at six feet five inches tall, and was a winner of a Bronze Star while fighting in Europe in World War II. He had also served as national commander of the American Legion from 1964 to 1965. After an unsuccessful run at the governorship of Iowa, Johnson became an ardent supporter of Richard Nixon. In return, Nixon nominated him to head the VA in June 1969. Despite his military background and post-service experience with veterans, Johnson—like many of his World War II brethren—proved an unreliable friend to the Vietnam veteran. Johnson insisted, as did Nixon, that Vietnam veterans were well cared for under their G.I. Bill. Claiming that benefits had kept pace with inflation, Johnson opposed any major congressional initiatives to provide increased education allowances. In April 1971, he testified before the inaugural hearings of the newly formed Senate Committee on Veterans' Affairs. Though he spent most of his time discussing perceived problems within the VA medical system, he cited increasing use of the G.I. Bill among veterans as evidence of the program's success and noted that among recipients of education benefits, "Three out of five are attending college. Comparable percentages under prior GI Bills were 29 percent for World War II and 50 percent for the Korea conflict."[74]

Repeatedly, Johnson used such participation rates and cost of living indices to cast the Vietnam G.I. Bill as an unqualified success. These statistics also found favor with lawmakers who saw no need to amend the program. The problem with using such figures, as many critics pointed out at the time, was that there existed as yet little statistical evidence to show how many veterans actually completed their courses and how many were forced to drop out because of financial pressures. Similarly, these numbers did not take into account the fact that higher education in the United States had become much more widespread since the original World War II G.I. Bill. Higher participation rates did not necessarily mean that the G.I. Bill was performing one of its intended functions of allowing veterans to catch up to their civilian counterparts in terms of educational opportunities. The original G.I. Bill gave veterans who might normally have not gone to college the opportunity to do so. But by the Vietnam era, far more Americans from diverse economic and racial backgrounds had made their way onto campuses. Without corroborating data, Johnson's claim that participation rates indicated that the 1966 G.I. Bill was having the same positive impact as the World War II bill remained tenuous. Moreover, Johnson expanded the argument made frequently in the past by Olin Teague that education benefits under the G.I. Bill should provide nothing more than a helping hand for the veteran. Even though the original G.I. Bill had provided a full ride for the vast majority of veterans, Johnson claimed that it was never intended to cover all of a veteran's education costs.

Further congressional testimony by VA officers highlighted the agency's ongoing and stubborn refusal to acknowledge any problems with the G.I. Bill. Olney B. Owen, the VA's chief benefits director, appeared before a subcommittee of the House Education and Training Committee on Veterans' Affairs in November 1971 to state the VA's position on several proposals to increase education benefits awaiting congressional action. His testimony revealed the surprisingly strong opposition within the VA to proposals that would have greatly benefited the veterans. As had Donald Johnson, Olney crowed that increasing numbers of veterans entering training signified the success of the G.I. Bill and added, "This impressive record results, we believe, from the motivation and drive of our veterans, encouraged by the active concern of the Congress and the President." Olney reiterated the VA's view that "[w]e recognize the GI Bill was not designed—and given the diversity of tuition charges among schools, could not be equitably designed—to cover all of a veteran's educational costs." Olney slated congressional proposals to increase veterans' benefits from $175 a month to $220 as inconsistent with Nixon's economic priorities. Ignoring the issue of rising tuition costs and the burden placed on the economically disadvantaged, he noted that the bills in front of Congress "propose rate increases far in excess of price increases" and affirmed, "we oppose the enactment of these measures." Teague's influence was then clearly present in Olney's next point, as he outlined the VA's opposition to direct tuition payments for fear of "returning to the inequities of the World War II GI Bill program and the abuses which occurred."[75]

In an attempt to answer some of the growing criticisms leveled against it, the VA commissioned Louis Harris & Associates to conduct the first nationwide survey of Vietnam veterans. The study analyzed responses from over two thousand veterans polled over two weeks in August 1971 as well as almost fifteen hundred members of the public and over seven hundred employers in an attempt to ascertain veterans' problems and the public's attitude toward veterans. One major focus of the report was on "the role of the Veterans Administration in facilitating veterans' readjustment after separation from the Armed Forces."[76] The VA published the results in January 1972 under the title *A Study of the Problems Facing Vietnam Veterans on Their Readjustment to Civilian Life.* The results were somewhat equivocal. Despite the widespread perception that veterans faced scorn and neglect upon their return to civilian life, the study found that overwhelmingly, "The public and prospective employers clearly feel that veterans are deserving of the same respect and the warm reception accorded to returning veterans of previous wars."[77] Moreover, 79 percent of veterans agreed that "[m]ost people at home respect you for having served your country in the armed forces," with only 19 percent disagreeing.[78] The Nixon administration received mixed responses for the assistance being offered returning veterans. Fifty-two percent of veterans agreed with the statement that "[t]he President and his Administration are doing all they can to help veterans readjust to civilian life," but 40 percent disagreed.[79] In their overall evaluation, veterans responded favorably to the VA. Sixty percent of Vietnam-era veterans gave the VA a positive rating against a 31 percent negative rating. The report concluded that veterans were "highly positive about the job the VA is doing."[80] Significantly, the report did not distinguish between veterans who had served in Southeast Asia and those who did not. Those who did not might well have had lower expectations of their government and of the VA.

Questions on education benefits elicited an ambiguous response from veterans. In general terms, education benefits ranked highest on the list of reasons given by veterans for their approval of the VA. Among veterans classified as "students" 66 percent gave the VA a positive score. But when asked specifically about the level of benefits, the response told a different story. When asked if their benefits provided "[m]ore than enough to live on comfortably," only 1 percent of student veterans replied affirmatively. Seventy-four percent agreed that money for schooling under the G.I. Bill was "[n]ot enough to live on comfortably."[81] "Nonwhite" veterans were more likely to give a negative assessment of the education benefits than their white counterparts.[82] These figures seemed to quantify many of the veterans' complaints that their benefits were insufficient. But Donald

Johnson could, and did, take solace from the response given by veterans to another question. When asked for their overall satisfaction with "GI education benefits for school training," 75 percent said they were "satisfied" compared with only 23 percent who were "dissatisfied."[83] The figures suggested, as Johnson had claimed, that most veterans did consider their education benefits a welcome and important part of their rehabilitation and that many found them to be very beneficial, even if they did not afford a "comfortable" living. Predictably, Johnson focused on the positive, declaring that the results of the study were "a real vote of confidence in the V.A. organization."[84]

The study did little to assuage the continued media criticisms of both the G.I. Bill and of the VA. Veterans' readjustment problems continued to be major news throughout the early and mid-1970s. Many of the media reports contained a degree of hyperbole. Newspaper and magazine articles continued to concentrate almost exclusively on the negative stories of the veteran homecoming experience. The scorned veteran had become a hot topic. Sometimes the media went too far. Responding to the *Life* article on the Bronx Hospital, Donald Johnson accused the magazine of "outlandish" journalism that "provide[d] an utterly distorted picture of VA care."[85] The director of the hospital, Dr. Abraham M. Kleinman, accused the magazine of staging the pictures in order to present a negative image of patient care. Even more outrageous, the *New York Times* at one point suggested that five hundred thousand Vietnam veterans had attempted suicide. Considering that roughly three million soldiers served in Vietnam and of them a small minority was exposed to combat on a regular basis, even a rudimentary application of logic should have revealed the error in the five hundred thousand figure. Several months later, the paper printed a retraction in which it admitted the figure had come from an unreliable source; by then, any damage inflicted on public perception of Vietnam veterans was already done.[86] The press was, perhaps, also guilty of reporting on *only* the negative stories of veteran hardship under the G.I. Bill. As the VA study had suggested, there were many returning veterans who were grateful for their benefits, and a large majority found them to be at least "adequate." Even the *Nader Report* concurred that most veterans could fare reasonably well under the G.I. Bill if they chose to attend lower-cost in-state public schools. But the problem of the Vietnam-era G.I. Bills was not that *everyone* was suffering. The problem that the VA refused to address was that there were many Vietnam veterans for whom the G.I. Bill was simply not enough. For the combat veterans, in particular, the fact that the government was playing politics with their future and not giving them the same opportunities offered their predecessors seemed like one more example of a country that had turned its back on its warriors. The bills were providing some education for most, but not a good education for all, as the previous bills had done.

Understandably, Vietnam veterans—those who could afford to go to college at all—began to wonder why they should have to compromise the quality of their education. While *Time* magazine could ask World War II veterans "why go to Podunk U if you can go to Yale," many of the Vietnam generation had to pick up odd jobs just to make it through Podunk U. With the 1944 and the Korea G.I. Bills, the government had set the precedent that military service during a time of conflict would be rewarded with a good quality of education. In some ways, the earlier bills had changed the equation of citizenship. Vietnam veterans might well have expected that when they returned home they would enjoy the same opportunities enjoyed by their predecessors. Any violation of this contract could be interpreted as a denigration of their service and their worth as citizen-soldiers. The lack of a welcome home had already made many feel as if they were carrying the can for America's ongoing failures in the war. Now the government seemed complicit in adding to this burden by not giving them the same recognition as their predecessors. The Vietnam generation was being told that their service was not worth as much now that they were getting nothing more than a helping hand in their education. Therefore, the veterans' fight over benefits was about more than just money: It was also a symbolic one to gain the appropriate recognition for their service.

Following the outcry from the press and the veteran community, Washington could no longer ignore the problems of the G.I. Bill. Unfortunately for the veterans, the next round of debates came at a time when the country was entering a severe economic downturn. Both Richard Nixon and Gerald Ford fixed veterans' benefits in their crosshairs as they attempted to combat federal spending and inflation. Having faced ideological barriers from Great Society liberals concerned with extending government assistance to those in greatest need, veterans now faced equally intractable opposition from fiscal conservatives in the White House.

4

Mr. President (Have Pity on the Fighting Man)

Nixon's Right Turn for America, Wrong Result for the Veterans

Our veterans have long known that they must be champions
of responsible government. They know the basic truth that a
veterans' program not good for the nation as a whole cannot
ultimately be of benefit to veterans themselves.
—President Richard Nixon, October 21, 1969

I do not believe that we should begin by depriving our
returning veterans of the just readjustment educational
training under the G. I. Bill. I cannot in good conscience
agree to lay this additional hardship on the backs of men
who have already served our nation with such great courage.
—Senator Ralph Yarborough, October 22, 1969

Like so many of his predecessors, Richard Nixon offered glowing public
expressions of support for the nation's veterans while working behind
the scenes to limit the assistance for which so many of them clamored.
However, many legislators, particularly in the Senate, continued the fight
to make the Cold War G.I. Bill a more effective readjustment program for
Vietnam veterans than it had been during its early years. The improvements to veterans' benefits that did occur at the start of the 1970s resulted
from intense negotiation among the House, Senate, and White House.
All agreed that the problems of the G.I. Bill needed addressing, but the
prescriptions for solving these problems varied greatly. Complicating
the negotiations, Vietnam veterans returned home to a far different economic landscape than their World War II or Korean War predecessors.

World War II veterans had returned home to an expanding economy that offered numerous opportunities. Even though their G.I. Bill

offered substantial benefits, many World War II veterans could afford to eschew its generosity and find meaningful employment in the private sector. More importantly, the strength of the economy meant that the government could more easily absorb the enormous costs of providing a generous benefits package. Many Vietnam veterans came home at a time when the economy suffered its most significant downturn in decades. During Richard Nixon's first term, unemployment climbed from 3.5 percent to 5.6 percent and inflation rose from 5.6 percent to 8.7 percent. Gross domestic product also slowed to its lowest levels since the Truman administration.[1] Factors such as the enormous costs of the Vietnam War and the federal programs created under the Great Society combined with external factors such as the oil crisis during Nixon's second term to compound the nation's economic woes.

Over the previous centuries of debates over veterans' funding, questions over the sheer cost of benefits had arisen frequently. In the face of the economic downturn at the beginning of the 1970s, the questioning grew louder as the outlay on veterans' care skyrocketed. When the Department of Defense reduced its manpower needs as the country began its slow extrication from Vietnam, large numbers of veterans came home to claim their share of federal benefits. From a high of 543,000 military personnel in South Vietnam at the end of 1968, the United States had only 24,200 by the end of 1972.[2] Many more servicemen and women who had not served in Vietnam also reentered society during the same period. Between 1969 and 1972, over a million new veterans per year reentered civilian life in what VA administrator Donald Johnson described as a "large scale demobilization."[3] By mid-1972, the presence of an almost continuous draft since 1940 created 28,804,000 veterans in society, with millions more dependents also eligible for benefits.[4] Now the costs of a universal Cold War G.I. Bill were becoming apparent. By 1972, the VA administered $1.7 billion in education funding. In contrast, despite all of the new education programs brought in under the Great Society, the Department of Health, Education, and Welfare administered only $1.47 billion in educational assistance.[5] Further draining the VA's resources, the aging World War I and World War II generations began to require increased medical attention. The VA's share of the federal budget rose from 3.8 percent in 1968 to 4.7 percent for the fiscal year 1972. The VA spent $6.9 billion on veterans' services in 1968; by 1973 this figure had risen to $11.8 billion.[6] The precarious state of the economy and the rising costs of veterans' benefits occurred precisely at the time when the calls for better treatment of the Vietnam veteran grew louder. This combination created a fraught economic and political landscape for the new president.

Nixon won a narrow election victory in 1968 by occupying the political center. In the eyes of many of those who voted for him, the Great Society had exceeded its legitimacy. The Vietnam War, urban unrest, and the expansion of federal power alienated many lower- and middle-class Americans and threatened the New Deal liberal consensus. Nixon won the Republican Party's nomination by campaigning as a moderate conservative candidate. During his first term, he maintained this centrist position, seeking a New Majority of Americans who believed that the government had neglected their needs and concerns. Like Eisenhower before him, Nixon initially sought a degree of fiscal responsibility without seriously threatening the social programs of his immediate Democratic predecessors. Early on in his administration, he prioritized a reduction in federal spending in an effort to slow down what he termed "the excesses of 1966, 1967, and 1968."[7] Less than a week after his inauguration, he circulated a memo to the heads of all executive departments and agencies, including the Veterans Administration, in which he called for "a careful and thorough review" of spending. In an effort to restrain what he termed the "present excessive rate of price inflation in our economy," he called on federal agencies to "identify activities of low priority which can be reduced or phased down and perhaps, over time, eliminated completely."[8] But his budget cuts were initially neither widespread nor drastic. Far from seeking to repeal the welfare state, he expanded it in many ways early on in his presidency.

Nixon's biographers point out that he was no great ideologue and no arch conservative in most political areas. Stephen Ambrose describes him as a "moderate" Republican, while Iwan Morgan calls him "the last liberal president" and the "most liberal Republican president in U.S. history."[9] Allen J. Matusow casts Nixon as an "enlightened centrist—a conservative man of liberal views,"[10] while Joan Hoff points to Nixon's impressive list of social legislation and federal regulations as evidence that he expanded and redirected the liberal goals of the previous four decades of social programs instead of challenging them.[11]

Such initiatives included continued federal support to education, an expansion of the National Park Service, and the creation of Amtrak under the Rail Passenger Service Act. He signed into law environmental initiatives, including the creation of the Environmental Protection Agency during a 1970 cabinet reorganization, and signed the Clean Air Act, the Noise Control Act, the Clean Water Act, and the Endangered Species Act. He also expanded the Bureau of Indian Affairs and signed the Indian Education Act of 1972. His proposed Family Assistance Plan would have expanded greatly the welfare state by guaranteeing a minimum income to the poorest families.

But there were certainly limits to Nixon's liberal leanings. In 1971, he opposed the Child Development Act that would have given free childcare to the underprivileged, and later on in his administration slashed funding to the EPA and many of the Great Society's social programs, such as the Office of Economic Opportunity. He proved equally equivocal in his education record. In 1972, he signed into law the Education Amendments of 1972, which liberalized the provisions of the Higher Education Act of 1965 and introduced new measures such as the Basic Educational Opportunity Grants (BEOGs), which offered an annual grant of fourteen hundred dollars to all students, with certain deductions made for parental contributions.[12] Early on in his administration, Nixon also called for federal assistance to be redirected to the needs of the poor through a series of additional grants and loans.[13] But Nixon also vetoed an appropriations bill for the Departments of Health, Labor, Education, and Welfare in January 1970 because of its cost, claiming, "it is in the vital interests of all Americans in stopping the rise in the cost of living." Later that same year he vetoed an additional appropriations bill for the Office of Education for similar reasons.[14]

Moreover, Congress remained the driving force behind many of the more liberal proposals signed by Nixon, including the 1972 Education Amendments Act. The BEOGs, for example, came from a Senate initiative. In addition, many of Nixon's environmental policies aimed to steal the thunder of potential presidential challenger Edmund Muskie, who had been at the forefront of the battle for environmental legislation long before Nixon became interested.[15] As Arthur Schlesinger Jr. noted, Nixon often just "rolled with the punches and went along with a reform-minded Congress."[16] And it was Congress—especially the

Senate—that landed the punches during the fights for higher veterans' benefits throughout Nixon's first term. As the public awareness of veterans' troubles grew, politicians from both parties joined Ralph Yarborough in pushing for increased benefits. Crucially, the focus of the new round of debates was changing. The passage of the 1966 G.I. Bill was hampered by the issue of providing benefits to noncombat veterans. But as increasing numbers of Vietnam veterans began returning from Southeast Asia, debates on education funding turned to whether the G.I. Bill was doing enough to help combat veterans. Even those lawmakers who had questioned generous benefits in 1966—such as Strom Thurmond—embraced the Vietnam veteran's cause because it was becoming clear that the nation's combat veterans were being let down. As had so often been the case, however, the government's efforts to correct the program's failings were neither uniform nor unified.

By the end of the 1960s, a clear order was emerging in how far the different branches of government were prepared to go in helping the veteran. The Senate regularly proved itself the more munificent with federal funds, and throughout the Vietnam era, Yarborough and other members of the Senate tended to be the best friends the Vietnam veteran had in government. Since the Eisenhower administration, the White House, for either ideological or fiscal reasons, continued to provide the strongest opposition to the Senate's efforts. Nixon continued that trend as he perpetually sought to keep benefit increases low. As with much of his social legislation, he never repudiated the idea of offering federal assistance to those in need; he just sought to place a lower ceiling on how far that assistance should go. In between the generosity of the Senate and the thrift of the White House, the House, still under the stewardship of Olin Teague's Veterans' Affairs Committee, sought a middle ground that generally pleased neither the veterans, nor the Senate, nor the White House, but that often proved to be the most politically palatable. All sides reverted to type during the first major round of debates over G.I. Bill rates during Nixon's term.

On August 4, 1969, exactly five years into the Vietnam era, the House voted on H.R.11959, a proposal to increase veterans' benefits by 27 percent, raising the monthly educational allowance to $165.[17] Concerns over the initial low usage of the 1966 G.I. Bill during its early years prompted this call for an increase. During the floor debate on the measure, several representatives claimed that passage of the increase would lead to many more veterans flooding into higher education. Further, Frank Annunzio (D-IL) boasted that "many words have been spoken in this Chamber about support for our fighting men overseas, and such words have not fallen on deaf ears."[18] Spark Matsunaga (D-HI) added, "In the face of today's rising tuition as well as rising cost of living, the undergraduate veteran can hardly be said to be going to school in lavish style on his VA allowance."[19] Others suggested that the need for the increase was "clear and indisputable" and that the bill was "long overdue" and "the very least that we in Congress can do for them."[20] A very self-satisfied House then passed the bill by a vote of 404–0. Predictably, the Senate moved with equal haste to correct the deficiencies of the 1966 bill. Yarborough and Alan Cranston (D-CA) introduced a bill (S.338) calling for a 46 percent increase in monthly education benefits. Before the House and Senate could work out their differences, the Nixon administration attempted to influence proceedings.

Shortly after Nixon took office, his administration expressed a genuine concern over the low usage rates of the G.I. Bill. Presidential assistant Bryce Harlow wrote Olin Teague of his desire to "keep the program dynamic" and added, "The President feels that as long as there are veterans with unfulfilled readjustment needs, greater efforts are required."[21] Nixon was also concerned about ceding control of the debate over education benefits to Congress. To explore potential solutions, in June 1969, Nixon created a President's Committee on the Vietnam Veterans to study the veterans' readjustment needs and to make recommendations on the new legislation. Donald Johnson headed the panel, which also contained then director of the Office of Economic Opportunity Donald Rumsfeld, Secretary of Defense Melvin Laird, and Secretary of Labor George Shultz. In their interim report published in October, the committee recommended a much lower education rise than those currently under consideration on the Hill; while acknowledging that the cost of living had risen 10 percent since the last benefits increase in October 1967 and that education costs had increased by approximately 15 percent in the same period, the committee recommended only a 10 percent increase. The authors of the report claimed that "[l]ong experience with previous educational assistance programs has demonstrated that when students have a stake in their own education they will avoid unwise use of the allowance provided by the government."[22] While Donald Johnson had previously acknowledged that such a low recommendation might "subject the Executive to criticism or ridicule," he believed that a cost-of-living increase was all that was needed until veterans' readjustment problems could be more fully studied.[23] Subsequently, Nixon proposed only a 13 percent increase, far less than was needed to bring the benefits in line with the World War II bill, even by his own estimation.

Before the House and Senate could thrash out their own differences, Nixon went on the offensive, attempting to persuade both lawmakers and the public of the need for frugality. On October 19, he addressed the nation on "the Rising Costs of Living." Criticizing the spending of his Democratic predecessors, Nixon claimed, "[t]he blame for the spiral of wages and prices falls fundamentally on the past policies of your Government. The Federal Government spent a lot more than it raised in taxes. Some of that spending was on the war in Vietnam, some of the spending was on new social programs, but the total spending was very heavy." He went on to laud the reductions in federal spending that had occurred over the previous nine months, noting that "hardly anything has escaped some reduction." Veterans' benefits had avoided cuts during this period, but they had not been elevated either, even as the president lamented the considerable increase in the cost of living. Although Nixon did not refer specifically to veterans in his message, he steeled all Americans for further "bitter medicine" that lay ahead and pledged, "We are going to continue to exercise that backbone in the face of criticism by a lot of powerful special interests." Nixon had laid down his economic marker, but was politically shrewd enough not to announce any sweeping attacks on veterans' spending. Privately, however, he made his feelings known to the politician he knew would cause him the biggest headache on this issue: Ralph Yarborough.[24]

Nixon wrote Yarborough to express his "deep concerns" over the costs of the proposed measures in the House and Senate. Citing that the bill would cost an additional $393 million over the next year that would have to be culled from other important programs, Nixon informed Yarborough,

I am in sympathy with a justifiable increase in educational allowances for post-Korean and Vietnam Era veterans. Yet, I consider the magnitude of the increases contained in H.R. 11959 to require reconsideration for two reasons. The proposed rates are excessive and their effect would be inflationary. . . . It is not easy to criticize the pending bill for it promises some appealing benefits to a most deserving group. But our veterans have long known that they must be champions of responsible government. They know the basic truth that a veterans' program not good for the nation as a whole cannot ultimately be of benefit to veterans themselves.[25]

Like Franklin Roosevelt, Dwight Eisenhower, and Lyndon Johnson before him, Nixon believed that veteran privilege ought not to come at the expense of the greater good. But whereas Roosevelt and Johnson sought to give everyone a share of the nation's wealth, Nixon expected everyone to sacrifice. This negative universalism did not play well with veterans who had already sacrificed so much for their country, nor with Yarborough. He immediately replied to Nixon to claim that the bill was not inflationary, "particularly compared with the cost of the War. The War is inflationary; these veterans' student allowances are minuscule in comparison." As to Nixon's point that the proposed benefits were excessive, Yarborough countered that the current rates were "not even on a level with those provided in the earlier [World War II] bill." He concluded his response by adding, "I shall support you in your goal of combatting inflation, but I cannot in good conscience agree to lay this additional hardship on the backs of the men who have already served our nation with such great courage."[26]

Predictably, Olin Teague shared many of Nixon's economic concerns and publicly expressed his reservations over Yarborough's attempts to escalate G.I. Bill benefits further. After Yarborough had continued to issue statements on the inadequacies of veterans' funding, Teague launched the following attack on Yarborough and on what he saw as "rabid press" reporting:

Recently, there were several news stories and editorials, based on the inaccurate statement of a misinformed critic of the GI bill that lamented the alleged low numbers of Vietnam era veterans taking training under the bill. The entire episode was unfortunate, first because there is no factual basis for such criticism. The current bill is a good, workable education measure that is attracting a larger percentage of trainees into

Richard Nixon surrounded by U.S. soldiers during his visit to Vietnam in 1969. *Courtesy of the Richard M. Nixon Presidential Library.*

higher education than either the World War II or Korean bill. . . . [S]uch unfounded, carping criticism serves only to do harm to a program that has proven one of the most successful and most beneficial to the eligible recipients, and to this Government.[27]

According to Teague, the low percentage of veterans taking advantage of the bill during the first two and a half years of the program still represented a greater raw number than had taken advantage of the

World War II bill in a comparable period. Once the program had run its course, he suggested, the numbers of participating veterans would increase to, and even surpass, the levels of the previous bills. Teague also praised the efforts of the VA for its outreach programs and Veteran Centers, which he described as a part of "the most widespread program of benefit information in its history."[28] Referring to Yarborough's public criticisms of the VA, Teague wrote Carl Albert, "Senator Yarborough's observations on this subject have always been a myth, and I cannot understand why he continues to make public statements which are not borne out by facts."[29]

But in his public comments, Yarborough's critique of the VA centered more on its obstruction to increased benefits than on the services it provided. On the floor of the Senate, he blamed the VA for being "largely responsible—probably under prodding by the Bureau of Budget—for keeping the veterans out of school."[30] And having spent over a decade fighting for veterans against stubborn resistance from three previous administrations and Teague's House Veterans' Affairs Committee, he was in no mood to lay down the sword. On October 23, after the bill had emerged from several months of tinkering in committees, the Senate voted on H.R.11959. Despite retaining the original name of Teague's bill, the Senate version bore little resemblance to the one passed by the House in August. When it left committee, the Senate bill had provisions from nine separate Senate proposals attached to it that drastically changed the nature of the bill. Title I called for a simple increase in the monthly education allowance to $190, up from the $135 for single veterans. On the Senate floor, Cranston defended the substantial rate increase, claiming that whereas the Korea G.I. Bill had paid approximately 98 percent of a veteran's total education costs, the Cold War G.I. Bill covered only 67 percent due to the increased costs of tuition. The $190 a month, he suggested, would equate to 98 percent of the veteran's needs compared with the House increase to $160, which equated to only 85 percent of a veteran's needs. He described Nixon's suggestion of a 13 percent rise as "wholly untenable" and called on his fellow senators to give veterans "the level of benefits which they need and deserve to help them in their education and training."[31]

Yarborough backed up Cranston's comments by suggesting that Office of Education figures revealed that his increase would make the benefits comparable to those offered under the 1952 G.I. Bill. He also reaffirmed the Senate's dedication to pushing for generous benefits by revealing the bipartisan support the bill gained in committee and further noting that "the only question was what could we do to give our veterans a fair chance in life." Highlighting the difficulties the Senate had faced in convincing the White House of the need for the increases, he lamented, "The goal of greater educational benefits for veterans has been pursued under three presidents and it has been a hard fight every step of the way."[32] In the Senate, at least, he met little opposition, and no one raised any significant objections to the proposed increases.

Title II of the Senate bill separated it even further from the original House measure by offering "Special Assistance for Educationally Disadvantaged Veterans." This section of the bill offered veterans the opportunity to take college preparation courses such as remedial reading at a local college without cutting into their higher education benefits. Veterans could also claim up to one hundred dollars a month for "special remedial, tutorial, or counseling assistance to enable the educationally disadvantaged veteran to perform satisfactorily in the course he is pursuing."[33] The VA would administer grants to participating schools to offset their costs. The Senate legislation also called for a Predischarge Education Program (PREP) under which the VA would pay for similar preparation courses in local schools for veterans before they left the service. The final measure called for the VA to increase its number of veterans' assistance centers to incorporate areas that were more rural, possibly by introducing mobile "vet centers."

Two main factors lay behind Title II's extensive and groundbreaking proposals. The first was a desire to increase the number of veterans taking advantage of the program. Department of Defense studies confirmed a widespread suspicion that educationally disadvantaged veterans were less likely to use their education benefits. By creating programs specifically targeted toward those veterans, the Senate hoped to increase participation of these marginalized groups in the G.I. Bill program. The second factor in the Senate's proposals reflected the enduring legacy of the Great Society. Lyndon Johnson may have vacated the White House, but Congress still contained plenty of adherents to his liberal goals of helping the most disadvantaged in society. World War II and Korean War veterans had received blanket benefits without consideration given to class or economic need. The new measures aimed to benefit those who needed additional help. The Senate passed the revised version of H.R.11959 by a vote of seventy-seven to zero. Once more, the Senate had given veterans a more generous benefits package than either the White House or the House envisioned.

Almost immediately, Nixon and Teague sought to undermine the Senate measure. White House aides had attempted to persuade Republicans to raise objections to the bill during the floor debate, but there was little stomach for such a fight in the upper house.[34] Few wanted the political risks of opposing such a popular cause. In a pattern that would repeat itself in the years ahead, Nixon lacked either the force or the finesse to impose his will on Congress in the way his immediate predecessors had done. Eisenhower, for example, had established a legislative liaison office in the 1950s to keep close contact with events in Congress. Lyndon Johnson brought his own special "treatment" to congressional relations. But Nixon put little effort into sweet-talking congressional leaders. Stephen Ambrose described Nixon as "the least effective President in dealing with Congress since Herbert Hoover."[35] White House congressional aide Bill Timmons noted that Nixon believed that pandering to the congressional egos was somehow beneath him and "[i]t was not in his personality to do it."[36] Nixon's Senate liaison, Patrick O' Donnell, confirmed that the president was "not comfortable dealing with Congress on a daily basis."[37]

Nixon could at least count himself fortunate that he had Teague in such an influential position in the House to restrain the more munificent Senate. After failing to block the bill's passage in the Senate, Nixon revealed that he might veto such an expensive package, prompting Senator John J. Williams (R-DE) to warn that if the bill went forward to the White House, "the President will have no choice but to veto it, and I think that veto will be sustained."[38] During House deliberations, Teague cited the threat of a presidential veto as reason enough to reject the Senate's measures, and instead he proposed a compromise 32 percent increase in monthly education benefits. After the House rejected the Senate bill, both houses then sent H.R.11959 back into conference to reconcile the significant differences in cost and type of their respective bills. A further three months passed before they could reach a compromise.

The report that finally emerged from committee in March 1970 proposed a monthly benefits increase of 34.6 percent, elevating a single veteran's payments to $175 per month. Alan Cranston claimed that Senate conferees "fought tenaciously" for higher rates but could do no better.[39] The House accepted most of the Senate's proposals to help the disadvantaged, albeit with some reductions. For example, veterans would receive a supplementary monthly benefit of fifty dollars for remedial courses instead of the Senate-proposed one hundred dollars. The House agreed to measures such as increasing the VA's outreach program and providing funds to schools participating in PREP. In return, the Senate dropped its calls to offer farm training under the G.I. Bill and acquiesced to the House request to deny payments for some more obscure vocational courses. After the House accepted the conference report on March 18 and the Senate on March 23, Cranston called the passage of H.R.11959 "a momentous day for all Vietnam veterans." Yarborough cautioned, "we must continue our efforts."[40]

At this point, Nixon and his staffers debated his taking the extraordinary step of becoming the first commander-in-chief to veto a veterans' education benefits increase. Nixon advisor Bryce Harlow argued for the veto, claiming that even if it were overridden, the administration would be sending a clear message to Congress that it was serious about spending cuts, and the American public could be told that "by this kind of spending, Congress is, in effect, preparing a new tax bill for the American people."[41] The disadvantages of such a move were obvious. The outcry from the public and lawmakers on the Hill would have been considerable and, as John Ehrlichman reminded Nixon, "the Administration could be pictured as anti-veteran."[42] Further, Donald Johnson warned that "a veto would have a catastrophic effect insofar as the veterans' community is concerned."[43] Even Harlow conceded that the veto would cause a "crisis relationship" with the veterans' organizations and predicted that "[i]f we do [veto], there will be blood knee deep running down Constitution Avenue."[44] Realizing the political pitfalls of a veto, Nixon promptly signed the bill without any public ceremony or qualifying remarks on March 26, 1970. White House press secretary Ron Zeigler noted that it would break the president's budget by $107 million and a further $186 million for the fiscal year 1971, but conceded that the extra money was for a worthy cause and that the administration believed that compared to costlier alternative proposals, "this is reasonable."[45] Here Nixon revealed his political pragmatism. Like Johnson in 1966, he realized that Congress held the upper hand in these debates and that the time for public opposition had passed. Moreover, he used the occasion to announce several new initiatives designed, in part, to preempt the measures to aid underprivileged veterans already suggested by Congress.

The President's Commission on the Vietnam Veteran finally submitted its report in March, just before the signing of the bill and almost six months after it was due. The commission shared Congress's view that the government ought to do more to aid veterans beyond simple increases in benefit levels. On the basis of their recommendations, Nixon liberalized the provisions for hiring veterans in federal positions. He also called for advanced payments of education benefits to help less well-off veterans attend school. Up to this point, veterans received their checks only after enrolling, which meant that they often required some up-front money to cover their initial school costs. The executive order also directed the VA to underwrite loans for mobile homes. As Congress had desired, he also expanded the in-service program to help veterans prepare for college. Such a service had already been available to servicemen and women who had served more than two years; the new measure opened up this opportunity for those who had served only six months. Finally, the executive order offered business loans and training for disadvantaged veterans. The new initiatives covered nearly four million veterans who had served since August 1964. In signing the order, Nixon affirmed, "This nation has an obligation to assist veterans of the armed forces in readjusting to civilian life."[46] The VA took some convincing before accepting the value of the new programs to aid poorer veterans. Some officials feared that the tailoring of benefits to specific social groups or classes might pervert the original intent of the G.I. Bill and make veterans' benefits a force for selective social engineering. But Donald Johnson was instrumental in the drafting of the report of the Veterans' Committee, prompting one official to state that the VA was now in theory "willing to go after—I mean really go after—the poor black kid who dropped out of high school to go fight in Vietnam."[47]

Even though he had initially opposed the increases, Nixon signed them into law and he added further initiatives designed to promote increased use of the G.I. Bill. These included a proposal from Robert Finch, secretary of health, education, and welfare, to provide special readjustment assistance to the first twenty-five thousand troops returning from Vietnam. Finch hoped that a well-publicized display of what the government was doing for these selected soldiers would provide a much-needed promotion of the benefits and services available to all.[48] The administration also called on comedian Bob Hope to promote the educational opportunities available to soldiers during his 1969 USO Christmas trip to military bases across South Vietnam. Administration officials credited the "Hope for Education" tour with generating significant interest in G.I. Bill programs.[49] Nixon's efforts seemed to suggest that he accepted the need for increased government assistance for veterans, at least in principle. But as with so many other episodes in Nixon's presidency, such generalizations do not adequately reveal the complexities and contradictions of his politics, for even as he gave with one hand, he took away with the other.

As he grudgingly accepted increases in education spending, Nixon slashed money from the VA's budget in other areas. He cut a proposal for four thousand new VA jobs suggested by Lyndon Johnson and impounded money earmarked for the VA, much of it for hospital improvements. In 1972, he pocket-vetoed the Veterans' Health Care Expansion Act, which would have provided an additional $85 million to the VA for health care. The act, he claimed, "unnecessarily adds hundreds of millions of dollars to the federal budget."[50] Throughout his term, Nixon attracted heavy criticism from the media, the veteran community, and Capitol Hill for cutting veterans' medical facilities. Nixon still had a long way to go before the veterans considered him a friend. Unfortunately for Vietnam veterans, they were about to lose the best friend they did have in government.

After the departure of Lyndon Johnson, Ralph Yarborough fought on for the liberal values they both shared. In 1969, he became chair of the Senate Labor and Public Welfare Committee. Having achieved so much in education, he turned his attentions to improving the nation's health care. As one of the nation's more progressive politicians, he launched regular verbal attacks on the Nixon administration, including frequent assaults on Nixon's Vietnam policy. Biographer Patrick Cox notes that at this time Yarborough "relished his role as a political maverick."[51]

The *Dallas Morning News* described him as the "least southern Senator" for his views on social policy. Unfortunately for Yarborough, the nation—and Texas politics in particular—was moving away from the idealism he, Kennedy, Johnson, and others had long shared. In the Texas primary for the 1970 senatorial election, Yarborough faced Democratic challenger Lloyd Bentsen Jr. Few of Yarborough's supporters expected a strong challenge, and the incumbent spent much of the campaign continuing his work in Washington and not courting his Texan constituents. But in the final few weeks, Bentsen ran Nixon-like television advertisements promising law and order while connecting his opponent with violent images of the 1968 Democratic National Convention in Chicago. The challenger also attacked Yarborough's calls for a Vietnam War moratorium, his failure to support Nixon's war policy, and his support of Eugene McCarthy in 1968. Teague saw an opportunity to twist the knife and threw his support behind Bentsen. In a close and often nasty fight, Yarborough lost his own party's nomination for reelection. Despite all he had achieved in his thirteen years in the Senate, the same tide of conservatism that had brought Richard Nixon to power and that had already begun to wash away some of the foundations of the Great Society swept Yarborough from politics. The veterans had lost their greatest champion on Capitol Hill.

Few individual politicians had done as much as Yarborough in promoting the veteran cause. The Cold War G.I. Bill had been one of his greatest legislative achievements in a career of fighting for worthy causes. He described the struggle to secure its passage as "the longest, hardest fight of my senatorial career."[52] Through his efforts, millions of veterans who had served since the end of the Korean War were able to return home and improve their lives through education and training. Although it was never as generous as he wanted, the consequences of Yarborough's bill were wide ranging. The nature of military service changed, making it possible for citizens to enter the military as a means of obtaining liberal benefits without ever having to serve during a time of war. Though he was always cognizant of the expense and civic implications of his bill, such concerns were secondary to Yarborough. His motivation was always to make sure that no veteran should be unduly disadvantaged through his or her service. The same sense of humanity, social justice, and crusading zeal he had carried throughout his public life and into his support for the more enlightened Great Society legislation had driven his fight for a new G.I. Bill. Few shared his views at first, but through his tireless work and against the backdrop of the war in Vietnam, he had prevailed. Perhaps one of the greatest testaments to Yarborough's achievements was that after his departure, former colleagues continued his fight as the culture of pushing for higher veterans' benefits that he had created in the Senate outlived his own tenure in DC. Alan Cranston was one of several lawmakers to ably step forward and fill the void. Cranston had been a stalwart supporter of Yarborough's fights over education benefits, but he also undertook his own veteran cause, one that gave further insight into the dynamics of veterans' politics for the Vietnam generation.

By the early 1970s, Cranston and others began to focus on the growing need for psychological counseling for returning veterans. As had been widely studied elsewhere, several eminent psychologists began holding "rap sessions" with returning vets and, upon hearing of the difficulties they were facing in their readjustment, launched a decade-long campaign to gain public recognition for the veterans' plight. Robert J. Lifton, Chaim F. Shatan, and Floyd "Shad" Meshad spearheaded a movement to raise awareness of post-service trauma and to get federal funding for psychological help. In a May 1972 op-ed piece for the *New York Times*, titled "Post-Vietnam Syndrome," Chatan identified the feelings of "terror and disorientation" some veterans were suffering long after service.[53] As awareness of these problems grew, Cranston attempted to pass legislation creating outreach centers to provide counseling and drug rehabilitation services. Five times in the 1970s his bill passed the Senate; five times it failed to make it out of the House.

The opposition to Cranston's bill came from a familiar source. After devoting a career to trimming any veterans' program that he deemed unnecessary, there was no way that Olin Teague was going to allow Cranston's bill to pass unchallenged. Veterans' activist Guy McMichael summed up the old World War II veteran Teague's attitude as "this is tough but we sucked it up, and we didn't need to go into . . . counseling and I am not sure that Vietnam veterans need this kind of thing."[54] When Shad Meshad confronted Teague over the need for new outreach programs, he recalled,

It was like pro wrestling, me against Olin Teague. When I came in [to his office] to talk to him, he wore his medal of honor . . . around his neck. He'd say "How can you little wimps be sick? A tour of duty only lasted twelve months! In World War II soldiers fought in the war for years. How could you be traumatized?"[55]

In Teague's mind, he had had his war and he had damn well won it. Now, the Vietnam veterans, having lost their war, were crying to Washington for the kind of help in overcoming their experience that his generation never had. As David Bonior, founder of the Congressional Vietnam Era Veterans Caucus, noted, "Abandoned by the major veterans' organizations, Vietnam veterans needed an ally among the barons, one who would stand with them against the major veterans' groups. The role was almost unintelligible to Chairman Teague."[56]

As Bonior's words testify, both the American Legion and the VFW also considered Cranston's bill an unnecessary drain on an already overburdened veterans' budget. Both organizations had provided cautious support for improving G.I. Bill benefits, but the outreach program was a step too far. They considered it a far worthier cause to fight for a pension for an uninjured World War II veteran than to assist the young Vietnam vet with a heroin problem. Max Cleland, Vietnam veteran and future head of the VA under Jimmy Carter, remembered that the Legion and VFW "fought tooth and nail" to kill Cranston's bill even while in public they "gave great lip service to Vietnam veterans, mostly because they wanted them to join the organizations and boost their ranks."[57] The fight for the outreach centers continued throughout the 1970s and only reached a successful conclusion for Cranston in 1979. With Teague retired by then, with Max Cleland pushing harder for Vietnam veterans' rights than any previous VA chief, and with a stronger presence of Vietnam veterans in Congress, the House Veterans' Affairs Committee finally ended its opposition, but not without extracting some final concessions from the Senate: The price of the committee members' acquiescence was greater influence in determining the location of future VA facilities, largely with a view to securing future construction projects in their own districts.[58] By the time of its conclusion, the fight over the outreach programs had heightened the sense of neglect from the government and estrangement from the World War II generation felt by many Vietnam veterans.

While the battle for counseling services raged, to the forefront of the G.I. Bill fight stepped Indiana Democrat Vance Hartke. Hartke, another World War II veteran who had served in the coast guard and navy, joined the Senate in 1959. Throughout the 1960s he had backed the domestic programs of Kennedy and Johnson, particularly in the areas of civil rights and Medicare. In the late 1960s, he openly broke ranks with Johnson over his Vietnam policy. Hartke considered the war in Vietnam to be unwise and immoral and publicly assailed the president's handling of the conflict. He continued his opposition under Nixon, casting himself as the "great dove." In 1972, he made a brief and unsuccessful run for the Democratic presidential nomination as an antiwar candidate. Prior to that, in 1970, he had become chairman of the newly created Senate Committee on Veterans' Affairs.[59] Despite his opposition to the Vietnam War, Hartke championed the rights of the men and women sent to fight it. As the next round of benefits proposals entered both houses in 1972, he stepped up to maintain the Senate tradition of pushing for the most liberal measure.

The House again acted first—but with Teague's usual caution—by proposing H.R.12828, dubbed the Vietnam Era Veterans' Readjustment Assistance Act of 1972. The name implied that this legislation was a new G.I. Bill, one that represented a chance to correct the failures of the past. The new bill proposed raising veteran benefits from $175 a month to $200. The bill also called for raises in vocational training from $108 a month to $160, a 48 percent increase, and liberalized the requirements for spouses and children to take vocational courses. Several of the bill's architects claimed that the increases would finally fulfill the promise of the 1966 G.I. Bill. John Saylor (R-PA) noted that the bill provides a "much needed increase," but maintained that the 1966 bill was only ever designed to "meet in part the cost of obtaining an education." John Hammerschmidt (R-AR) reaffirmed, "It will carry out the purpose of the original GI bill which was designed to provide an educational assistance allowance to meet, in part, the expenses of subsistence, tuition, fees, supplies, books, and equipment."[60] But other representatives recognized the continued shortcomings of the bill. Elwood Hillis (R-IN) lamented, "I thought our Vietnam era veterans deserved tuition payments. . . . I think we can do better."[61] Marvin Esch (R-WI), himself a recipient of the World War II G.I. Bill, said, "I believe that we should offer the same benefits to our veterans today."[62] Again, Teague presented the bill under the Suspension of Rules procedure, which prevented any amendments. Esch ended his attack by issuing a plea to the Senate to correct the deficiencies of the House bill in a way that he could not. The Senate duly obliged.

The Senate waited until August 3 to vote on its version of the bill, and once more, its proposal was far more generous than that offered in the House. The Senate kept the House designation H.R.12828 but attached the central features of Hartke's own proposal, S.2161. Hartke's bill offered veterans a 43 percent increase in the monthly allowance, raising the benefit from $175 to $250. As with all of the G.I. Bills, the amount increased proportionally with the number of dependents a veteran claimed. The bill also created work-study programs for veterans, allowing them to earn up to three hundred dollars in an advance payment for undertaking up to 120 hours of work for the VA. The bill also loosened the eligibility requirements for spouses of veterans to receive remedial training without affecting their entitlements for secondary education. Other features included increased farm training benefits, the option for veterans to use their benefits for overseas schools, and greater assistance to disabled veterans in obtaining federal employment. The most controversial feature of the Senate bill was the provision for low-interest loans to veterans. Under Title V of the bill, veterans could claim up to $1,575 to cover costs not covered by other federally available loan programs. Although the provision of loans was not as generous as offering outright grants, veterans could at least have another option to ease their financial concerns.

The architects of the bill clearly believed that these proposals would bring the much-needed and widely sought parity with the benefits offered World War II veterans. Cranston asked his fellow senators, "who would argue that the Vietnam era veteran should not, at long last, receive a rate of assistance under the present GI bill which is comparable to the level of assistance under the World War II GI bill?" He called the need for comparable benefits "a moral imperative for the Nation."[63] Hartke claimed that his increase would "provide true parity of benefits with the World War II GI bill." He conceded that the costs of the bill would have been considerable, but added, "the cost of the war which created these veterans is more expensive. . . . [T]he question that we face today is not: 'Can we afford to do it,' but rather 'Can we afford not to do it.'"[64] The other senators clearly shared his views and passed the bill by a vote of eighty-nine to zero. Not for the first time, and not for the last, the Senate had passed a generous G.I. Bill and now had to wait for the House to launch its anticipated and by now almost inevitable counterattack.

Indeed, after Teague got his hands back on the bill, H.R.12828 once more became a far less generous measure than the one sought by the Senate. Conferees offered a monthly allowance increase of only 25.7 percent, elevating payments to $220 a month. The maximum amount of extra income a veteran could earn from work-study programs dropped to $250. Significantly, the Senate "reluctantly" agreed to drop their provision to offer loans. The House and the Veterans Administration claimed that such loans were not necessary because of other universal student loan programs veterans could utilize. Hartke pledged to "monitor" veteran loan claims to see if they were using the other loan programs.[65] After several other compromises on secondary issues, the Senate passed the bill and sent it to the White House.

Through the VA and at the urging of the Office of Management and Budget, Nixon's administration had advocated an increase to only $190 a month, but he knew that proposal would gain little traction. His strategy to keep benefits low was twofold: The first was to ask for as little as politically feasible on the understanding that, as Nixon staffer John Evans put it, "whatever we ask for Congress will increase."[66] The second was to back Teague's maneuverings in the House, knowing that the Texan would attempt to restrain the Senate's generosity. According to Evans, "we decided to throw in with Teague, ask him to hold the line as low as he could, and tell him the President was counting on him to keep the costs down."[67] Although the compromise bill, in essence, amounted to little more than a simple increase in the monthly allowance, Hartke claimed, "the results we have obtained represent a substantial and perhaps even historic movement forward . . . [and] a giant step toward recognizing the enormous debt we owe to our Nation's veterans."[68] Although Hartke seemed quite satisfied with his efforts, the veterans still had to wait for the kinds of benefits they hoped for and thought that they deserved.

Once more, Nixon used the passage of a bill he had attempted to thwart to reaffirm his commitment to the Vietnam veteran. In a radio

Olin Teague (center) relaxing with his personal friend and commander of U.S. military operations in Vietnam from 1964 to 1968, General William Westmoreland (right), alongside Richard Nixon (left). Teague frequently worked in unison with the president to reduce federal spending, including veterans' benefits. *Courtesy of the Cushing Memorial Library and Archives, Texas A&M University.*

address given just two days before the signing of the 1972 G.I. Bill he proclaimed,

> As President I have done everything I can to see to it that this gratitude and respect is reflected by the Government's treatment of American veterans. Dollars, health care, educational opportunities can never fully repay the sacrifices our veterans have made, but they can at least serve as a beginning. I am happy to be able to report that America is doing more for its veterans today than ever before.

Failing to mention his own continued opposition to higher benefits and the slashing of VA funds for medical care, he boasted that "we" had raised education benefits, increased hospital treatments by four million patients, and doubled the number of participants in the G.I. Bill program.[69] Continuing to fawn over the soldiers in public, Nixon invited eighty Vietnam veterans to the signing ceremony in the White House State Dining Room. They had been carefully selected for their support of Nixon's Vietnam policies, so that the president could be seen standing tall with "the real heroes of America, the ones who have chosen to serve rather than run away."[70] Nixon informed them that the bill "will allow you to get that education and that training so essential to get the jobs that you will later want."[71] The Vietnam Era Veterans' Readjustment Assistance Act of 1972 became Public Law 92-540 on October 24, 1972.

Thereafter, and as with many previous White House occupants, Nixon continued his pattern of working behind the scenes to cut veteran funding in many areas while lauding the veterans in public. In March of 1973, in a "Statement About the Vietnam Veteran," Nixon proclaimed, "No group of American fighting men was ever called on to demonstrate their bravery, their endurance, or their love of country under more trying circumstances than those gallant Americans who served in Vietnam." Promising to "honor them," he went on to claim that no other generation of veterans had ever enjoyed such a wide range of government benefits. He then called on all employers to look favorably upon Vietnam veterans in their hiring practices.[72] But he also used one of his favorite tactics to undermine one of the education programs he had signed into law the previous October. Upsetting the constitutional balance, Nixon regularly impounded money appropriated by Congress for federal programs, effectively killing the program. He did this on over one hundred occasions, most notably for the Clean Water Act of 1972.[73] He refused to release $25 million for the Veterans' Cost of Instruction Program, authorized under the 1972 G.I. Bill, designed to give money to institutions that encouraged veteran enrollment. It took court proceedings brought by the National Association of Collegiate Veterans (NACV) to release the money in May of 1973. The NACV president called it "pathetic that the Vietnam veteran must seek court action to gain the same benefits afforded veterans of past wars through congressional action."[74]

Donald Johnson continued to stubbornly support the administration's line, even as the public and political pressure on him increased. In March of 1973, he defended the hospital cutbacks in front of a House Appropriations subcommittee. In April, he wrote a stinging reply to a *New York Times* editorial that had accused Nixon of using "selective statistics" and that had attacked education benefits as "pitifully short."[75] Johnson asserted, "A compassionate concern for these young veterans has long had top priority in Administration considerations." After citing the numerous measures signed by Nixon to assist veterans, he claimed that Vietnam veterans could claim "nearly three times the World War II allowance" and that the G.I. Bill "gives most veterans more monetary assistance than after World War II, even allowing for inflation and increased school costs."[76] Johnson's claims contradicted many of the studies undertaken on the G.I. Bill, making any objective evaluation of the success of the program difficult. There remained a lot of confusion, misinformation, and hyperbole in the public debate over the G.I. Bill. Congressional leaders such as Teague and Yarborough had offered differing views of the success of the benefits while the press continued to paint a damning picture of the program. A March 1973 editorial in the *Washington Post* claimed, "The Viet vets have found that their GI bill dollars buy only one-fourth the education that their fathers got for the same money after World War II."[77] In light of such wildly contradictory claims, Congress sought additional quantification of the effectiveness of the program before taking any further legislative action.

Even though the two G.I. Bill increases in 1970 and 1972 went some way to alleviating the veteran's burden, they did not extinguish the overall criticisms against the program that persisted in the press. The backslapping and puffed-up speeches emanating from the White House and from some on the Hill indicated that lawmakers were becoming increasingly content with the efforts they had made thus far for the Vietnam veterans. But many veterans continued to feel that the government could do a lot more to aid their return home. Congress, therefore, included a proviso on the 1972 G.I. Bill that commissioned an independent study to analyze the effectiveness of the program. The study aimed to provide a comparison of the post–Korean War G.I. Bills "with similar programs of educational assistance that were available to veterans of World War II and of the Korean conflict."[78] The Education Testing

Service (ETS) of New Jersey won the contract to conduct the study on May 25, 1973. On August 30, they submitted their results, but a VA advisory committee rejected it for not fulfilling the requirements. The revised report arrived on September 8.

The ETS report offered the most thorough analysis yet of the post–Korean War benefits and revealed significant flaws in the statistics being used in Washington to either support or decry the program. The report noted that veteran participation under the 1966 G.I. Bill—and following the subsequent raises—had surpassed Korean-era levels and would soon surpass World War II levels. However, the report suggested that usage levels were an imperfect indicator of success because no statistics existed in the VA or in other agencies that revealed how many veterans actually completed their courses. The VA had only collected data relevant to the administration of the program and did not keep track of dropout rates. No one knew if Vietnam veterans were using the G.I. Bill as a temporary cash boost without ever completing their course of study. A further problem in using participation rates was that they did not reveal how the veterans had fared relative to their nonveteran peers. Therefore, there was little indication of whether Vietnam-era veterans had received proper readjustment benefits that compensated them for time lost from civilian life, one of the main goals of all G.I. Bills. The report also confirmed that minority and underprivileged veterans were less likely to use their benefits for higher education, even though no other generation of veterans had had so many programs aimed at helping them. Federal efforts to assist these groups, the report concluded, needed expanding. No comparable data existed on disadvantaged veterans of the World War II era.

Perhaps the most significant issue addressed in the report, the one that had been at the heart of the debates since 1966, was the adequacy of funding levels. Here the report suggested that "the average Vietnam veteran attending a 4-year public or a 2-year public institution has educational benefits slightly higher than his World War II counterpart when adjustments for changes in the Consumer Price Index are made."[79] But the report raised several variables that affected the "real" worth of the benefits to the veteran. When raises in the costs of tuition were considered or, for example, the fact that colleges did not make low-cost housing available for Vietnam-era veterans as many did for World War

II veterans, the Vietnam veteran's "'real' ability to purchase postsecondary education has diminished with respect to his World War II counterpart."[80] Based on an average budget of a veteran's annual expenses, including all living, medical, educational, and other costs, the average single veteran needed an additional $628 a year or roughly fifty-two dollars a month on which to live. The available benefits, suggested the report, covered only 68.2 percent of the average single veteran's annual expenses. The average married veteran required an additional $1,644 a year to cover expenses. The benefits offered in 1973 provided for only 50 percent of their needs.[81] There were, of course, variables from this average. A veteran attending a lower-cost public school fared much better than one attending a private school. Moreover, the report confirmed that the differing costs of education in different states made a considerable impact on how far a veteran's money went.

Ultimately, the report revealed that variations such as geography, class, and marital status made the kinds of broad generalizations about the program heard in Washington and in the press difficult to quantify. Many veterans did benefit from their G.I. Bill, but many more were in need of additional aid. If, as the VA claimed, the G.I. Bill was designed to do nothing more than *assist* a veteran achieve his or her education goals, then the G.I. Bill did provide a welcome injection of funds and covered a significant amount of the veteran's costs. The VA explicitly stated that the veterans ought to contribute something to their education, either from their own savings, from employment, or, in the case of married veterans, from their spouse's employment. Indeed, the report noted that when one added a spouse's income to the basic benefits, a married veteran with no dependents might have had enough to cover his or her expenses. In addition, the veterans could still claim other federal benefits such as BEOGs, National Defense Student Loans, or federally insured student loans (the report found that veterans had not made use of these other resources in significant numbers). If, however, the G.I. Bill aimed to provide the same levels of coverage as previous G.I. Bills, the Vietnam-era legislation was falling well short.

The ETS report met with mixed responses from those parties most affected by its findings. Sections of the media and the veteran community jumped on the report's conclusions as further evidence for their familiar refrain that the government and the VA were ignoring the veterans' needs. The *Washington Post* used the report to call for "A Fair Shake for Vietnam Veterans."[82] In its monthly newsletter, the NACV informed its readers on the front page that "Educational Testing Service Reports Vietnam Veterans Get Less Aid."[83] Predictably, the VA took issue with some of the report's more negative assessments of the program. In testimony before the Veterans' Subcommittee on Education and Training, Odell Vaughan, chief benefits director at the VA, focused on the positive aspects of the report and maintained, "the majority of Vietnam era veterans are better off today."[84] Further, he suggested, "no general restructuring of the educational program seems necessary or advisable, especially with reference to the present benefit system."[85] Few were surprised when Donald Johnson criticized the report for its methodology and its conclusions. Moreover, he suggested that most of the variables raised in the report that stretched the veterans' resources lay beyond the scope of the VA's mandate. He believed the VA should not, for example, fully compensate veterans wanting to attend higher-cost schools or those wanting to start a family. Johnson thought that the government was doing enough by paying more on average per head in adjusted dollars than it had done for the World War II veteran. This view offered little comfort to those veterans who suffered because of their own geographical or familial status or who did not want to compromise the quality of their education. Johnson believed the report demonstrated that the Vietnam veteran "does have availability to educational assistance benefits . . . that are comparable to those extended to veterans of World War II and the Korean conflict."[86] The VA refused to endorse any further benefit increases in the wake of the report.

Although it confirmed many of the previous observations made in private reports on the G.I. Bill, the ETS report, which was the largest federal attempt to quantify the effectiveness of the program, made a few waves on Capitol Hill. Bolstered by the new evidence contained in the report, Congress moved forward with new proposals to increase the veterans' monthly allowance. At the end of October, the House Veterans' Affairs Committee considered a new proposal to give veterans a 13.6 percent increase, raising the monthly allowance from $220 to $250. The proposal also sought to tie veterans' benefits to the Consumer Price Index. Significantly, the proposal also sought to increase the length of time a veteran could claim his or her benefits from eight years to ten years. This would allow veterans who had faced problems on coming home to have additional time to readjust before returning to higher education. In the Senate, Vance Hartke introduced a bill that would provide a 23 percent increase in benefits and provide up to two thousand dollars in low-interest loans for veterans in higher-cost schools. Nixon began to apply pressure as soon as Congress began to move. He suggested that veterans should receive no more than an 8 percent increase and threatened to veto more costly legislation.

The House did not vote on its bill until February of 1974. Their final measure, H.R.12628, promised veterans a far from generous 13.6 percent increase in their monthly allowance. By 1974, Teague had stepped down from his position as chair of the Veterans' Affairs Committee. The space program had been another of Teague's pet interests, and in 1973 he chose to serve as chairman of the House Committee on Science and Astronautics. It was not a decision he took lightly, but he ensured that he would still continue to influence House actions on veterans' legislation by serving on the Subcommittee on Education and Training of the Veterans' Affairs Committee.

William Jennings Bryan Dorn succeeded Teague as chair of the full committee. Dorn, a Democrat from South Carolina, was another World War II veteran. He denounced Nixon's calls for a mere 8 percent increase and called the House proposal "fully justified in view of the very significant increase in living costs and school expenses."[87] Every member who rose in the debate over H.R.12628 accepted the need for a benefits increase, but most raised concerns that the bill did not go far enough. John P. Hammerschmidt (R-AR) noted that the Consumer Price Index would rise to an estimated 13.2 percent by May, meaning that the proposed 13.6 percent increase would barely keep pace with the cost of living. Margaret Heckler (R-MA), one of the architects of the bill, added that food prices would rise by 16 percent in 1974 and called the increase "hardly generous—it is merely adequate."[88] Silvio Conte (R-MA) called for a bill that would pay 80 percent of a veteran's tuition costs. He conceded, "I intend to vote for the veterans' educational benefits package . . . even though it falls somewhat short of the mark."[89] Teague, of course, saw no such problems with the bill. Referring to a more costly measure introduced in the Senate, he protested, "I am distressed . . . that the public is being subjected to the steady barrage of propaganda calculated to support a bill which has been introduced in the Senate." Teague also resurrected the specter of the overly privileged veteran when he added, "After the passage of this bill, the position of the Vietnam veterans will be distinctly preferential."[90] Once again, when the bill went to vote, it received unanimous backing. Despite the misgivings of many over the shortcomings of the bill, most considered any increase better than none. The final vote was a crushing 382–0.

H.R.12628 did retain the provision to raise the amount of time a veteran could claim benefits from eight years to ten. Previous G.I. Bills had an eight-year limitation, but after World War II and Korea, veterans had received their generous benefits immediately. In part, Vietnam veterans did not enter the program in high numbers early on because of the low benefits offered under the 1966 bill. Only after the rates were elevated did significant numbers begin to claim their benefits. The problem that those who had left the service in 1966 but who had entered school in 1970 or 1972 now faced was that their eligibility would expire in 1974 under the existing bill. In the debates over H.R.12628, many politicians revealed that they had received floods of letters from concerned veterans as their eligibility was about to expire. A two-year extension would offer veterans the opportunity to complete their degree; it would also carry particular significance for one group of veterans.

Nearly twenty thousand women served in Vietnam in such capacities as nurses, clerical staff, or advisors to South Vietnamese clerical support staff. The scope and nature of military service for women had expanded considerably over the course of the twentieth century. By the mid-1970s, female veterans were given equal access to federal benefits such as the G.I. Bill, but that had not always been the case. In 1901 women had been welcomed into the fold of military personnel with the creation of the Nurse Corps of the Army. The navy followed suit in 1908. But servicewomen were not yet given equitable pay, rank, or the veteran status that would have given them post-service benefits. During World War II, women continued to serve as nurses in combat theaters across the globe. Their role in clerical support was expanded greatly by the creation of the WACS (Women's Army Corps), the navy's WAVES (Women in Volunteer Service), the coast guard's SPARS (a combination of the U.S. Coast Guard motto "Semper Paratus" or "Always Ready"), and the Women Marine Reserves. Service in these roles guaranteed veteran status and made women eligible for programs such as the G.I. Bill. However, the WASPS (Women's Airforce Service Pilots) were inexplicably denied veteran status until 1977, despite excelling in ferrying every type of front-line combat aircraft in the United States' arsenal during World War II. The Women's Armed Forces Integration Act of 1948 cemented women's roles as enlisted personnel in the postwar era, meaning that for the first time women could serve in peacetime and still have access to post-service benefits. The benefits were not always granted equitably, though. Only in 1972 were women allowed to claim their husbands as dependents under the G.I. Bills (thereby increasing their monthly educational allowance) in the same way that men had been able to since the 1944 bill.

For female veterans, the G.I. Bill offered a similar promise of self-improvement and much-needed assistance for civilian readjustment as it did to male veterans. Although women were withheld from direct combat during the draft wars of the twentieth century, many female veterans suffered the same rigors of military life that necessitated post-service assistance. In all roles, they underwent similar issues such as the separation from family, inculcation into a military environment, and the potential difficulties of readjusting to the comparative banality of civilian life. Those serving in combat theaters also brought home the psychological burden of bearing witness to the devastating effects of war. Nurses, in particular, who went to Vietnam were likely to walk in the shadow of death far more frequently than even the most battle-tested of male combatants. One female nurse who worked in an evacuation hospital recalled the gruesome task of having to match body parts of the victims of one enemy attack so that the victims' families were presented with remains that contained parts that "were the same color, and [that] there would not be two left feet, to two right hands."[91] On a regular basis, nurses suffered the trauma of watching their patients suffer and die. This trauma was true of all wars, of course, but in Vietnam, with the enemy's use of booby traps and the advent of rapid evacuation from the battlefield, the wounds could be particularly horrific. When they came home, women who had served in Vietnam also carried the same stigma of serving in an unpopular war. Despite their service, few of their civilian counterparts wanted to hear of their experiences and cared little for their sacrifice. A common question might have been,

"Was it like *M*A*S*H* over there?" but most veterans just kept their experiences to themselves. One army nurse veteran who had volunteered for service in Vietnam hid her military background when campus riots erupted at the University of Maryland where she was enrolled. "Things got rough at times," she recalled, "We military people stuck together and didn't tell anyone we were in the military."[92]

In crafting G.I. Bill legislation, the lawmakers and the VA paid little attention to the specific needs of female veterans. In part, this failure was due to the fact that—up until the creation of the All-Volunteer Force in 1973—women had always constituted a small minority of the armed forces. Approximately 250,000 women—roughly 2.3 percent of the armed forces—for example, served during the Vietnam era.[93] The VA assumed that a blanket program covered all veterans adequately and did not even keep records on the numbers of World War II or Korean–era female veterans who used their G.I. Bill. But up through the Vietnam era, one consistent complaint from female veterans was that they struggled to use their G.I. Bill benefits in the limited time allotted. By 1972, female veterans could claim the same benefits as their male counterparts, but they tended to use their benefits much later after discharge from service, sometimes seven or eight years later. According to one VA report, 20.1 percent of male veterans were still in school seven years after service compared with 40.1 percent of female veterans.[94] One major reason for this delay was that many left the service because of pregnancy or due to a desire to start a family. Given the gender mores of the 1960s and 1970s, this process meant the female veteran tended to be the one who had to take several years out of her life to raise children. Many, therefore, found it difficult to complete a four-year college course within the allotted eight-year window to claim benefits. One veteran interviewed for a 1983 study on women's post-service lives joined the marines in 1964. She delayed going to school to raise her children and ended up losing her benefits after her eligibility expired. Another veteran from the same study had accumulated one hundred hours of college credit toward her degree, but for similar reasons her benefits expired before she could complete her course of study.[95] The two-year extension offered by the House bill would, therefore, have allowed more female veterans an opportunity to complete their degree before their eligibility expired—helping correct a major problem of previous legislation.

The Senate bill contained a similar two-year extension to the House bill, but also went much further in what it offered veterans. The Senate Veterans' Affairs Committee reported out their bill, S.2784, on May 22. The Senate bill retained the central features of Hartke's earlier proposal by offering an 18 percent increase in benefits and the option of two thousand dollars in loans. In addition to the two-year extension, a veteran could also receive forty-five months of benefits instead of thirty-six. No previous G.I. Bill had offered veterans as long a period of time in which to claim their benefits. As had the House bill, the Senate bill increased vocational training benefits for disabled veterans. The Senate bill also contained many other measures to liberalize the veteran's entitlements, including offering greater assistance for tutorial programs and significantly raising the amount a veteran could earn in work-study programs. The most contentious element of the Senate bill was a proposal to pay 80 percent of a veteran's tuition, up to one thousand dollars per year once a veteran had paid an initial one hundred dollars. Unlike with the World War II G.I. Bill, the tuition payment would go directly to the veteran.

The American Legion, the VFW, and other veterans' organizations offered widespread support for the Senate bill. They had come a long way from their early days of equivocation on Cold War education benefits. Robert Eaton, national commander of the American Legion, expressed his hopes to Hartke that "S.2784 will be passed by the Senate without amendment and that the House will agree to its provisions at the earliest possible moment."[96] The VFW made it a priority in 1974 to support "the enactment into law of comparable readjustment assistance for Vietnam veterans, as was provided for veterans of previous wars." Francis W. Stover, the VFW's director of National Legislative Service, informed Hartke that "the prompt approval of S.2784 by the full Senate will be deeply appreciated by the more than 1.8 million members of the Veterans of Foreign Wars."[97] The Disabled American Veterans offered Hartke their "heartfelt thanks and appreciation" for the bill, while the American Veterans Committee noted that "the benefits of this important bill to the Vietnam-era veterans, to education and to society itself, far outweigh possible abuses."[98] The National Association of Concerned Veterans' Timothy Craig informed Hartke, "The NACV believes that you and the members of the Committee have performed [an] excellent service to Vietnam Era veterans in formulating the bill which you have reported to the Senate."[99]

The Senate bill clearly went further than any previous measure to offer Vietnam veterans the kinds of liberal benefits offered veterans of previous wars. Hartke claimed, "In many ways this bill exceeds the measure under which many of us in Congress went to school after World War II."[100] Alan Cranston added, "I believe that finally . . . we will have provided a true measure of comparability of GI bill educational assistance for Vietnam-era veterans with the level of benefits provided after World War II and the Korean conflict."[101] Even the press responded favorably to the Senate bill. The *Washington Post* described the measure as "generous and fair."[102] But whether the House would accept such a generous bill remained in doubt. It took a long and arduous summer of negotiation before House and Senate conferees reached an agreement.

While Congress moved slowly toward an accord, 1974 was fast becoming Richard Nixon's *annus horribilis*. While his political career was crumbling amid the Watergate allegations, his erratic record on veterans' affairs continued. In public, he took his praise of Vietnam veterans to new heights. On January 28, he sent a "Special Message to the Congress Proposing Veterans Legislation" in which he reiterated his call for an 8 percent raise in education benefits "to keep pace with inflation" as well as increased funding in health care and pensions. He claimed that his administration had "done our best" to assist Vietnam veterans and that "[w]e owe these men and women our best effort in providing them with the benefits that their service has earned them."[103] Two days later in his State of the Union Address he reiterated, "We must also be concerned for those veterans and veterans' families who remain in need." On February 26, as he signed legislation proclaiming March 29 "Vietnam Veterans Day," he pledged, "we do owe a great debt of honor to those who served."[104] On the day itself, he commented, "We can be thankful that America produced such men, and we can be thankful that in the future these men, their courage, their continued service, will make it possible for us to achieve the goal that all Americans are dedicated to, peace for ourselves and for all mankind."[105] Four senators, McGovern, Inouye, Dole, and Mathias, called a press conference on Vietnam Veterans Day at which they described the celebration as "an empty gesture without action to fulfill the nation's debt to Vietnam-era veterans."[106]

The bills circulating in Congress to increase education benefits represented the government's best and perhaps final chance at fulfilling that debt. The Vietnam era was now almost ten years old. The last combat veterans had already been home for almost a year, and the government was still squabbling over how much they were owed. Even as his presidency unraveled around him, in the final months of his administration, Nixon and his staffers worked hard to ensure that the debt the nation owed to these servicemen and women would not be paid in full. A White House memo laid out the administration's objections to the Senate bill. The memo claimed that the Senate measure "[s]ubverts the purpose of the GI Bill program" by encouraging those who might have only a casual interest in higher education and are "primarily interested in augmenting their own income without working." The memo suggested that the costs of the bill would also discriminate against veterans attending lower-cost public schools by diverting VA funds to veterans wanting to attend more expensive schools. Fears of tuition abuse also fueled the administration's opposition. The final objection was that the Senate bill "Balloons GI Bill costs unnecessarily" by "converting a cost-sharing program to an income-attractive program."[107]

Nixon again hoped to enlist Teague in the fight against the Senate bill and wrote him to reiterate the main White House objections. Teague seemed more than willing to comply. He informed White House staffers that he was attempting to bypass Hartke's more expensive bill by taking up the cause of one of the alternative, less expensive Senate bills, attaching the House version, and returning it to the Senate. But Teague warned that—in the words of one administration aide—"Hartke is completely berserk on this one," and he asked the White House for assistance "on the Senate side to trim the monster back."[108] Nixon's aides then attempted to pressure Senate Veterans' Affairs Committee members Strom Thurmond and Cliff Hansen to reduce the costs of the "monster" bill in conference. The main feature of the Senate bill that the White House wanted removed was the proposal for tuition payments, described by Nixon aide Bill Timmons as an "obnoxious provision."[109]

In one of his last acts in office, Nixon offered a further suggestion that he might veto any measure approaching the costs of the Senate bill. On July 30, just eight days before resigning the presidency, he wrote Hartke and Teague to attack the Senate bill, warning of the "'suction' effects of converting the G.I. Bill from an educational cost-sharing to an income attractive program."[110] The *Washington Post* described Nixon's letter as a strong suggestion that he might veto the bill.[111] But Nixon had offered similar opposition to education increases throughout his presidency, so there was certainly no guarantee that he would follow through on his veto threat. Ultimately, the decision was not his to make. By the end of the summer, the Watergate investigations forced his resignation. One of the most significant bills in the history of the G.I. Bill remained in conference as Nixon boarded Marine One and lifted off the White House lawn for the last time. Nixon's successor, Gerald R. Ford, would be the one to face Congress and the veterans in a tumultuous fall in Washington. Pressure on Ford to pass the bill would come from many areas. However, conspicuously absent was any concerted, nationwide, and broad-based lobbying pressure from the Vietnam veterans. Their failure to organize on a large scale, in the same way that the American Legion had after World War I, left them vulnerable to the political whims of Washington. So where had all the veterans gone?

5

On the Streets and in the Schools

The Veterans Come Home

Most of us were not walking around publicizing the fact that
we were veterans. . . . I just think many of us wanted to get
on with our lives.
—Dave Hollingsworth, April 2005

While the calls for an improved G.I. Bill echoed in the halls of Congress and in the press, the group of citizens for whom the calls rang out remained relatively quiet. There seemed to be either a reluctance or an inability among Vietnam veterans to organize into a coherent force capable of bringing meaningful pressure to bear on those legislators still putting up roadblocks to their readjustment. In contrast to the American Legion and VFW's actions on behalf of returning World War I and World War II veterans, few large-scale national organizations existed to promote the specific needs of returning Vietnam veterans. In part, this void was a consequence of some veterans' initial unwillingness to embrace their veteran identity. They seemed particularly averse to putting their uniforms back on and fraternizing with other veterans. Daniel Ellsberg alluded to the differing mindset of the Vietnam veteran in a speech at Columbia University in October 1971. According to Ellsberg, the Vietnam veteran represented a new kind of veteran, one less concerned with organizing for benefits and more concerned with "resistance to legitimate authority" and bringing an end to the war.[1] As one staff member of the Senate Veterans' Affairs Committee noted, "Today's vets, for better or worse, are not a highly organized group, unlike the World War II men. . . . They come home, and don't think of themselves as veterans and don't organize themselves."[2]

As has been widely studied, many Vietnam veterans returned home to a tepid welcome. World War II veterans could expect a degree of adulation once they donned their uniform. Military service, for them, was a badge of honor in a society that revered their sacrifice. For Vietnam veterans, whatever personal pride they might have felt in their service, putting on their uniform was unlikely to draw the same approbation. Proud boasts of military adventures in Southeast Asia were unlikely to attract the same kind of personal or political capital in a nation that had grown increasingly wary of the war and, in some quarters, had begun to raise questions about the conduct of the troops. The combination of their own mixed feelings over the war and the lack of a welcome home they had received led some veterans to want to put away their uniforms and forget their military experience. As one veteran recalled, "I remember that when I returned from Vietnam, the first thing that we did was shed the uniform and get into civilian clothes. This is in stark contrast to the veterans of World War I, World War II, and Korea, who wore their uniforms to their hometowns, and were received with welcome arms."[3] The result of this lobbying void was that, as the author of one study of the politics of Vietnam-related issues concludes, "As the 1970s began, Vietnam veterans lacked a national organization dedicated to their interests and had no effective advocate in Congress."[4] There were some notable exceptions to this relative lack of action.

By the beginning of the 1970s, the organization most dedicated to lobbying Congress for higher education benefits was the National Association of Concerned Veterans (NACV). Although never as powerful or influential as the older and more established veterans' lobbies, the NACV emerged during these troubled years as one of the more consistent advocates of Vietnam veterans' rights. Formed in Mankato, Minnesota, in 1968 by a group of G.I. Bill users, and initially called the National Association of Collegiate Veterans, the NACV was one of the few Vietnam veteran organizations with a national focus.[5] When pushing for benefit increases in the summer of 1974, the NACV complained that "[c]urrently not enough grass roots support has hit reluctant Congressmen to press them into influencing fellow Congressmen who are blocking Senate proposed improvements in the G.I. Bill."[6] The NACV attempted to fill this void. They organized lobbying campaigns for several veterans' initiatives, including the establishment of Upward Bound programs, and brought lawsuits against the government to free up funds to support the federally mandated veterans' programs. The NACV also promoted job fairs across the country to help veterans find employment and pushed for greater sensitivity in the VA to the plight of minority veterans. NACV representatives also testified before several House and Senate hearings on veterans' benefits. As noted in one NACV newsletter from 1974, whenever new veterans' legislation was being debated, the NACV sent members "flying, driving, and hitch hiking in to see their individual Congressmen."[7] By 1973 the NACV claimed over thirty thousand dues-paying members and had established 130 chapters nationwide. That same year, Vance Hartke, chairman of the Senate Committee for Veterans' Affairs, praised the organization on the floor of the Senate for its efforts. He noted, however, the difficulties the organization faced in attracting members. "Too often" he claimed, "some people would like to forget the Indochina war and would also like to forget those who fought that war. . . . This has meant tough sledding for NACV."[8] Even though it still represented a tiny fraction of the veteran population, the NACV remained at the forefront of the fight for better benefits for Vietnam veterans. There were, however, far more vocal and high-profile veterans' organizations.

Perhaps the most visible Vietnam veterans' group was the Vietnam Veterans Against the War (VVAW). A small group of veterans formed the organization in April 1967 after a protest march demanding U.S. withdrawal from Vietnam. The VVAW went on to organize some of the most notable acts of veteran antiwar activity of the Vietnam era. VVAW tactics included "guerilla theater," which involved dressing in fatigues, carrying replica weapons, and acting out combat scenes in order to bring the chaos of war to America's streets. One notable target of the guerilla treatment was Strom Thurmond, who, on account of his hawkish attitudes toward the war, was accosted by VVAW activists on one of the Capitol building's underground transportation cars. When he dismissed the veterans' calls for sweeping hearings on the war, Thurmond was subjected to verbal assaults and the thrusting of toy M-16s in his face. Thurmond's reaction, recalled one participant, was to spew "every cliché he could think of about the antiwar movement. . . . 'Commie asshole pinko bastards get a job' shit. . . . He was just going off his nut."[9]

Then, over Labor Day weekend 1970, the VVAW conducted Operation RAW (Rapid American Withdrawal), a protest march that culminated in a rally at Valley Forge with speeches by high-profile antiwar activists. The following January, the organization sponsored a three-day gathering in Detroit, Michigan, aimed to highlight the brutalizing nature of the war for all participants. Dubbed the Winter Soldier Investigations, the event included graphic testimony from recently retuned veterans on U.S. atrocities and misconduct in Vietnam. The event inspired Senator William Fulbright to begin further hearings on ending the war in his Senate Committee on Foreign Relations in April 1971. That same month, the VVAW descended on Washington, DC, for Operation Dewey Canyon III. The operation derived its name from Dewey Canyon II, the South Vietnamese U.S.–backed incursion into Laos of some weeks earlier, and was styled as a similar strike at the heart of American power. In one of the more poignant displays of protest during the gathering, hundreds of Vietnam veterans renounced their participation in the war by tossing their medals and other emblems of service onto the steps of the U.S. Capitol building. Then, toward the end of the year, fifteen VVAW members briefly occupied the Statue of Liberty.[10]

At its height, the VVAW counted almost fifty thousand members. Invariably, the group supported calls for improved education benefits whenever such calls arose. When Nixon was equivocating over the 1972 G.I. Bill improvements, for example, the VVAW collected signatures for a petition to "Extend and Expand the G.I. Bill." Reflecting the radical and often anticapitalist nature of their organization, the preamble to the petition proclaimed, "A lot of promises were made to vets. American corporations needed us to fight their wars. We were forced to do their dirty work—to get killed, wounded or disabled in wars like Indochina only so that they can continue to bring profits from foreign plunder." Following up with a call for increased monthly payments and tuition guarantees, they continued, "We say enough! We're not going to let the rich give us the shaft again. Once they made us fight for them, but our fight's against them." The solution offered by the VVAW for funding the proposed increases revealed the main thrust of the organization's activism. Instead of increasing the "already heavy burden of taxes on the poor and working people," they argued, "the additional cost can be covered by the cessation of the war in SE Asia and by a reordering of U.S. priorities in a more humane direction."[11]

From its very inception, the VVAW's mission was to end the United States' involvement in the war. The group's tactics and organizing activities, from the guerilla theater and the attack on Thurmond to the veterans' testimonies, had been geared toward convincing the public of the need to end the war. Highlighting the devastating effects of the war on all participants, including both the victims and the perpetrators of atrocities, was an effective means to this end. This single-minded focus meant that the VVAW rarely devoted itself fully to such prosaic matters as education benefits. Indeed, in his study of Vietnam veterans' activism, Gerald Nicosia speculates that the VVAW's open hostility toward the government's continued prosecution of the war may have made it even more difficult for Nixon to be sympathetic to the readjustment problems faced by Vietnam veterans. Nixon, suggests Nicosia, "never a cheerful loser, was determined to get back at the Vietnam veterans in every way he could."[12] Rusty Lindley, one-time VVAW officer and participant in Dewey Canyon III, recalled that the VVAW's action led to "a radical change in attitude in the White House." Pending legislation, such as Alan Cranston's counseling bill—which gave special consideration for veterans' readjustment difficulties—might have reaffirmed the VVAW's focus on the destructive nature of the war. According to Lindley, because Nixon was so determined to build a positive narrative of the war, his administration became "adamantly opposed to the provision of any assistance that would indicate that the war was adversely affecting veterans."[13] For Nixon, the long-haired and disheveled interlopers sporadically invading DC served as an unwelcome and public reminder of how the war had gone so terribly wrong.

After the last combat troops came home in 1973, the VVAW lost much of its momentum. Stripped of its original raison d'être, the organization rapidly lost members and focus. In particular, the increasing influence of anticapitalist and Marxist ideas among the organization's leadership turned off many veterans and hurt its public image.[14] One of the organization's last hurrahs of the Vietnam era was an additional march on Washington in July 1974, dubbed Operation Dewey Canyon IV. With the war fading into most Americans' rear view mirror, the turnout this time was greatly diminished. Reflecting the group's more diffuse postwar goals, its banners read "Universal and Unconditional Amnesty," "Implement the Peace Agreement—End All Aid to Thieu and Lon Nol," and "Kick Nixon Out."[15] This time, their presence on the National Mall made little impact in the press or on Congress. In June 1976, VVAW members rallied once more to reoccupy the Statue of Liberty in order to protest, among other things, the expiration of veterans' eligibility for G.I. Bill benefits. The protesters were quickly arrested by park police, but the banners draped from Liberty's crown certainly presented a dramatic spectacle.

With the war over, toward the end of the 1970s the VVAW did devote more of its efforts and many pages of its newsletter, *The Veteran*, to raising awareness of the lingering G.I. Bill issues. The "Extend and Expand the G.I. Bill" banner draped from the Statue of Liberty was part of a wider campaign to draw attention to the fact that many veterans risked losing their benefits because their eligibility was running out. Further, the organization continued to bring attention to such issues as the problems of the VA's bureaucracy, the ongoing failure of the government to provide full tuition coverage, and the inequities between past G.I. Bills and the Vietnam iteration.[16] On a local level, the VVAW also worked with individual veterans wherever possible to help them overcome problems with the VA.[17] Indeed, the VVAW was—and long after the war continued to be—one of the strongest advocates for veterans' rights. Their ability to influence G.I. Bill legislation, however, was somewhat diminished by their initial focus on bringing American soldiers home when their membership and profile was at its zenith. Understandably, the VVAW saw ending the war as the most important issue as the big battles over benefits raged in Washington at the end of the 1960s and in the early 1970s. Their increased focus on the issue came mainly after the war was over and after the dye had been cast for the Vietnam generation.

Other attempts at organizing Vietnam veterans into a coherent national political force provided even more muted results. In July 1974, while Congress seemed on the verge of passing new G.I. Bill benefits, Ron Kovic hoped to bring one hundred thousand veterans to DC for a new Bonus March. The organization he spearheaded, the American Veterans Movement, was numerically minuscule, but it had created something of a stir earlier in the year when some of its members

Members of the
Vietnam Veterans
Against the War
occupy the Statue of
Liberty in June 1976.
Their "Extend &
Expand the G.I. Bill"
banner reflected
their increased focus
on veterans' benefits
from the mid-1970s
onward, while the
other banner, "We've
Carried the Rich
for 200 Years, Let's
Get Them off Our
Backs," alludes to
the organization's
frequent anticapital-
ist tone. *Courtesy of
the Vietnam Veterans
Against the War.*

occupied and staged a seventeen-day hunger strike in Alan Cranston's Westwood California office. They demanded a showdown with the senator and with the VA's Donald Johnson to discuss the VA's perceived indifference to Vietnam veterans. But throughout its short lifespan, the AVM remained chronically short on numbers, financing, or organizational acumen, and only a handful of veterans showed up to the DC march. While Kovic remained one of the more visible veterans' activists and would gain international notoriety as author of the 1976 memoir *Born on the Fourth of July,* the American Veterans Movement crumbled in the wake of the DC debacle.[18]

The veterans' organizations with the greatest ability to influence education legislation remained, of course, the American Legion and the

VFW. The Disabled American Veterans regularly joined the fight but maintained their focus on assisting those veterans in greatest need. In theory, Vietnam veterans could have found an outlet for their political activism in these traditional organizations, but immediately after service, many Vietnam veterans seemed hesitant to join. Later in their lives, as more Vietnam veterans came to terms with their service and as the nation began to show a greater appreciation for their sacrifice, many did embrace their veteran status more fully. But in the early years after their discharge from the service, veterans' organizations seemed like places where old guys sat around, drank, and reminisced about what they did in the war. Understandably, this held little appeal for Vietnam veterans, many of whom were in no rush to relive their wartime experience. Fred Hart, a veteran who served through the Tet Offensive during his tour of duty as a truck driver in Vietnam, never really felt his participation in the war was "worth something" until decades later. Hart never joined a veteran organization and recalls, "the country didn't much want to bother with us, so we really didn't feel a part of the veteran community. . . . I don't know why. I never had a desire to join."[19] After returning home from service in a combat engineering battalion in Vietnam and Germany in 1972, Dave Hollingsworth took several years to come to terms with his veteran status and never considered joining a veteran's organization. He notes, "there was a bit of a climate in those years that . . . with some of the traditional service organizations that we may not fit in. . . . And the other thing was that if I had joined a service organization, I would have had to realize my 'vetness.'"[20]

There existed an especially strong tension between some members of the older generations of veterans and their more radical Vietnam counterparts. Certainly, there was no love lost between the VVAW and the established veterans' organizations. While the VVAW was decrying the capitalist overtones of the conflict and acting out the brutality of the war on Main Street U.S.A., the VFW and Legion were regularly publishing articles in support of the war in their monthly magazines. Further, the generally conservative politics of both the Legion and VFW would have been anathema to the more militant Vietnam veterans. One Legion article claimed to be "exposing the communist blueprint for the American negro" and warned of China's plan to mobilize the Black Power movement to "burn America to the ground."[21] The VFW also promised to "leave no stone unturned in support of Lt. Calley" when the sentencing for the officer convicted of committing atrocities in the My Lai massacre was handed down.[22]

The VFW was also openly critical of the VVAW's antiwar activism. In the wake of Dewey Canyon III, VFW commander-in-chief H. R. Rainwater excoriated the organization in front of the Senate Committee on Foreign Relations when he called out what he saw as the "pettiness of their own pride and their own menial political aspirations." Recoiling at the VVAW's "single issue" devotion to ending the war, Rainwater thundered, "the all-encompassing and self-righteous finger of condemnation with which they point at the heart of our nation is leveled by the hand of betrayal."[23] During the VVAW's Operation RAW, representatives of the VFW's Douglas A. MacArthur Post confronted the Vietnam veterans with a counter-protest, carrying signs with such slogans as "In God We Trust" and "Why Lose?" One VFW participant cried, "We won our war. You see, these fellas didn't . . . and from the looks of it they couldn't win." Another added, "This ground has been desecrated by these people . . . and we wanted to make sure a few good Americans stood on it today."[24]

For their part, many in the VVAW saw the VFW and Legion as little more than organizations full of jingoistic hawks more concerned with aggrandizing their own pensions than with supporting the needs of the Vietnam vets. In promoting the VVAW, Al Hubbard wrote that, "These younger veterans are not content with a para-military, pro-war organization representing them."[25] Their suspicions would have been confirmed by the Legion's and the VFW's sustained opposition to Alan Cranston's counseling programs throughout the 1970s. For while the older organizations could take some credit for pushing for G.I. Bill improvements, their neglect of other issues left a bitter taste. As the actions of the NACV, VVAW, and—to a far lesser extent—the AMV suggest, Vietnam veterans were certainly neither apolitical nor apathetic, but there was little unity or cohesion in their activism. Some veterans just wanted to put their military experience behind them while others might have found little in common with the methods or goals of the organizations founded in their name. Others found little solace in the political culture of the established older organizations. In addition, relative to World War II veterans, proportionally few had entered

Congress by the end of the 1970s. Only three years after the end of World War II, there were ninety-seven World War II veterans on the Hill compared with only eleven Vietnam-era veterans as late as 1978.[26] There was, therefore, a lack of consistent, organized pressure applied on lawmakers from the Vietnam veterans as the fights over education funding reached their conclusion.

As a consequence of the lack of organization and a muted public welcome home, Vietnam veterans tended to make a low-key return to civilian life. Notwithstanding some sensational stories of suicide, drug use, and crime that appeared in the press, most of them quietly went about rebuilding their lives. One area of public life where this silent transition was most apparent was the nation's college campuses. Even though so many veterans were struggling to make ends meet under their G.I. Bill, at the end of the 1960s they started making their way to school. The story of the Vietnam veterans in higher education reveals an often-ignored aspect of the Vietnam homecoming experience. It also reveals the strength of character displayed by many in overcoming both the financial burdens under which they labored and the personal difficulties encountered by entering a campus environment in which they may not have always been welcome.

In stark contrast to their World War II predecessors, when the Vietnam veterans did return to the nation's campuses it was with little ceremony or fanfare. There were few stories of proud G.I.s marching from the battlefield and into the classroom. The World War II veterans had unquestionably transformed campus life when they returned home under their G.I. Bill. Long lines for registration, overcrowded classrooms, and rows of temporary housing units became the norm in many institutions and became part of the mythology surrounding the first G.I. Bill. In Madison, the University of Wisconsin used temporary trailers at their Camp Randall stadium to house married veterans. Similar "G.I. villages" cropped up across the country. World War II veterans became highly visible and eminent members of their university communities, assuming leadership roles in campus organizations and fraternities. Seventy percent of the University of Michigan Rose Bowl–winning team of 1947 went to college on the G.I. Bill, as did the Heisman trophy winner that same year, Notre Dame's Johnny Lujak.[27] Their sheer weight of numbers ensured that the World War II veterans maintained a notable presence on campuses throughout the late 1940s and into the 1950s. At Rutgers University, by 1948 veterans comprised nine thousand of the school's sixteen thousand students. At the same time, Stanford's enrollment reached seventy-two hundred, up from forty-eight hundred. In 1947, veterans comprised 49.2 percent of all enrolled students across the nation and nearly 70 percent of all male students.[28] Vietnam veterans would make nothing like the same impact on higher education when they came back to school.

The most obvious reason why Vietnam veterans did not have the same dramatic impact on higher education was their relatively diminished numbers. Although numerically more Vietnam and Vietnam-era veterans than World War II veterans went to school on the G.I. Bill, they made up a smaller percentage of students. The expansion of higher education opportunities meant that higher education had become a far more commonplace feature of American life by the late 1960s than it had been at the end of World War II. In addition, the relatively lower benefits on offer for the later generation ensured that the nation's more elite schools saw few veterans in their classrooms. By one estimate, out of the 1,751 students enrolled at Johns Hopkins in the 1948–48 school year, 1,083 were World War II veterans. In the 1971–72 school year there were 25 veterans out of 2,020 students. Similarly, at Harvard, 3,326 of the 5,600 students enrolled in 1948–48 were veterans, compared with just 89 of the 6,073 enrolled in 1971–72.[29] In schools across America, Vietnam veterans tended to have a lower profile on campus. When he decided to attend the University of Tennessee, Dave Hollingsworth remembers that on campus, "Most of us were not walking around publicizing the fact that we were veterans. . . . I just think many of us wanted to get on with our lives." Hollingsworth grew out his beard and his hair "to just try to blend back in" and adds, "I think that's what many vets did."[30] Hollingsworth did not even realize that he shared a classroom with about ten other veterans until one cold spell when they all wore their field jackets to class to keep warm. When Morocco Coleman returned to Atlanta's Morris Brown College in 1977, he noted that veterans had "very little presence" on campus. He recalls that his fellow students "didn't know I was a vet. I wanted to put all that behind me and catch up with my peer group in the life experience."[31]

Some veterans, even if they felt unequivocal pride in their service, were often reluctant to flaunt their military backgrounds given the antimilitary milieu on some of the nation's campuses. Throughout the 1960s and into the 1970s, college campuses remained the focus of much of the nation's antiwar protests.[32] From Berkley's Free Speech Movement and the nationwide Students for a Democratic Society's activism to the widespread teach-ins and student strikes, campuses seemed ablaze with unrest. By the end of the 1960s, many of the students who had agitated for civil liberties at the start of the decade directed their ire toward the war in Vietnam. Students helped fuel the Vietnam Summer in 1967, a movement to "educate" the public about America's Vietnam policy. Riots broke out at Oakland in the fall of 1967 in protest to the draft. Soon after, violent clashes erupted between police and students at Madison's University of Wisconsin when protesters blocked a recruiter from napalm and Agent Orange manufacturer Dow Chemical.[33] Three years later protesters exploded a bomb at a research facility at the same school, killing a graduate student. By 1969, a Gallup poll indicated that 69 percent of students considered themselves "doves" and opposed the war. Protest marches and student strikes became more commonplace as the decade wore on, many of them turning violent in nature. During the academic year 1969–70, police had to intervene and arrest students in 731 separate incidents nationwide. Four hundred and ten of these incidents incurred property damage and 230 resulted in physical violence.[34] The 197 attacks on ROTC buildings confirmed the antimilitary timbre of some of the protests.

The most dramatic and violent student protest took place in the aftermath of Richard Nixon's announcement of the Cambodian incursion on April 30, 1970. Almost immediately, demonstrations broke out on campuses throughout the country. Protesters attacked thirty ROTC buildings in the first week of May alone. One of those included the ROTC building at Kent State University, Ohio.[35] On May 4, as the turmoil continued on the Kent State campus, Ohio National Guardsmen opened fire on a crowd of students, killing four and wounding nine others. Soon after, police opened fire on students at Jackson State, Mississippi, killing two. The combined outrage over Cambodia and the subsequent campus killings turned up the heat in schools across the nation throughout the month of May.

Against this backdrop of protests and antimilitarism, few veterans showed up to class with a chest full of medals, wary of the reception they might receive. Although most protests targeted the war, not the soldiers, occasionally, veterans did feel some backlash for their service. Lane Cooke was drafted into the army in 1966. After serving as an electronics specialist in Vietnam, he returned to school in San Diego in 1968. He heard "derogatory statements and demonstrations" over the war and recalled his unease when he thought about "having gone through what I did for my country and thinking, my gosh, all my friends and buddies who didn't come back [and] for the same people that were now deriding them."[36] In August 1968, Douglas Zwank returned to Madison's University of Wisconsin having previously dropped out in 1966 to join the marines. He soon discovered that his fellow classmates cared little for what he had endured. With campus protests "going on daily," Zwank recalls that when he talked about his service,

> not only didn't they support it, they resented you for doing it and you became the target of their rage. . . . [I]t didn't take me more than a couple of weeks and I realized that this thing I accomplished that I had this pride in was something to be ashamed of by their standards and that I had to hide.[37]

Doug Simon, an air force intelligence officer in Vietnam from April 1965 to May 1966, recalls one student at the University of Oregon yelling "Baby Killer" at one of his classmates, even though the recipient of the abuse had only served in Europe and had never set foot in Vietnam. Simon also narrowly avoided being blackballed from the university after one professor feared he might use his military intelligence background to inform the CIA or Pentagon on antiwar activities.[38] One former nurse who had volunteered for service in Vietnam hid her veteran status when campus riots erupted at the University of Maryland, where she was enrolled. "Things got rough at times," she recalled. "We military people stuck together and didn't tell anyone we were in the military."[39]

Charles Thompson, president of the veterans' club at Detroit's Wayne State, offered some timely advice to returning veterans. When interviewed in 1972 for a *VFW Magazine* piece titled "Today's Student Veteran," Thompson revealed, "The first thing I tell any new vet on campus

is 'never discuss the war unless it's with someone who was there.' . . .
[Y]ou get in these discussions of the war and you find yourself on the
defensive. . . . I don't have to defend myself." Thompson also warned
veterans to avoid the pitfalls of drugs and alcohol as a way of dealing
with feelings of isolation or societal rejection. He did not experience
any open hostility toward his service, and noted that "the attitude a veteran meets on campus is not open resentment but a kind of intellectual
snobbery, as though we were real suckers to enlist or to allow ourselves
to be drafted instead of finding a way out of our service commitment."[40]
Indeed, testimonies from Vietnam veterans from all across the nation
suggest that most did not face overt hostility from students during their
time on campus.

In part because of their low profile, many carried on their studies
without raising their classmates' ire. Doug Simon recalls that overall
he "was treated well" by the Oregon students.[41] Similarly, when Fred
Owens used his G.I. Bill to attend Columbia State University in 1975
and later finished up his degree at Troy State in Georgia, the students
never questioned his service. Most never knew the horrors he had witnessed fighting in the Central Highlands in 1965 and 1966, because
most never asked. As many veterans discovered throughout society,
even if people did not treat veterans with outright hostility, most simply
did not want to hear about the veterans' wartime experience.[42] Roger
Stephen Boeker also suffered no adverse reaction from students when
he attended Santa Ana College in 1975 and City College of Seattle from
1976 to 1977, although he concedes, "I was aggressive enough that most
persons did not dare to share their feelings about my very personal and
traumatic experiences in Vietnam."[43] Robert Ficks left the University of
Wisconsin–Milwaukee after one year to serve as a marine in Vietnam
from 1964 to 1966. He returned to finish his studies at Wisconsin's Milton College and found that there was "[n]o spitting on vets, things were
generally fairly cordial. There were a couple of . . . Bolsheviks who were
a little strident in class debate or let's say at the student union. But, no,
there was no overt behavior."[44] Tom Crane, a former air force intelligence veteran, feared that when he returned to Michigan State, his fellow students might "consider me a 'Fascist Pig' because I was a vet."
Crane's worst fears never materialized and he enjoyed a quiet and successful first semester back in school.[45]

Vietnam veteran Dave Hollingsworth experienced first-hand the fallout from the most notorious of all antiwar protests. Before returning to the University of Tennessee, he traveled to the Ohio State campus the day after the Kent State shootings. He recalls watching students running across campus with handkerchiefs over their faces, and then "[a]ll of a sudden, the tear gas started drifting our way. . . . The bells and whistles went off and I knew there had to be some sort of demonstration nearby."[46] The unrest led the authorities to evacuate Ohio State and send national guardsmen to patrol the campus.[47] Although he bore no grudge against the protesters, Hollingsworth feared that many of them had blurred the line between the war and the warrior. But if he had anticipated a rough reception when he returned to Knoxville, he need not have worried. The University of Tennessee, like most southern schools, saw few widespread protests against the war or against veterans. The most celebrated protest at the university occurred several weeks after the Kent State shootings on May 28 during a Billy Graham crusade at Neyland football stadium. Richard Nixon decided to attend the event in what was his first public appearance since the Kent State shootings. The Nixon administration considered Knoxville one of the nation's few "safe" campuses. After visiting the campus for a football game, one *Los Angeles Times* reporter described UT as "another world, a place where kids listen instead of shout."[48] Several hundred students and staff did use Nixon's visit to protest his Cambodia invasion. The protesters marched from the University Center into the stadium, held signs aloft, and chanted antiwar slogans as Nixon gave a speech. Although many arrests followed in the coming days, Knoxville authorities dropped the charges against most of the protesters. The protest caused a few waves on campus for several months, but thereafter the campus remained quiet. Some veterans may have experienced individual acts of opposition at UT, but Hollingsworth was never confronted over his veteran status.

Even at the University of Wisconsin, hostility toward veterans was not commonplace. When Tom Deits returned to law school in Madison in 1970, he suffered no backlash from his fellow students. Deits served as a combat infantryman in Vietnam in 1969 and 1970 and won the Bronze Star and a Purple Heart after suffering wounds from a fragment grenade. He chose to wear his fatigue jacket every day and recalled that he "never received a second look." Again, as with the general response many Vietnam veterans received from society at large, Deits's fellow students treated his veteran status with a resounding, "'So what?' You're a veteran of a war but it's not that big of a deal."[49] Another veteran, a combat engineer wounded in Vietnam in 1967, did think that the Madison campus was "not very friendly" toward veterans when he attended from 1969 through 1974, but personally never experienced any problems.[50]

Temporal and geographic factors dictated, in large part, the reception Vietnam veterans received on campus. The South, for example, saw few violent, large-scale antiwar protests, although southern students did attempt to offer up some antiwar resistance. After 1966, the Southern Student Organizing Committee (SSOC), the southern counterpart to the Students for a Democratic Society, diverted some of its attentions from the civil rights struggle to organizing numerous antiwar activities across the South, including a Peace Tour across southern campuses between February 1967 and December 1968. But southern antiwar activities never reached the same intensity as in some other regions of the nation. Indeed, the SSOC encountered much hostility on several campuses. At the University of South Florida, students seemed ready, as one SSOC member recalls, "to rip us apart." At Erskine College, South Carolina, one student pulled a gun on an SSOC member and told him, "I just might kill you" because "those damn gooks" had killed his brother in Vietnam.[51] The experience of the SSOC serves as a reminder that—contrary to popular mythology—many campuses retained a strong conservative presence throughout the 1960s. Such schools were unlikely to give returning vets a hard time.

Time, in addition to location, would also have affected the veteran's campus experience. Veterans choosing to attend school at the end of the 1960s would clearly have expected more opposition than the veterans returning to school either before 1966 or in the mid-1970s. With the war winding down rapidly, violent student protests subsided after reaching a crescendo from 1969 to 1970.[52] Doug Simon returned to Drew University in 1972 and encountered a "post-sixties depression. There was a period of enormous activity," recounts Simon, "from about 1968 to around 1971, and then I think it began to get old. . . . The counterculture was getting tired. . . . This campus didn't have a great deal of vitality to it."[53] With the potential for such variation, every veteran's experience may have been unique.

A 1980 VA-commissioned Louis Harris & Associates poll on Vietnam veterans adds further credence to the suggestion that veterans returned to campus without too much disruption. In addition to interviewing Vietnam veterans and the public, the poll also included the views of over five hundred educators in colleges and campuses across the country. The educators overwhelmingly agreed that other students associating veterans "with the war in Vietnam" represented "not a problem at all" (66 percent) or "not much of a problem" (23 percent). Similarly, students associating veterans "with the military" represented "not a problem at all" (73 percent), or "not much of a problem" (18 percent). None of those polled considered the military association to be "a great problem" for returning vets or to campus harmony in general.[54]

Faculty members at institutions of higher education seem also to have avoided confrontation with returning veterans. Dave Hollingsworth recalls that professors "were sensitive on things that could push our buttons . . . and really, if anything, leaned over backwards to try to be accommodating."[55] The Louis Harris & Associates poll confirmed that 89 percent of educators believed that faculty associating veterans with their participation in the Vietnam War represented "not a problem at all" (73 percent) or "not much of a problem" (16 percent). The educators also believed that veterans being "so changed by their military experience that they don't fit in on campus" represented "not a problem at all" (61 percent) or "not much of a problem" (20 percent).[56] Most veterans, therefore, returned to campus with relative calm.

Once Vietnam veterans did decide to return to campus, most made excellent students. In excelling in the classroom, they shared a common heritage with their World War II predecessors. Following the announcement of the original G.I. Bill in 1944, many educators feared the effects of millions of veterans flooding the nation's campuses. In a famous *Colliers* article, University of Chicago president Robert Hutchins called the G.I. Bill "a threat to American education," and argued that an influx of veterans with low education levels and little preparation for the academic life might lead to "[c]olleges and universities . . . converted into educational hobo jungles."[57] Harvard's Seymour Harris agreed that the G.I. Bill "carried the principle of democratization too far."[58] Veterans soon proved the naysayers wrong and became some of the more mature and academically proficient students of their generation. In 1947, the *New York Times* education editor wrote about "the most astonishing fact in the history of American higher education. . . . Far from being an educational problem, the veteran has become an asset to higher education."[59] In 1949, *Fortune* magazine called the class of 1949 the "best, . . . most mature, . . . most responsible, . . . [and] self-disciplined" in the history of higher education. *Life* magazine praised Harvard's veterans as the "the best in Harvard's history." James Conant, the Harvard president who initially expressed doubts about the potential of veterans as students, described them as "the most mature and promising students Harvard has ever had."[60] Several factors contributed to the quality of veterans as students, including their age, level of maturity, and the perspective on life they had gained from military service. Living through the horrors of war led many to dismiss the traditional high jinx of campus life and, as a group, veterans tended to be far more focused and dedicated to their studies than their nonveteran peers.

In the 1960s and 1970s, the education community geared up for another massive influx of veterans under the Vietnam-era G.I. Bills. But this time, academics offered far less public debate over the potential impact of this new cadre of veterans on higher education and offered far fewer frightening statements on their potential quality as students. Because, by the 1960s, higher education had already become democratized and was far more an established part of American life than it had been in 1944, few observers expected the Vietnam veterans to have the same dramatic impact on higher education as did the recipients of the original G.I. Bill. Tim O'Brien took a more cynical view of the lack of academic attention to returning veterans. With the widespread press reporting of maladjusted veterans, he commented, "Perhaps the educators' silence is rooted in fear. After all, who wants a swarm of smelly junkie-weirdo-killer freaks invading their serene campuses?"[61]

The Veterans Administration attempted to warn educators of the potential problems they might encounter when the veterans returned to school. In an April 1972 commentary in the *Journal of Higher Education*, VA officials E. Robert Stephens and Charles A. Stenger wrote of "The Opportunity and Challenge of the Vietnam Era Veteran to American Educators."[62] Stephens and Stenger noted that the veterans' presence could easily be overlooked because they did not return en masse as did the World War II veteran. On the basis of a 1970 survey of the interaction between VA officials and Vietnam veterans, the authors highlighted five distinct characteristics of Vietnam veterans of which educators ought to be aware when dealing with them in the classroom. Each one suggested that the Vietnam veteran might make a rather volatile classmate. The characteristics included the following:

- The young veteran is less willing than earlier veterans to accept authority in a compliant manner.
- An expectation that authority in any form will be unresponsive to his intense desire to be treated as an individual.
- A general sense of uncertainty and pessimism toward the future with a resultant greater concentration on immediate gratification.
- An intense, positive identification with his own age group that is more than the typical sharing of common interests and activities.
- A tendency to exercise less control over emotions and feelings and to react with impatience and impulsivity.

The commentary went on to suggest that although many students suffer from similar dispositions, military service, especially service in Vietnam "adds a special type of reality experience" that can lead to "doubts and fears about the worth of society and the meaning of life that he had earlier shared with others his age."[63]

The 1973 VA report on veteran funding, conducted by the Education Testing Service (ETS) of New Jersey, also carried a warning about how military service might manifest itself differently in the Vietnam veteran than in the World War II veteran. The ETS suggested that the World War II veterans returned home with a more conservative devotion to their country and their family and with their religious faith reaffirmed by their experience. The Vietnam veteran, the report cautioned, had a greater propensity toward "deep-seated psychological damage" and a far weaker devotion to their country or their family and were generally unsure of their position in society.[64] The warnings of the VA and the ETS suggested that Vietnam veterans would face difficulties fitting in on campus. No doubt, some veterans may have had some difficulty relating to their peers, but despite some fundamental differences in outlook and life experience, Vietnam veterans never became the "smelly junkie-weirdo-killer freaks" some may have feared.

Military experience invariably has a profound effect on most veterans, but in the area of academic performance, the effect on Vietnam veterans was not always negative. Because of their years of military service, Vietnam veterans were likely to be several years older than their fellow students, were more likely to be married, and were probably more eager to finish their studies to make up for lost time. This extra level of maturity often manifested itself in a constructive way because when the Vietnam veterans did return to the classroom, many brought with them the same positive qualities displayed by World War II veterans. Douglas Zwank recalled that "when I left to go in the service I wasn't motivated to go to school. When I came back I was very motivated to go to school 'cause I saw the difference in what your life has to offer after you graduated as opposed to if you don't."[65] John Finneran, a former helicopter pilot in Vietnam, remembered steering clear of "the kids" at college who seemed more interested in the frivolities of campus life and less concerned with studying.[66]

The 1980 Louis Harris & Associates poll confirmed the high level of maturity displayed by returning veterans. The educators surveyed in the poll placed the quality and commitment of Vietnam veterans as higher than their peers. Sixty-one percent of those polled stated that Vietnam veterans displayed more "emotional maturity" than other students in their classes.[67] Twenty-nine percent placed them "about the same," while only 6 percent considered veterans less mature than their peers. Forty-eight percent considered veterans more "conscientious about their coursework"; only 8 percent considered them worse.[68] Vietnam veterans scored higher than their peers in "seriousness with which they take their coursework," "knowing what they want out of life," "prospects for completing the program," "motivation to learn," and "commitment to education." In all categories less than 11 percent of respondents regarded Vietnam veterans as worse than nonveterans in terms of classroom performance. While the educators did not believe veterans possessed any greater "innate intelligence," the veterans' grades tended to be better than those of nonveterans. Twenty-eight percent of educators considered veterans' grades superior, 59 percent considered them to be about the same, and only 7 percent perceived them as worse. The only area of classroom performance where veterans scored worse than their nonveteran peers was—as the VA had cautioned—their "tolerance for unpopular ideas." Vietnam veterans, therefore, while not attaining the same profile or notoriety on campus as World War II veterans, demonstrated a similar devotion to their studies and a similar academic excellence. Whatever problems the government created by their foot dragging over education benefits, the veterans themselves seemed dedicated to trying to improve their lives through higher education.

The years of legislative neglect may have hampered the ability of many veterans to return to school, but they did little to dampen the veterans' desire to do so or their performance when they got there. Once on campus, they showed a commitment to learning that equaled or surpassed that of their World War II counterparts. What was different was that Vietnam veterans had additional financial burdens to overcome. The low levels of G.I. Bill benefits meant that many had to hold down jobs or rely on income from their spouse or family to stay in school. Thus, during the early years of the program, the numbers of Vietnam veterans returning to school remained relatively low and the ability of many veterans to finish their education remained compromised. Eight years of legislative struggles had failed to provide Vietnam-era veterans with the same levels of benefits as World War II veterans. But when Richard Nixon left office in August 1974, Congress seemed on the verge of passing legislation that might finally correct this problem. By then, the nation's Vietnam combat veterans had already come home and had begun planning their futures. For many, particularly the economically disadvantaged, the 1974 bill represented their last realistic shot at an affordable education. This time, there seemed genuine optimism that the government would come through. The momentum on the Hill seemed overwhelming, and with a new school year looming, the veterans waited anxiously.

6

Denouement

Ford's War on Inflation and Teague's Last Stand

We went, some willingly, the rest regretfully, right or wrong
we went. We watched our brothers die or . . . be maimed for
what? . . . We believe the time is now to heal our Countries
[sic] awful wound of Vietnam but first we ask that the MEN
who fought and served their country be taken care of first.
—Joint statement by three Pennsylvania college veterans'
associations, October 17, 1974

We are all soldiers in the war against brutal inflation. . . . I
will not hesitate to veto any legislation to try and control
inflationary excesses.
—President Gerald R. Ford, August 19, 1974

Just ten days after being sworn in as president, Gerald Ford spoke at
the annual convention of the Veterans of Foreign Wars in Chicago. His
speech contained the usual politically expedient platitudes toward veterans as he pledged, "As a veteran, I want good relations with all veterans. We all proudly wore the same Nation's uniform and patriotically
saluted the same flag. During my administration, the door of my office
will be open to veterans just as it was in all of my 25 years as a member
of congress." Ford served as naval gunnery officer and assistant navi-
gator on board the *U.S.S. Monterey* in the Pacific during World War
II, so he certainly sounded sincere when he promised, "If we can send
men thousands and thousands of miles from home to fight in the rice
paddies, certainly we can send them back to school and better jobs at
home." But the new president's speech also contained ominous signs for
veterans hoping for some respite from their financial struggles. Ford

revealed a side to his political outlook that appeared to contradict his professed affiliation with the plight of veterans. Alluding to the benefits proposals tied up in Congress, Ford commented, "your Government, of necessity, has to be constrained by other considerations as well. We are all soldiers in the war against brutal inflation. . . . I will not hesitate to veto any legislation to try and control inflationary excesses."[1]

Throughout his brief term as president, Ford surpassed Nixon's attempts to bring a culture of economic sacrifice to government spending. Three days after taking office, he identified inflation as "public enemy number one." As a former member of the House Appropriations Committee, Ford brought a keen interest in and knowledge of economics to the presidency.[2] From day one, he met with his economic advisors and launched a series of "Inflation Summits" throughout the fall to discuss ways of tackling the inflation problem.[3] His administration also launched a voluntary "Whip Inflation Now" campaign whereby concerned citizens could express their support for beating inflation by writing to the White House and requesting "WIN" pins. Over one hundred thousand people signed up, but the new program represented little more than a symbolic gesture and attracted mild ridicule from some.[4] Ford's more serious solution for tackling inflation put him immediately at odds with the Democrat-controlled Congress. Ford believed that the decades of wide-ranging government spending on social programs, begun under the New Deal and given renewed impetus under the Great Society, had led to America's economic woes. In his memoirs, Ford outlined his vision on the ideal role for government when he espoused the conservative mantras of "less government intervention in the affairs of citizens and corporations, greater reliance on individual initiative and a free market economy, and increased local responsibility for overcoming adversities."[5] To implement his economic philosophy, Ford sought to introduce extensive cuts in federal spending on social programs. Not surprisingly, during the 1976 presidential election a poll of Keynesian economists gave the president a grade of "D" for his handling of the economy, whereas fiscal conservatives gave him an "A-."[6]

Much to the president's chagrin, more often than not Congress proved reluctant to share in his vision of economic retrenchment. During his first few months, Ford vetoed the Railroad Retirement Act, which he claimed would cost over $7 billion over twenty-five years,

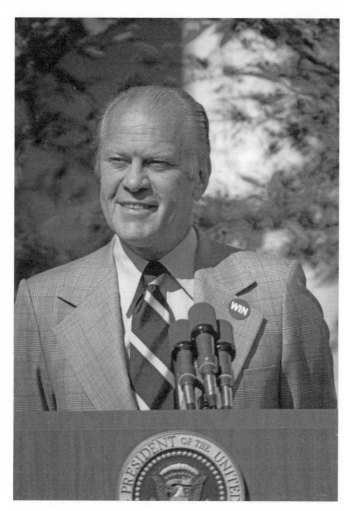

Gerald Ford proudly displaying his "Whip Inflation Now" pin. *Courtesy of the Gerald R. Ford Presidential Library.*

only to have his veto overridden by Congress. Congress also refused his request to defer a federal pay raise for three months. In total, Ford vetoed sixty-six bills, with Congress sustaining fifty-four of his vetoes.[7] In part, the opposition on the Hill was philosophical. Steeped in the activist government traditions of the New Deal and Great Society, many Democrats saw federal investment in social programs as a way to ease unemployment and inflation concerns. On a more mercenary note, 1974 was also an election year for many in Congress, so the kinds of cuts in popular programs envisioned by Ford could hinder the reelection prospects of some if they compromised the interests of their constituents.

As a part of his economic plan, Ford hoped to slash around $5 billion from the federal budget that Richard Nixon had already submitted for the fiscal year 1975.[8] As it stood, the legislation then circulating on Capitol Hill to increase veterans' education benefits jeopardized that budget target. The veterans waited to see if Ford's commitment to helping them was stronger than his dedication to beating inflation.

One possible crumb of comfort for them was that Donald Johnson was no longer around to fight them every step of the way. Throughout his tenure as VA chief administrator, Johnson had stubbornly refused to acknowledge the need for meaningful increases in the G.I. Bill and had been lukewarm, at best, toward programs geared to the specific needs of Vietnam veterans. One of Johnson's final letters to Richard Nixon in the summer of 1974 was an impassioned plea to the president to hold the line against increased education benefits. He claimed that the proposed increase in the monthly allowance was "a clear case of being over generous" and that "the added features in the bills are truly Christmas tree items and are totally unwarranted." "Putting it in rather blunt terms," he added, "I believe these bills to be irresponsible legislation." Signing off from his five years of service, Johnson proclaimed, "The record of this Administration in veterans' affairs is unsurpassed in its accomplishments; and, when the quiet and solitude of history scholars prevails, the accounting will be on the positive side."[9]

Given Johnson's prevailing attitude, most Vietnam-era veterans welcomed any change in the VA leadership. In his place, Ford appointed a new and potentially more accommodating leader for the political battles that lay ahead, former Indiana congressman Richard L. Roudebush.[10] Roudebush certainly seemed to possess the credentials to make an effective VA administrator. He had fought in the North African and Italian campaigns of World War II and immediately following service worked in the Indianapolis Regional Office of the Veterans Administration. In 1957 he served as commander-in-chief of the VFW. During his five terms in the House from 1961 to 1971 Roudebush remained a keen veterans' advocate and served as ranking Republican on the House Veterans' Affairs Committee. From January 1971 through January 1974 he served as a deputy administrator in the VA, after which he served as

Donald Johnson's assistant deputy, the second highest position within the VA. Although some Vietnam veterans feared that Roudebush might be just "another good ole boy," most welcomed his appointment.[11] Timothy L. Craig, president of the National Association of Concerned Veterans (NACV), expressed his hopes that Roudebush "will demonstrate a solid commitment to reversing many VA policies toward Vietnam-era veterans that have been operative for the past five years."[12] But before either Ford or Roudebush had the opportunity to demonstrate their commitment to veterans, Congress first had to agree on an appropriate package of benefits to present to them for consideration. As usual, this proved no easy task.

By mid-August, Senate and House conferees reached a fragile compromise between the House and Senate bills introduced during Nixon's tenure, and on August 9, William Jennings Bryan Dorn announced that the House conferees had sent forward their compromise bill, still under the title H.R. 12628, to the Senate for approval. The House had struck the Senate's desire for direct tuition assistance from the bill. To compensate, they agreed upon a 23 percent increase in the veteran's monthly allowance, raising it to $270 (up from $220) for a single veteran. The compromise plan also allowed eligible veterans to claim up to a thousand dollars in loans to offset tuition discrepancies. Veterans would also be given forty-five months in which to claim their benefits, a nine-month extension. With the deadlines for fall enrollments looming, Dorn noted that it was "important that the Congress act immediately so that veterans know what to expect in making their plans for the fall term."[13] It appeared as though an accord had been achieved in Congress. Attempting to allay fears of the costs of the program and, perhaps, preempting the anticipated challenge from Ford, Vance Hartke noted, "The measure we have agreed upon today is not inexpensive. . . . But past G.I. Bill expenditures have been repaid many times over in the higher taxes of those whose education gave them greater earning power. It's the best kind of investment we can make in people and our economy."[14]

If passed, the bill would represent a significant increase in veterans' education benefits. The provisions for loan payments to offset tuition discrepancies would address one of the biggest criticisms leveled against the previous Vietnam-era G.I. Bills. Even under the new bill, the Vietnam-era veterans' benefits remained less liberal than those offered the World War II veteran in terms of tuition payments, but the new option of low-interest loans did at least give the veterans a new source of funding to help abate their financial troubles. The increase in the monthly allowance, while barely outstripping the rising costs of education, would make higher education a more attractive and feasible option for millions of veterans who might have been dissuaded by the stories of veteran hardship and poverty emanating from campuses over the previous few years. One issue had already been resolved. In July, the House and Senate passed a separate act giving veterans their two-year extension. Congress had separated this provision so that veterans would know if they were eligible to receive benefits in the forthcoming school year. This act gave veterans ten years to claim their benefits, longer than any previous generation of veterans had received.

The veteran community responded with cautious optimism to the new G.I. Bill. The NACV expressed disappointment over the omission of direct tuition assistance, but welcomed the overall increase in allowances.[15] Therefore, reasonably satisfied that Congress had, at last, done its part in the fight to increase education benefits, veterans' advocates steeled themselves for the next anticipated battle, getting the awaiting president to sign the bill into law. On August 21, the Senate passed the bill unanimously with a voice vote and with very little debate. All that remained was for the House to follow suit. No one expected too many surprises there. As one *New York Times* editorial noted, "Given the amount of patriotic speechmaking in Congress about Vietnam in particular and war veterans in general one might think that this measure would be about as controversial as Mother's day."[16] But in light of the recent history of veterans' policymaking in the House, the veterans could take nothing for granted.

The vote went to the House on August 22, the eve of a congressional recess. With a passing vote, the bill would have been sent to Ford for his consideration and millions of veterans would have had a much clearer understanding of their financial prospects for the forthcoming school year. On August 21, Ford paid a visit to his "old friends" on the Hill and called for a spirit of unity between Congress and the White House. Putting pressure on the House to pass a less expensive bill, he stated, "Together we have a big job ahead, and I emphasize 'We' on the basis of togetherness."[17] Ford's words should have had little impact. With minor amendments, the Senate had essentially agreed to the House bill and all that remained was for the House to rubber stamp its own legislation.

All seemed calm when Speaker Carl Albert and William Bryan Jennings Dorn introduced the bill for a vote until Iowa Republican Harold Royce Gross spoke up and proclaimed that the "conference report violates clause 3 of rule XXVIII in that the conferees exceeded the scope of the conference."[18] On a point of technicality, Gross had declared the conference compromise report invalid on the grounds that the agreed-upon 23 percent benefit increase exceeded the 13.6 percent agreed by the House back in February and the 18.2 percent agreed in the Senate in June. Gross's actions left Carl Albert with no choice but to sustain the point of order and declare the compromise bill null and void. Technically Gross was correct, but his actions violated the spirit of accord that had been reached in conference. Gross was no maverick. He was a World War I veteran who had served in Congress since 1949 and was ineligible for reelection in 1974. He could afford to carry the can for more powerful forces who wanted to pull the rug out from under the veterans' feet.

Unbeknownst to most lawmakers, Ford had been working behind the scenes to kill the bill. William Jennings Bryan Dorn had been onboard the presidential flight back from the VFW convention in Chicago on August 19. Ford had informed Dorn that he would veto the compromise bill if the House passed it as it stood.[19] Dorn then made the decision to yield to Ford's wishes so that veterans could at least have *some* sort of increase before the new academic year began. In a hastily arranged meeting at 6:00 a.m. on the morning of the vote, Republican leaders crafted the strategy to kill the compromise bill, instantly wiping out months of negotiation. Gross's actions drew immediate criticism from his fellow legislators. New York representative Lester Wolff protested, "What about these Vietnam veterans? If we bow to the White House, we are not meeting our responsibility to them. . . . Where are all those who so strongly supported this war now that these men have come home?"[20]

The debate on the floor then took another turn when Dorn produced an alternative bill on which the House could vote. His new bill offered only an 18 percent increase in benefits and completely removed both the loan provision and the nine-month extension for eligibility. With the congressional recess looming and lacking credible alternatives at such short notice, many in the House felt compelled to vote for Dorn's bill. Pennsylvania representative John P. Murtha had a particular interest in the proceedings. Murtha had volunteered for service in Vietnam and served there in 1966 and 1967. He became the first Vietnam combat veteran elected to the House. He agreed with Dorn that "the overwhelming priority at this time is that we agree on a bill, and that we pass and the president sign it before September so the veteran knows what he can count on as another school year begins. This is not a perfect bill. But it is an acceptable bill. And it will help."[21] The revised measure passed the House by a vote of 388–0.

Almost immediately, many in Congress expressed their concern over the way the matter had been handled. One member of the House Veterans' Affairs Committee even thought that House members were voting on the original conference report and claimed that he did not even know they were voting to kill key measures of the compromise bill.[22] A letter to Ford signed by fifty-nine lawmakers later pointed out, "When voting on [Dorn's substitute] conference report, some members were not aware that these provisions had been removed at the last minute. Others supported the [reduced] bill because it would offer some assistance, and it was the sense of the House to keep the bill alive."[23] Colorado representative Patricia Schroeder wrote Dorn, Carl Albert, and the other members of the Veterans' Affairs Committee to express her disgust and proclaim,

> quite frankly, on August 22, Vietnam era veterans were shafted by the technical parliamentary move mounted by opponents—including some of our own House conferees—of the Conference report. . . . [T]he outcome of the backroom maneuver by senior House members at the urging of the White House is to leave Vietnam era Veterans slowly, slowly twisting in the wind—to use a recently popular political phrase.[24]

Ford claimed to have played no direct part in the House decisions beyond raising concerns with members of the House and Senate over the "$780-some-million over and above the budget for this year" that the compromise bill would have added. But he also expressed his hope that, when the bill went back into conference, Congress would retain the "good provisions" of the revised House bill "because it was inflation-ary the way it was."[25]

Not surprisingly, a chorus of disapproving voices arose from all cor-ners over the House's actions. In the Senate, an outraged Vance Hartke charged, "it is evident that this point of order was made with full knowl-edge and active participation of the House Leadership and the Admin-istration. Had the House had the opportunity to vote on the full con-ference report I am confident that it would have overwhelmingly been approved."[26] A *New York Times* editorial asked a question that must have been in the minds of many at the time: "Why is it politically cor-rect to treat Vietnam veterans in this shabby and inadequate manner?" Timothy Craig of the NACV stated, "Once again Vietnam veterans have been lied to. . . . The House conferees have gone back on their word by failing to approve the conference report they unanimously agreed to on Aug. 19."[27] Carl Albert received a host of letters from concerned veterans and veterans' counselors lamenting the actions of the House and urging corrective action. The director of the Office of Veterans Affairs at Okla-homa City Southwestern College expressed his "dismay and surprise at the failure of the House to approve the Conference Report," having personally witnessed "numerous veterans drop-out because they had to work overtime just to make ends meet."[28] Joseph L. McCarter, veter-ans' counselor at San Diego City College, forwarded Albert a petition of veterans' names, imploring the speaker to "act on their behalf . . . [and] for their and our sake, be generous, they deserve it."[29] Warren John-son spent fifteen months in a support role for C-130 Hercules aircraft in Southeast Asia. He implored Albert to look favorably on the more generous Senate bill when Congress reconvened. Johnson wrote, "I and many other veterans look at the Senate version of the new GI benefits as a Godsend. It looks at the needs of the Vietnam veteran in a realistic manner."[30] Following Congress's recess, a September 30 voice vote in the Senate rejected the parsimonious House bill and so the G.I. Bill went back into conference. With the new school year now well underway, the veterans still waited.

It took several more weeks of political bargaining before the House and Senate conferees could once more agree on a new version of H.R. 12628. Negotiations survived an eleventh-hour attempt by Ford to agree to a bill that limited the benefits increase to 20 percent while removing the loan provision and allowing veterans up to forty-five months to claim benefits. Ford also wanted payment of any benefit increases to be delayed until January 1, 1975. The conferees knew they risked a veto by drafting a new bill that, in many respects, resembled the original compromise agreed to on August 19 and rejected by the House. The new bill retained the 23 percent increase in the veterans' allowance. The new bill also cemented the increase in veterans' eligibility to a forty-five month period, with the added proviso that the extra time must be used only to complete undergraduate work. The provision for loans to veterans remained in the new bill, but the conferees reduced the maximum amount allowed from a thousand to six hundred dollars per year and stipulated that the veteran must first attempt to secure loans through generally available federal student loan programs. If passed, the benefit increases would be retroactive to September 1. Dorn commented that in conference, "We had no difficulty agreeing on most major points."[31] But Senator James McClure indicated in a letter to White House aide Bill Timmons that the new conference bill might have resulted from some politicking from the Democrats. Specifically, he charged that Olin Teague had "suddenly changed completely" from his opposition to tuition assistance and "not only conceded to the Senate point of view but insisted that we go beyond what had been discussed in previous conferences." But Teague had not suddenly become the Vietnam veteran's new friend. According to McClure, Teague seemed to be "following Democrat strategy to force the President to veto this bill."[32] The implication here is that the Democrats wanted to hand Ford a political time bomb by giving him a bill that he would refuse to sign, thus casting him as a foe of veterans.

The second conference report reached the House and Senate on October 7, with the vote set to take place on October 10. Dorn began proceedings in the House by outlining the "conferees' philosophy as to the fiscal impact of this legislation."[33] He agreed that the 18 or 20 percent increase proposed by the White House was consistent with the increase in the cost of living but argued that it ignored rising tuition costs in private and public schools. He also stressed that the loan provision was in no way designed as a handout and that veterans could expect "consequences" for default of payment. New Jersey representative Henry Helstoski called the bill a "reasonable compromise," but Connecticut congresswoman Ella Grasso described it as a "mixed blessing" and lamented, "I believe we should have done better."[34] This time, there were no background dealings to thwart the vote. The measure sailed past the House by a vote of 388–0. In the Senate, Jennings Randolph, standing in for the absent Vance Hartke, began the debates by noting that the compromise bill had shaved almost 46 percent off the cost of the original proposal passed in the Senate on June 19. He added, "The committee does not believe that we can compromise further on this crucial measure."[35] Alan Cranston spoke of the government's "moral obligation" to its veterans, and urged Ford to "put a stop to the waiting game veterans have been forced to play since late last spring by signing this much needed bill into law."[36] The Senate then passed the bill with a unanimous vote.

Finally, after months of political wrangling, Congress could present the president with a new G.I. Bill for his consideration. The Senate held on to the bill for several weeks to avoid a pocket veto by Ford, but on November 18, the Vietnam Era Veterans' Readjustment Assistance Act of 1974 arrived at the White House. Only Ford's anti-inflationary convictions stood between the Vietnam veterans and their long-overdue increase. On the same day the bill arrived at the White House, Ford sent an ominous message to Congress in which he stated, "while acknowledging the debt to those who served during the Vietnam era, I must insist on a fiscally responsible bill on behalf of all Americans."[37] With one political battle over, another one loomed.

The new G.I. Bill garnered almost universal support from Congress, veterans' organizations, public officials, and the general public. Throughout the debates over education assistance for veterans from August to November, the White House received a flood of letters urging Ford to sign the bill into law. From the House, fifty-nine congressmen and women signed a letter to Ford, stating, "While we agree that government spending should be cut, we do not think it fair to further burden the men and women who served in our armed forces in recent years. . . . One of our national priorities even in battling inflation must be to compensate our country's veterans."[38] All members of the New York State congressional delegation called on Ford to accept the increases in benefits, time limits, and loan provisions cut from the House bill on August 22.[39] Margaret Heckler wrote Ford to proclaim, "we owe these veterans the same benefits which we provided those who returned from previous wars."[40] John Murtha wrote the president,

> As you probably know, I was in South Vietnam with the 1st Marines. Consequently, many of the young fellows who served in Vietnam come to me with their problems. . . . These young fellows who, in many cases, did not believe in the war served honorably under very adverse conditions. While Congress sat in their air-conditioned offices and debated the efforts and the righteousness of the war, they fought in the mud and jungles of Southeast Asia. . . . I believe it would be a real injustice to veto any legislation which is so important to the young men who fought for our country and are now trying to get started again.[41]

The Senate proved equally firm in its support of H.R. 12628. Sixty-two senators from both ends of the political spectrum, including Bob Dole, George McGovern, Bob Packwood, Joseph Biden, Hubert Humphrey, Edward Kennedy, and Sam Nunn, wrote of their deep concern "about the plight of Vietnam veterans" and sought Ford's "help in avoiding further delays in the enactment of an improved Vietnam-era veterans education bill." They noted that "[t]housands of veterans have contacted us to express their frustration and anger over the delay which has held up enactment to date."[42] In a separate letter, Strom Thurmond joined with other members of the Senate Committee on Veterans' Affairs to inform Ford that "[w]e believe this country should be able to provide as comprehensive an education program for the Cold War and Vietnam Era veterans as it did for their fathers. H.R. 12628 goes a long way to accomplishing this end."[43]

Pressure on Ford to sign the bill came from many other sectors of society. Predictably, veterans on campus were among the most vocal advocates of the new G.I. Bill. Although Ford had called on all Americans to be "soldiers in the war against brutal inflation," the Vietnam veterans had already had their war and, for some, the new call to arms was every bit as unwelcome as the first had been. Over thirty-five hundred veterans and nonveterans from the University of New Orleans petitioned Ford to inform him, "The passage of these additional benefits is essential to the welfare and the continuing education of all veterans who have given so much to keep this country great and free."[44] The *New*

York Times reported that veterans at the University of California had recruited students to donate blood "as a demonstration of their need for increased educational benefits."[45] Speaking on behalf of over three thousand veterans enrolled at California's Grossmont College, the on-campus veterans' affairs director let the president know that he considered H.R. 12628 "a good solid piece of legislation, and very supportive of the veterans at our campus and throughout the nation."[46] The president of California State University sent a letter along with the signatures of seven hundred veterans notifying Ford that "[t]his new G.I. Bill will help us keep faith with the veterans of the Vietnam era who served at a very difficult period in American history. It is a great step forward in providing the necessary financial assistance to veterans who are attempting to complete their educational goals."[47] From Pennsylvania, veterans' activists from three colleges reminded the president that "[w]e went, some willingly, the rest regretfully, right or wrong we went. We watched our brothers die or . . . be maimed for what? . . . We believe the time is now to heal our Countries [sic] awful wound of Vietnam but first we ask that the MEN who fought and served their country be taken care of first."[48]

Ford also received telegrams from Malcolm Wilson, governor of New York, to "respectfully urge" him to sign the bill to "help provide our Vietnam veterans with a greater opportunity to achieve their educational goals."[49] Brendan Byrne, governor of New Jersey, told Ford that "[t]here can be no doubt that the increase in benefit payments, in addition to the other provisions of this legislation, is critical to veterans living in the New Jersey area."[50] Finally, the VFW's Ray Soden informed Ford, "The Veterans of Foreign Wars believes compassion dictates that those who have served honorably and have already made a sacrifice in the national interest by their service in the armed forces should not be compelled to make a second sacrifice in the battle of inflation."[51] In one of the more colorful expressions of support for the new bill, three veterans confronted Ford in what the Associated Press described as a "finger waving debate" at the University of Utah after Ford had just given a speech on campus. The three veterans, all members of the University of Utah Veterans Association demanded to know whether Ford intended to approve the new bill. Ford informed them that he was "not in a position to say yes or not until it gets down to the White House." When pressed further for an opinion, the cornered president claimed that the bill would give Vietnam-era veterans greater entitlements than any previous generation of veterans and that the bill still "had some problems that are to be analyzed." After being led away from the fray, Ford told a group of journalists on board Air Force One, "I hope they understand that this bill raises some legitimate questions. It involves substantial amounts of Federal dollars. I haven't made up my mind yet as to what to do about the bill."[52]

Given such an outpouring of political and public support, Ford would have been left in no doubt as to the level of criticism he might expect if he chose H.R.12628 to make his stand in the fight against inflation. Before deciding on the most prudent course of action, Ford sought advice from many different agencies and concerned parties within his administration. As director of the Office of Management and Budget (OMB), the recommendations of Roy L. Ash would have a considerable bearing on Ford's decision. Veterans' advocates had long criticized the disproportionate influence of the OMB (and previously the Budget of the Bureau) in dictating White House attitudes towards veterans' legislation. Too often, they charged, the financial conservatism of these agencies had led the government to ride roughshod over the genuine financial concerns of veterans. Given his commitment to cutting costs, Ford would pay particular attention to Ash's views on the inflationary nature of H.R. 12628. Ash solicited the views of the VA before making his recommendation to the president. On October 17, VA administrator Richard Roudebush wrote Ash in some detail outlining the VA's position on the specific provisions of the bill. Noting that since 1972 the cost of living had "increased approximately 19.5 percent," Roudebush considered the tuition increase of nearly 23 percent to be "within reasonable reach of those increases which the president has indicated are acceptable." He also agreed with the loan program and the nine-month extension for receiving entitlements. Roudebush concluded that "I am convinced that despite the large increase in cost engendered by the enrolled enactment, it represents the best compromise that can be reached and, on balance, is realistic. . . . For the foregoing reasons, I recommend that the President approve H.R. 12628."[53]

Other agencies proved more equivocal in their responses to Ash. Peter J. Brennan, secretary of labor, outlined the Department of Labor's view "that the maximum feasible efforts are needed to help returning veterans find a useful and productive place in the society which they have helped to defend," but ultimately deferred their recommendation to "other agencies more directly concerned."[54] Similarly, the Department of Health, Education, and Welfare, despite expressing reservations over the loan programs, informed Ash that "the bill contains many other features of direct and substantial impact on programs administered by the Veterans Administration. We therefore defer to that agency as to the desirability of the enactment of the bill."[55]

Ash made his recommendation to Ford on November 22. While acknowledging the VA's arguments in favor of approval, he countered that the G.I. Bills "were not intended to be an educational income security program," and that increasing participation rates under the Vietnam-era G.I. Bills indicated that they had served their purpose adequately as a means of providing "readjustment assistance." Ash also noted that the new bill would add an additional $502 million to the 1975 budget sought by the administration. In the final analysis, Ash informed Ford, "Because these costs are clearly unacceptable, and because of the other unnecessary and undesirable provisions . . . we recommend that you disapprove the bill and reaffirm your recommendation that the Congress enact a proposal providing a simple 18.2 percent rate increase effective January 1, 1975."[56]

Roy Ash was not the only moneyman to express his disapproval of H.R. 12628. Since July 1974, Alan Greenspan had headed the Council of Economic Advisors.[57] Ford would later write of Greenspan, "Whenever I was under pressure to add funds to a program and he thought I might be influenced by the political aspects of the decision, he would caution me to hold the line. Usually, he won because he was right."[58] Greenspan shared Ford's belief that many of America's economic woes could be traced back to the growing influence of government in economic affairs since the 1930s.[59] Ford met with Greenspan several times during the final week of November to "discuss potential spending cuts."[60] On November 25, Greenspan informed presidential aide Warren Hendriks of his position on the proposed veteran benefits increase when he wrote, "We are concerned with easing the transition to civilian life for members of the armed forces. However, we oppose the creation of public programs to provide long-term subsidies to nondisabled veterans, necessarily at the expense of non-veterans." Denouncing the new

G.I. Bill as antithetical to the administration's "well-publicized policy of budget restraint," Greenspan declared it "in the public interest for the President to veto H.R. 12628."[61]

Ash and Greenspan reaffirmed Ford's fears of the inflationary nature of the bill. But in addition to the VA, Congress, veterans, and the public, several of Ford's advisors reminded him of the political dangers of such an action in the final days leading up to his decision. William J. Baroody Jr., assistant to the president for public liaison, urged Ford's approval on the grounds that "sustaining a veto is impossible, there is no benefit to be gained by alienating a large number of Veterans organizations."[62] Bill Timmons, assistant to the president for legislative affairs, recommended approval, again noting that Congress would probably override the veto. If Ford did veto, added Timmons, his veto message must challenge Congress to "practice what is [sic] preaches in campaign oration; it must join in making the tough decisions if we are to combat inflation."[63]

As he prepared to make his final decision, Ford should have been left in no doubt as to the consequences of his actions. The new G.I. Bill would have given veterans a much-needed increase in education assistance, bringing their benefits more in line with those of their World War II predecessors. By signing it, Ford would carry through on his promise of caring for veterans. The overwhelming majority of the public would, without question, greet his actions with approval. But the new bill severely tested his dedication to "Whip Inflation Now." His decision would be a litmus test for where the new administration's priorities lay. At 3:00 p.m. on November 26, Ford announced his decision and sent the following message to Congress:

I am returning today without my approval H.R. 12628, a bill which would provide what I consider an excessive increase and liberalization of veterans' education and training benefits.

Instead, I urge the Congress to send me a veterans' education bill along the lines that I have proposed. By doing so, we can avoid adding another half billion dollar load to the already overburdened taxpayer. Failure to do so will mean that the Congress will in the aggregate—Federal Pay deferral, Railroad Retirement and Veterans Education—add over one and a half billion dollars to the Federal deficit in 1975.

This bill which I am returning to the Congress provides benefits that are greater than those granted World War II and Korea veterans. It would cost taxpayers half a billion dollars more in fiscal year 1975 than is appropriate in view of the country's current economic circumstances.

The decision not to sign this bill has not been an easy one. But it is necessary if all of us are to operate with essential budgetary restraint. The Nation must reduce Federal spending if we are to stop the inflation spiral.[64]

Following the announcement, the veterans' organizations immediately made their disappointment known. The VFW accused the president of doing "a disservice to those who performed a service for their country when called upon to fight."[65] John J. Stang, the recently elected commander-in-chief of the VFW, wrote to House Speaker Carl Albert to assure him "that the more than 1.8 million members of the Veterans of Foreign Wars and its more than 500,000 members of the Ladies Auxiliary are in total agreement that the veto of this Veterans education Bill must be promptly overridden by the Congress."[66] James Wagonseller, national commander of the American Legion, accused Ford of favoring "draft dodgers and deserters" while undercutting much-needed assistance for the Vietnam veteran.[67] Charles Huber of the Disabled American Veterans informed Carl Albert that "[w]e view the President's action with a deep sense of regret; and urge you, on behalf of the 450,000 members of the DAV, to vote to override the veto of H.R. 12828."[68] An override of Ford's veto now represented the last chance to get the bill passed.

Congress had already demonstrated its willingness to challenge Ford in its battles over the Railroad Retirement Act and federal pay increases. White House press secretary Ron Nessen told reporters that Ford made his decision to veto the veterans' bill with the full expectation of an override. On November 30, Richard Roudebush told reporters, "I have no question in my mind that Congress will take the necessary action to override the veto. I'm sure the President is just [as] aware of it as I am."[69] Republican leaders on the Hill immediately let it be known that they intended to override the veto. Republican senator John G. Tower stated, "There was virtually no sentiment for sustaining [the] President's veto, and I would predict there would be very little support for it."[70] Strom

Thurmond added, "It is not my view that those who bit the bullets in Vietnam should be the first ones to bite the bullet back home."[71]

The vote to override the veto took place on December 3. Just hours before the vote, Ron Nessen reiterated the White House's position that "when Congress votes, the President feels that it will not be voting simply to uphold or override a veto, but what it will be doing is voting on whether to increase the Federal Budget by over a half billion dollars above the Administration's proposal."[72] But that afternoon, on Capitol Hill, a succession of lawmakers stood up to make forceful arguments in favor of the override. On the floor of the House, William Jennings Bryan Dorn opened the deliberations by systematically attacking the key points contained in Ford's veto message. He called the president "simply misinformed" for claiming that the new benefits package would give Vietnam-era veterans greater benefits than their World War II predecessors.[73] Henry Helstoski followed Dorn, arguing that it would be "grossly unfair to our Vietnam veterans to provide a penny less than that called for in the bill now before the House."[74] No one spoke up in defense of the veto.

In the Senate, Vance Hartke began the assault on the veto message. In addition to echoing the criticisms made in the House, Hartke noted that Ford had ignored the considerable compromises already made in conference to the original bills. Hartke also pointed out that despite the veteran population increasing by about six million in the previous few years, federal expenditure on veterans' benefits had remained around 5 percent and would remain the same under the new proposals. Attacking Ford's economic philosophy, he continued, "to focus on Government spending as the principal cause of inflation is to indulge in a fantasy that may comfort traditional mythology, but does little to deal with its true causes."[75] Strom Thurmond followed, adding, "I think he [Ford] is going to be a great leader for this country. However, I feel he is in error in vetoing this particular bill."[76] In between comments from Alan Cranston, Bob Dole, Edward Kennedy, George McGovern, and others in support of the override, Charles Mathis Jr. reminded his fellow senators that this bill was not "some vast pork barrel program, . . . [but] a commitment to the men and women who fought in our most recent war."[77] By late afternoon, both houses were ready to vote. In the end, the outcome was not even close. The House voted for an override by a margin of 394–10, with thirty representatives not casting votes. Nine of the ten dissenters were lame ducks following the November elections. The Senate passed the measure by an equally crushing 90–1, with nine not voting. Only Michigan senator and deputy Republican leader Robert P. Griffin sided with the president.

With palpable relief, the veterans began to express their appreciation for the override. June A. Willenz, executive director of the American Veterans Committee, told Carl Albert, "A victory for justice and equality was won last week with the override of the veto of the GI Bill for Vietnam veterans. Your leadership helped make this GI Bill a reality."[78] In a December 12 meeting with Richard Roudebush, Timothy L. Craig, president of the NACV, thanked the new VA administrator for his support of the benefits bill. Craig also noted that "during the brief period in which Mr. Richard L. Roudebush has been the Veterans Administrator, there has been a marked change in the VA's attitude and policy toward Vietnam era veterans."[79] H.R. 12628, the Vietnam Era Veterans' Readjustment Assistance Act of 1974, became Public Law 53-508 on December 3, 1974. On December 15, the VA started mailing out over 1.2 million checks for benefits retroactive to September 1 in the hope that most of the eligible veterans would receive them before Christmas. For the single veteran claiming no dependents, the checks amounted to $200; a veteran claiming one dependent could expect $240. While still far from generous, the bill represented a significant improvement, and Ford had to look elsewhere in his effort to reduce the federal budget.

Although many at the time viewed Ford's obstructionism as a sign of callousness and indifference, Ford saw the fight over veterans' funding as an earnest crusade against an inflation problem that he genuinely believed could undermine the fabric of American society. Ford saw the use of the veto as one of the few options open to him if he was to stand any chance of pushing his economic agenda. More than any previous president, Ford pursued a deliberate veto strategy to counterbalance the overwhelming Democratic majorities he faced in Congress. In the aftermath of the November elections, the Republicans had lost forty-three seats in the House, giving Democrats a 291–144 majority, and three seats in the Senate, giving Democrats a 61–39 majority. Ford's own political approval ratings had plummeted by 30 percent between August and December of 1974, with much of his already-scant political capital burned up by his pardoning of Richard Nixon.[80] Through frequent use of his veto power, Ford hoped to both reinvest the executive office with a power that political circumstances denied him and also to encourage Congress to reduce its spending.[81] Of the veto, Ford stated, "[it] is not a negative, dead-end device. In most cases, it is a positive means of achieving legislative compromise and improvement—better legislation in other words."[82]

In making his decision, Ford joined the cast of previous twentieth-century presidents who, despite the political drawbacks, opposed veterans' benefits in what they considered to be a stand vital to the national interest. For Ford, the most pressing issue for the nation in 1974 remained inflation. He later wrote that he had hoped that "[i]f the executive branch could set an example of fiscal restraint by trimming its own proposals the Congress might be persuaded to follow suit."[83] Congress did not. Indeed, Ford's attempts to thwart the will of Congress—in this and in later veto decisions—placed a significant strain on his relationship with Congress. When he first entered the White House, Ford promised to heal the relationship between the executive and the legislature that Richard Nixon had left so soured. Instead of the disdain Nixon had repeatedly showed Congress, Ford promised "communication, conciliation, compromise, and cooperation."[84] At the beginning of Ford's presidency, one Democratic congressman recalled a widespread "physical dislike toward Nixon. Ford, in contrast, was trusted, even among those who strongly disagreed with him."[85] Ford's continuous use of the veto ensured that his honeymoon period was short-lived. One Ford assistant recalled, "Each veto crippled future opportunities for success; each veto eroded the president's already limited base of support. No president can afford to veto twenty-five bills a year. . . . It's too damn much, and Congress won't stand for it."[86] By the time of the 1976 presidential election, the veto strategy had alienated many political allies on the Hill, leading one White House assistant to suggest that had he won the election, "Congress wouldn't have listened to Ford. The constant flood of vetoes had angered too many potential allies."[87] But whatever the ramifications were for Ford, the main outcome of the political battles that took place in Washington in the fall of 1974 was that the G.I. Bill finally made higher education a more attractive proposition for Vietnam veterans. Although the costs to the government of the 1974 G.I.

Bill exceeded Ford's worst fears, the benefit to the lives of veterans was potentially far greater.

And if Ford remained concerned about the inflationary effects of the cost of the new benefits, the news was about to get worse. Roy Ash resigned as director of OMB in December 1974. It was left to his successor, James T. Lynn, to inform Ford early in 1975 that

> [the] VA has alerted us to a recent spurt in veteran benefit applications. By the end of February, the GI Bill education program was paying 91,000 trainees over that estimated in the FY 1976 President's Budget. . . . However, the increases seen thus far are just the tip of the iceberg. From the sparse data thus far available in March, it appears that the trend may go even higher.[88]

Vietnam veterans had waited a long time—too long—to be offered a reasonable reward for their service and to gain an opportunity to return to school. Now they seemed determined to seize the new opportunity.

The numbers of veterans in higher education had increased gradually since 1966 as a natural result of more veterans reentering society, but the upward curve spiked noticeably after the passage of the 1974 G.I. Bill. In 1967, fewer than five hundred thousand veterans were using their benefits for higher education. In 1971, the number stood at one million. In 1976—fully ten years after the first eligible veterans came home—over 2.9 million veterans were claiming some form of education benefits under the G.I. Bill. About one-third of veterans in 1976 used their benefits for vocational training, leaving almost two million in institutions of higher education across the country. The number of veterans enrolled in 1976 alone exceeded the number of veterans who attended schools during the entire course of the Korean War G.I. Bill (1.2 million) and almost equaled the entire number of World War II veterans who entered higher education under the original 1944 program (2.2 million). The percentage of Vietnam-era veterans claiming education benefits reached 63.6 by 1973. Already, this number was far above the 50.5 percent of World War II veterans who participated under the original program. Moreover, whereas only 2.2 million out of 15.6 million World War II veterans used their benefits for higher education, 3.6 million out of 6.5 million eligible veterans used their benefits at the college level after the passage of the 1966 bill.[89] As earlier critics of the program had pointed out, however, usage percentages remained an imperfect test of the program's success or failure.

The Ford administration clearly believed the 1974 G.I. Bill had gone far enough in compensating Vietnam veterans. In 1975 Ford even proposed scaling the time frame in which veterans could claim benefits from ten years back down to eight. VA administrator Richard Roudebush agreed. Outlining the administration's justifications for the proposals, he resurrected the old argument that the G.I. Bill constituted a temporary readjustment tool and not an ongoing entitlement program. He also noted, correctly, that Vietnam veterans enjoyed far more generous eligibility terms—ten years instead of eight—than had veterans of previous wars. The current bill, suggested Roudebush, "has the effect of discriminating against veterans serving in earlier periods."[90]

The established veterans' groups seemed to concur that the government had finally done enough to compensate Vietnam veterans with the 1974 bill. When Congress debated a 1976 proposal to allow Vietnam veterans even more time to claim their benefits, they made their opinions known. The 1976 proposal sought to provide an additional year of eligibility. Proponents of the extension argued that benefits had been so low at the start of the program that many needed the extra time because they could not have previously afforded to go to school. For the American Legion, VFW, and DAV, which still had the interests of the aging World War II generation at the forefront of their concerns, this extension went too far. Thomas C. Walker, commander-in-chief of the VFW, called on Carl Albert to oppose the measure and added, "We believe, all things considered, the current GI Bill is the most generous of all three GI Bills and, again, there is no tenable justification for a further extension of the delimiting period."[91] The American Legion supported only a cost-of-living increase for disabled veterans and education benefits but opposed the eligibility extension. The Legion urged Albert to "insist that these funds be directed to higher priority programs for millions of war veterans and their dependents, which in addition to needed costs of living increases in education programs would include improved compensation and pensions, and sorely needed changes in medical and hospital programs."[92] The Disabled Veterans of America's constituents had a more obvious reason to oppose excessively liberal education payments. The DAV had expressed initial opposition to the original 1944 bill for fear that it would divert funds away from disabled veterans whose needs clearly exceeded those of the returning able-bodied veteran. A similar fear guided the thinking of DAV national director of legislation Charles L. Huber when he expressed the organization's concern that the proposed increase "will make it impossible for the Congress to pass legislation of a much higher priority within the limits of the budget for Veterans' Benefits and Services." Specifically, Huber called for increased disability payments, pensions, and medical treatment and added, "We believe there is no justification to reduce funding for these programs in favor of an extension of educational benefits."[93]

In 1976, Congress did pass an 8 percent cost-of-living benefits increase, but the momentum behind any significant further increase for veterans seemed to be ebbing.[94] By the late 1970s, it is questionable as to how much a new or improved program would have helped Vietnam veterans. By then, most of the Vietnam generation would have either found a way to go to school or would have been so far along in an alternative life course or career that education benefits might have had less appeal than they would have had five or ten years earlier. However, in 1977 a new group of legislators steeled themselves for one final push to provide direct tuition relief for the remaining Vietnam veterans still interested in higher education. They found a familiar foe in their way.

By 1977, Olin Teague's body was ailing. On doctor's orders, he had dropped forty-eight pounds to help with his diabetes, and in February he had his war-damaged foot amputated after gangrene had set in. Thereafter, he shuttled around the halls of Congress on an electric cart.[95] But as he entered the final few years of his life, Teague remained as adamant as ever that the government had done enough for Vietnam veterans and as steadfast as ever in rebuking attempts to offer more generous education allowances. Legislators introduced over a hundred bills in 1977 designed to help correct some of the difficulties veterans still faced in meeting tuition costs. Proposals ranged from direct tuition payments—similar to those passed in the Senate in 1974—to an accelerated payment program that would allow veterans to compress their full 45-month entitlements into a shorter period of time if they could complete their degrees sooner.

After the 1974 G.I. Bill increases, few legislators were willing to out-right condemn the education benefits as wholly inadequate; instead, at the heart of the new round of proposals lay the desire to help veter-ans attending schools in states with higher tuition rates. The continued struggle of those veterans remained the one outstanding injustice of the Vietnam-era G.I. Bills that warranted legislative action. Congressmen Leon Panetta and John Murtha sent letters to their colleagues on the Hill in support of the legislation, pointing out that "[i]n many states with less generously funded public education systems, veterans have difficulties using their GI Bill benefits, and many of these men feel anger about their lack of recognition for national service."[96] They wrote Teague directly to proclaim, "Today's GI Bill legislation is grossly inade-quate for the veterans, particularly in high-cost-of-education states. . . . [W]e urge you and the Subcommittee to give careful consideration to corrective legislation."[97] The *Washington Post*, in one of a series of edi-torials focusing on the plight of Vietnam veterans, highlighted a report from the National League of Cities and the U.S. Conference of Mayors that claimed that "a California vet, who may have served in the same company with the Philadelphia vet, has to spend only 15.1 percent of his yearly GI Bill benefits for education costs—while the Philadelphia vet has to spend 57 percent of his benefits."[98] The following week an editorial in the paper attacked the House leadership over a proposal that Teague favored that would have provided only a simple cost-of-living increase to the monthly educational allowance. Such a proposal, the editorial opined, would do nothing to help veterans in high-tuition states, and "the effect of this [bill] would be to spend much of the avail-able money on veterans who are comparatively well off."[99]

Despite his failing health, "Tiger" Teague sharpened his claws to repel one last charge. In over forty years of public service, Teague had remained steadfast in his political views and was in no mood to waver. Reflecting back on the development of his personal philoso-phy, he told a reporter in 1977 that his parents had told him to "love God and love work . . . and they gave me the opportunity to do both." When challenged that his policies might have led to the neglect of the disadvantaged, he snapped back, "I guess we're all influenced by the type of life we've lived. My life proved to me we give people an oppor-tunity. . . . Every person should do something for everything they get from the taxpayers."[100] For the Vietnam veterans, this belief had translated repeatedly into obstructing any legislation that offered direct tuition relief. To Teague, such proposals went beyond offering a mere opportunity and veered into handout territory. The latest rounds of veterans' bills allowed him to dust off some all-too-familiar refrains.

Teague went on the offensive against both his House colleagues and the editors of the *Washington Post*. In response to the letters from Leon Panetta, John Murtha, and others, he wrote to his colleagues to outline the enormous and ongoing costs of liberalizing veterans' benefits. He also claimed that any provision that brought relief to veterans in high-tuition states would be unfair to taxpayers who already subsidized public education in low-tuition states. "Should the taxpayers of States such as California," he asked, "be taxed again to pay more money to veterans attending schools in States who do not have low-cost public education? I fail to see the equity in such a proposal."[101] He called out the editor of the *Washington Post*, asking him to testify before Teague's committee and adding, "I would suggest before you testify, that you do your homework, which obviously you have not done."[102] After the editor declined the invitation, Teague wrote back to clarify his position. Again, he highlighted what he considered to be the fairness of the existing program and also emphasized all of the additional programs available to Vietnam veterans that previous veterans did not enjoy, such as outreach programs to help with their employment needs. When Teague's committee held hearings on the various proposals in the fall of 1977, no amount of contrary testimony was going to sway his views. His questions to one of the tuition bill's sponsors, Minnesota representative Albert Quie, for example, contained lengthy preambles that merely reiterated his long-held views on veterans' benefits. He repeated the line that the G.I. Bill was only ever intended to help veterans "meet *in part* his educational expenses, and to not serve as a tuition grant," and that any direct tuition assistance would serve only the needs of educational institutions and not the taxpayer or the veterans.[103] The result of Teague's largely symbolic hearings was a bill that contained no direct tuition relief to veterans in high-tuition states. Moreover, Teague ensured that the desires of many House members for a more full and open discussion of the bill would be crushed.

Teague's bill, backed by House Veterans' Affairs Committee chairman Ray Roberts (D-TX), offered a simple 6.6 percent increase in educational allowances. Much to the chagrin of many of his fellow representatives, Teague circumvented a full discussion of the measure in the Veterans' Affairs Committee where the members could have discussed tuition provisions more fully or debated a compromise with more generous proposals circulating in the Senate. Teague also sent his bill to the floor, again, under the Suspension of the Rules procedure that denied any amendments and prevented any representative from bringing the tuition issue to a vote. The House bill, H.R.8701, passed, but not without protest. One representative called Teague's measure the "anti-Vietnam-era veteran" bill.[104] In one final twist of the knife, Teague also convinced Senate and House staffers to thrash out any compromises with the Senate proposals in informal talks and without a full conference committee. The compromises were made "around a breakfast table," noted Teague. "It's just quicker and easier . . . without a whole lot of people."[105] Over coffee and pastries, the last chance for Vietnam veterans to get widespread tuition relief died.

The final bill contained modest proposals for tuition relief, but nothing close to the liberal provisions called for in the Senate. Teague got his scant 6.6 percent across-the-board increase, barely keeping benefits in step with inflation. The amount of loans available to veterans rose to twenty-five hundred dollars. Veterans could also claim loans for an additional two years after their ten-year eligibility expired if they needed the extra time to finish their degree. But states were now required to match every federal dollar paid for tuition over seven hundred dollars. The rationale behind this provision was that it would either encourage or force high-tuition states to invest more heavily in public education. The practical consequences, as New York Republican senator Jacob Javits noted, was "tantamount to saying there will be no help for veterans. Few, if any, states can afford to meet the current costs of higher education much less come up with additional appropriations."[106] The widespread disquiet notwithstanding, Jimmy Carter signed the G.I. Bill Improvements Act into law on November 23, 1977. One of the bill's other provisions of note, adopted by a voice vote from an amendment by Republican senator Barry Goldwater, finally granted veteran status to Women's Airforce Service Pilots of World War II. Though pitifully late and practically irrelevant, this provision finally gave a symbolic acknowledgment of the vital contribution of the WASPs to the war effort.

Following more than a decade of fighting, the Vietnam veterans seemed resigned to this latest knockback. The *Washington Post* reported the views of one veteran who had made his way to Teague's hearings in September and who related that the veterans had grown weary of making pointless treks to the nation's capital only to be put through a "heartless routine" of "seeing their hope rise as they made the rounds but then going home to seethe at the inaction that inevitably followed." What ire they could muster was reserved mostly for Olin Teague. The *Post* reported that "[f]rom Vietnam veteran groups . . . Teague receives the weakest of salutes, if any at all. He is seen as being so out of touch as to not understand even the obvious: that Vietnam was a different war that led to different readjustment problems in a different America." Further, the report noted that during the hearings, Teague repeatedly pointed to the lack of veterans' letters or lobbying pressure as a sign that corrective legislation on tuition was not needed. For one veteran, Teague's actions represented "vanity gone wild: Unless his subjects beg him for relief, he ignores them. But the veterans are past begging. It had gained little, so why continue?"[107] The president of the New York City Community College Veterans Association lashed out at Teague's obstructionism, telling the congressman,

Your recent comment on not hearing from Vietnam Veterans on their needs is a joke. On our journey to Washington last spring, we met with you [and], as expected, we were given a deaf ear. For us to repeat the farcical nature of our education benefits here in New York City and the North East is a joke. [The] Vietnam Veteran knows the game that is being played. Please don't ease your conscience at our expense. I can't believe you don't know what damage you are doing to thousands of veterans in our city.[108]

The pleas, as they had done for many years, made little impact on Teague. Teague had made no secret that he was sick of hearing such sob stories from supposedly neglected veterans. After Jimmy Carter had given a speech at Arlington Cemetery in which he claimed his own son was part of a generation of Vietnam veterans who had come home "unappreciated, sometimes scorned," and were owed "a special debt of gratitude," Teague wrote the president to tell him that Vietnam veterans were not "scorned" and that such sentiments "distressed" him.[109] And as he had done in most of his thirty years of passing veterans' legislation in Congress, Teague had won the day, ensuring that many veterans were left feeling that the "special debt" had not been repaid. Teague's stand in 1977 was to be his last. He left Congress in December 1978, and in January 1981, at the age of seventy, he died at Bethesda Naval hospital of renal failure and a heart attack.[110]

Teague's departure coincided with the Vietnam veterans finally gaining a stronger voice in Congress. After being elected as Democratic representative for Michigan in 1976, air force veteran David Bonior formed the Vietnam Veterans in Congress group. By 1980, the caucus had nineteen members, all Vietnam veterans, from both parties and from both Houses. Decrying previous government treatment of Vietnam veterans, Bonior stated that "[p]art of the problem lies in under-representation. Although 19 of the 28 members of the House Veterans['] Committee are veterans, only one is a Vietnam-era veteran. Anyone claiming that the Vietnam vet has been adequately cared for simply ignores the facts."[111] The Vietnam veteran caucus continued to decry the geographic inequalities of the G.I. Bill, but increasingly began to focus on the lack of assistance for veterans facing drug-abuse, psychological issues, and employment difficulties.

Similarly, there were promising signs that the White House might be more receptive to addressing veterans' problems. Jimmy Carter had incurred the wrath of some of the older veterans' groups with his blanket pardon of Vietnam War draft deserters and his attempts to streamline the VA medical system. Carter also questioned the practice of giving veterans preferential treatment in federal employment.[112] But Carter was the first president to so openly acknowledge the severity of problems faced by some Vietnam veterans in his speech at Arlington Cemetery. He also made sure that Vietnam veterans had one of their own in one of the most important federal positions on veterans' affairs.

Carter appointed Max Cleland to head the VA from 1977 through 1981. Cleland earned Bronze and Silver Stars while serving in Vietnam. He had survived the siege at Khe Sanh in 1968, but days later lost both legs and one arm attempting to pick up a dropped grenade. He described the incident as a "freaky war accident" and downplayed his bravery in trying to shield other soldiers from the blast.[113]

In congressional hearings in 1969, Cleland had criticized the VA medical establishment over his struggles to receive artificial limbs or even a wheelchair.[114] The *Washington Post* described him as "handsome and articulate. Imaginative and tough, a hell-raising witness on Capitol Hill for GI rights, driving his own car to work despite his physical handicaps, surrounding himself with other Vietnam veterans as advisors, fanning the fire in his gut to fulfill a passion for public service."[115] He became the youngest-ever head of the VA at the age of thirty-four, and promised to "institutionalize hope, caring, [and] sensitivity" that had been starkly absent under his predecessors.[116] Speaking of his own disability, Cleland saw himself as "a public reminder of the price that's been paid."[117] Cleland helped steer through much-needed legislation for Vietnam veterans, including a new psychological counseling program that the Senate had passed repeatedly only for the House and previous administrations to cut down.

Cleland and his fellow Vietnam veterans in Congress fought for better benefits and services for Vietnam veterans as the 1970s drew to a close, but their influence came too late to have any major impact on the G.I. Bill. By the end of the decade, most Vietnam veterans were in their late twenties or thirties and had either already used their education benefits or exhausted their eligibility. Many more might have started families or embarked on careers and were not at a stage in their lives where more schooling ranked high on their list of priorities. The fight for education benefits faded into the background as more immediate issues such as post-traumatic stress disorder and the use of Agent Orange began to dominate the attention of lawmakers, the veteran community, and the press: The G.I. Bill no longer represented the hot topic it had been during the preceding two decades. Several cost-of-living increases followed in 1980, raising the monthly allowance to $327 for the single veteran, and in 1981 increasing it to $342, until the last major increase in education benefits for the Vietnam-era veteran became law on October 17, 1984. The 1984 law gave the single veteran $376 a month on which to live and was to be the last significant G.I. Bill legislation for the Vietnam generation.

Conclusion

"A Chance for Learning" Missed

In the summer of 1968, Stephen Piotrowski's life was at a crossroads. With high school graduation looming, a succession of rejected grant and scholarship applications had dashed his immediate hopes of going to college. His brother was close to returning home from a tour of duty as an air force mechanic in Vietnam and, with the risk of his draft number being called, Piotrowski decided to enlist in the army. He was well aware of the controversial nature of the war and of the risks involved in volunteering, but several factors dictated his decision. Failure to secure funding for college meant that the prospect of a G.I. Bill held great appeal. "I didn't have the scholarships," he recalled, "[so] I went down and saw the recruiter and said, look, I want the G.I. Bill." Piotrowski also felt a strong sense of civic duty to serve. With his father and uncles being World War II veterans, service "was part of the family history, part of what you did." In addition, he still held a firm conviction that the Vietnam War was a righteous cause and that the government would not send its citizens to fight in an immoral conflict. He still believed that "the war was something . . . where we must be right." Three days after graduating high school, Piotrowski was in uniform. He completed his basic training in Fort Campbell, Kentucky, and advanced infantry training in Fort Lewis, Washington. Following airborne training in Fort Benning, Georgia, he was sent to Vietnam as part of the 173rd Airborne Division in January 1969. Piotrowski's plane touched down in Tan Son Nhut airport amid the mortar attacks and enemy fire of the Tet '69 offensive. Though less well known than Tet '68, the Tet '69 Communist attacks were intense enough that Piotrowski was convinced that he would not survive his tour of duty. A feeling of calm came over him at that point, he remembers, which gave him a sense of acceptance of whatever fate lay ahead.

After surviving several close encounters with enemy forces over the next twelve months of patrolling the Central Highlands—including a run-in with a Viet Cong women's brigade—Piotrowski headed home. He was finally able to begin his undergraduate studies at the University of Wisconsin–Stevens Point in the summer of 1970. He had hoped that his G.I. Bill would give him the opportunity he believed he had rightly earned, but like so many other veterans, Piotrowski was sorely disappointed with the results. Over twenty years after graduating he notes, "It still makes me bitter that my G.I. Bill, when I started college, was only $15 more than a World War II vet got when he started college. And he got room, board, and tuition. . . . Inflation was a bit more than $15 over that period." Contrasting his experience with that of his father's generation, he notes, "World War II vets really had stuff handed to them on a silver platter because the World War I vets took care of them. And it was a good war. Everybody was behind it." Although several increases in educational allowances followed for Vietnam veterans in the 1970s, Piotrowski recalled "only getting $340 a month on the G.I. Bill in 1977. That's outrageous." His experience was not uncommon, and his sense of injustice was far from unwarranted.[1]

By the time the Vietnam-era G.I. Bills finally expired on December 31, 1989, the Veterans Administration estimates that 76 percent of eligible veterans had claimed some form of education benefits.[2] Further, according to the 1984 VA annual report, Vietnam-era veterans had attained an average education level of 13.2 years compared with 12.9 years for nonveterans. As the report notes, "greater educational attainment results, almost without exception, in increased earnings." Indeed, the median earnings for male Vietnam-era veterans reached $21,670 a year, compared with $18,730 for nonveterans. The report also found that Vietnam-era veterans had attained a slightly higher percentage of college degrees than their nonveteran counterparts. According to the VA, 24.4 percent of Vietnam-era veterans earned a college degree by 1984 compared with 24.2 percent of nonveterans in the same age group.[3] Superficially, these numbers seem impressive; however, the VA figures did not take into account the many variables among veterans of the Vietnam era, such as where or when they went to school, their race and economic background, their branch of service, whether they were drafted or volunteered, or the overall quality of their education. Further, and most importantly, the VA figures did not distinguish between those veterans who had served in Vietnam and those stationed elsewhere during the Vietnam era. As with Piotrowski, it was the combat veterans who most acutely felt the sense of neglect.

The figures also mask some very real problems that continued to compromise the program's effectiveness right up until its demise. As long as the government failed to pay tuition in full or directly to institutions, many veterans faced significant restrictions on the education they could attain. Where veterans lived and how much additional income they could muster dictated the type of school they attended and ultimately the quality of education they could afford. Veterans' education benefits went much further in some states than in others, so some veterans could go to school without much financial worry if they lived in a state with lower tuition rates and chose a cut-price school. Those that lived in higher-tuition states tended to have to find additional work just to make ends meet. Other studies reveal a much more nuanced and less-than-glowing portrait of the quality of education offered under the G.I. Bills than the VA figures suggest.

Veterans tended to select lower-cost institutions over more expensive four-year degree programs, despite having a higher level of high school education than their nonveteran peers. Sharon Cohany's analysis of a 1989 Bureau of the Census survey of veterans' households concluded that Vietnam-era veterans were "more heavily concentrated in the middle-level educational attainment categories."[4] Further, Cohany noted that veterans tended to be more educated going into the service—a product of the selective nature of military service—with only 7 percent of veterans being high school dropouts compared with 20 percent of comparable civilians. Yet, only 26 percent of veterans had completed a college degree compared with 31 percent of civilians. Moreover, 28 percent of veterans tended to have completed only one to three years of college compared with 17 percent of nonveterans.[5] Significantly, Cohany also noted that 23 percent of veterans who served in the Vietnam combat theater attained a college degree compared with 29 percent of noncombat veterans. Similarly, Josefina Card's 1983 comparison of the lives of five hundred civilians, five hundred Vietnam veterans, and five hundred non-Vietnam veterans—all of whom finished high school in 1963—found that over 32 percent of nonveterans had completed a college degree compared to 28 percent of non-Vietnam veterans and 26 percent of Vietnam combat theater veterans. Both Vietnam and non-Vietnam veterans were much more likely to have attained a vocational or less-than-four-year degree. Among the Vietnam veterans, 23.3 percent had completed a vocational degree compared with 21.7 percent of Vietnam-era veterans and only 11.5 percent of nonveterans.[6] These studies suggest that Vietnam combat veterans—those who were calling most loudly for equitable benefits—were indeed most adversely affected by military service in terms of their educational attainment.[7]

Jay Teachman's more recent study of Vietnam-era veterans' educational attainment reveals that a lot of the discrepancies in education levels tended to diminish over time; that is, the further away veterans were from the time of their discharge, the more likely they were to have caught up with their civilian counterparts. Even so, and with some variations, he concludes that "[i]n the broadest terms . . . Vietnam-era veterans attained less education than did their non-veteran counterparts."[8] Teachman also notes that because of the low level of benefits on offer to Vietnam veterans, their G.I. Bill gave nothing like the same boost as the 1944 G.I. Bill had given World War II veterans. Because higher education was still an exclusive realm in 1944, education benefits offered veterans a chance for learning not open to civilians. By the Vietnam era, higher education had become far more commonplace as a result of the proliferation of higher education funding and lower-cost schools, with the consequence that veterans faced a struggle just to achieve parity with civilians.

Many veterans felt compelled to attend lower-cost schools, a sacrifice in their futures that previous generations did not have to make. A 1975 VA study for the Senate Committee on Veterans' Affairs confirmed that "trainees under the G.I. Bill tend to seek the lowest cost schools" at whatever level of training they sought.[9] When asked if the provision of a separate tuition payment—one that would cover their tuition costs at a school of their choice—would have encouraged them to seek education at a more expensive school, 40 percent confirmed that it would. Further, a 1976 General Accounting Office *Report on Veterans' Responses to VA Educational Assistance Programs* revealed that 44.2 percent of veterans who had started a degree program under the G.I. Bill "did not achieve their primary training objective" of earning a degree or vocational skill. Therefore, although 76 percent of Vietnam-era veterans may have claimed education benefits, the type of education they received fell far short of what many expected and thought that they had earned through their military service.[10]

Studies that examine the impact of education benefits on the life earnings of Vietnam-era veterans offer further qualifiers to the VA's statistics. Joshua Angrist, in two articles written in the early 1990s, suggests that white Vietnam-era veterans had earned 15 percent less than their nonveteran counterparts ten years after service.[11] Other studies have found similar results: Two articles by Jere Cohen, David Segal, and Lloyd Temme claim that Vietnam-era veterans have not achieved the same educational and employment levels as nonveterans.[12] While future research might provide more definitive answers on the overall impact of the Vietnam-era G.I. Bills on veterans' lives, the wealth of veterans' testimonies, such as Stephen Piotrowski's, and the sheer volume of outrage that accompanied the legislative battles over education benefits reveals unequivocally that a great many veterans of the Vietnam generation suffered under their G.I. Bill in a way that World War II and Korean Conflict veterans did not.

If their G.I. Bill had been as generous as the 1944 version, veterans such as Piotrowski could have gone to school and, perhaps, had the same kind of positive outcome from their service as that enjoyed by World War II veterans. But for many Vietnam veterans, going to college under their G.I. Bills often added one more struggle to the sacrifice of military service. The 1944 and 1952 G.I. Bills held out the promise that veterans could expect the government to provide them a chance for self-improvement by providing tuition coverage and a generous monthly stipend. The 1966 G.I. Bill—because it covered so many Cold War veterans whose noncombat service was deemed unworthy of generous reward—was less than adequate for the needs and desires of returning Vietnam veterans. Arguably, the bill represented a reasonable return for veterans serving in peacetime conditions as their sacrifices and expectations might have been far lower. But for those who had put their lives on the line more directly or had served in a theater of war, the 1966 bill fell far short of what they believed they had earned. The precedents set by the previous G.I. Bills *had* elevated military service far beyond a mere obligation of citizenship. For the government to then offer the Vietnam generation only a partial reward for their service, and to have so many politicians fighting almost every step of the way to prevent significant increases, seemed to many veterans like a denigration of their sacrifice.

In the years following the passage of the 1966 bill, several lawmakers attempted to introduce measures to increase educational benefits. As the war in Vietnam heated up, debates veered away from what the government owed noncombat veterans toward making the benefits more appropriate for Vietnam combat veterans. Significant improvements were made to the program. But repeatedly, such attempts were compromised by a succession of legislators wedded to particular economic or political philosophies. Further undermining the generosity of the program, throughout most of the Vietnam era the Veterans Administration kept insisting there was no problem with the levels of funding, despite evidence to the contrary. The veterans also lacked the support of an organization with the same lobbying influence provided for World War II veterans by the American Legion and VFW.

Several senators made laudable efforts to challenge the federal inertia. Ralph Yarborough did perhaps more than any other politician in the 1960s to assist Cold War veterans. Yarborough began his push for a peacetime G.I. Bill long before hostilities in Vietnam escalated into a full-blown conflict. An unfortunate and unintended consequence of his attempts at providing assistance to all Cold War veterans was that his G.I. Bill placed Vietnam veterans at a significant disadvantage relative to veterans of previous conflicts. Although his efforts stemmed from a genuine concern over the injustice of having a small number of citizens bear the burden national defense, the failure of his bill to recognize the distinct readjustment needs of combat veterans resulted in legislation that failed to meet the expectations of Vietnam veterans. Yarborough remained acutely aware of this problem and in the final years of his tenure on Capitol Hill worked hard to increase the level of education benefits offered. Vance Hartke, Alan Cranston, and others continued his work during the 1970s. Without their efforts, the benefits on offer would have been even more miserly. These lawmakers did succeed in improving the benefits, but their attempts at passing a more generous G.I. Bill were thwarted at nearly every turn by some formidable foes on Pennsylvania Avenue and in the House.

Successive presidents offered differing reasons for opposing liberal benefits. In the 1950s, Eisenhower feared the economic consequences of an ongoing and wide-ranging slate of obligations and, under the aegis of the Bradley Report, reaffirmed the notion that military service was more of a civic duty than a basis for ongoing benefits. Although this principle was more directed at the provision of pensions to World War I and World War II veterans than to peacetime Cold War veterans, it introduced an element of thrift into federal funding to able-bodied veterans that greatly influenced the debates over the first Vietnam-era G.I. Bill in 1966. Lyndon Johnson then provided a new reason for keeping benefits low as he believed that there were other more impoverished sectors of society that needed federal assistance far more than the average Cold War veteran. He did not want his broader education goals for the Great Society jeopardized by a program that privileged only those in uniform. The resulting 1966 Cold War G.I. Bill fell well short of the 1944 and 1952 G.I. Bills. Attempts to raise the educational allowance then ran afoul of Richard Nixon and his attempts to scale back federal funding at the start of the 1970s. Finally, Gerald Ford's determination to "Whip Inflation" led him to veto a more generous G.I. Bill in 1974.

The failure of the House of Representatives to provide a generous G.I. Bill resulted in large part from the ideas and actions of Olin Teague. Teague had played kingmaker for seventeen years as chair of the House Committee on Veterans' Affairs—by far the longest-serving chair on the committee—and had been the most influential legislator on veterans' issues in Congress. Throughout his tenure he was an unfailing champion of those veterans he considered to be in greatest need such as disabled veterans and dependents of deceased soldiers. Those groups had unquestionably benefited from having him fight in their corner. But in other areas of veterans' legislation, he consistently and successfully imposed his own conservative views of fiscal responsibility and civic duty. As self-appointed guardian of the gates of the treasury, his positions resulted in legislation that was far from generous to those veterans who had left the service with no physical impairments. His actions helped limit the generosity of the 1966 Cold War G.I. Bill, and he continued to fight against increases in the political battles over benefits that followed.

Teague was not as heartless as some of his more vocal critics in the veterans' community sometimes cast him. He expressed a deep appreciation for the Vietnam soldiers' sacrifice during the second trip he made to Southeast Asia in February 1966. The purpose of his visit, which he undertook alongside VA head William Driver, was to help the South Vietnamese establish their own veterans' programs and to assist them in the care of widows and orphans. After returning home, he made an effort to ensure that the South Vietnamese received wheelchairs and crutches for their injured veterans. Just before he left Da Nang Air Base, he wrote the following words about his experiences:

> Tired, dirty, sore all over. I wish I could describe all I have seen. A war is so terrible. I walked through wards . . . about 40 to a tent, bleeding, groaning, trying so hard to stay alive. Blood everywhere, and everyone too busy to clean it up. Faces burned off, legs off, about 10 temporary operating rooms—all working. Doctors, nurses, corpsmen, going quietly about their business—few words—facing a steady stream of ambulances going back and forth to the pad—taking loads to big planes—bringing back wounded. Sixty to a plane on their way to Japan, Clark Field or Oki-nawa—and it will all become much worse before it is better.
>
> It is such a sad situation, just as we at home know that someone at home will be hurt or killed in a car wreck. We get in our cars and know it won't be us. They know many will be killed or wounded one way or another, but they all know it will not be them. . . . Old men should fight our wars—not our kids.[13]

In World War II, Teague had experienced first-hand the horrors of war and had carried the physical and psychological scars for the remainder of his life. As his heartfelt testimony revealed, he was not oblivious to the suffering that combat could cause. But he could not, and would not, uncouple himself from his commitment to fighting the growth of federal power. Ultimately his actions had very real consequences for the Vietnam veterans whose suffering he witnessed in 1966.

When the weight of Teague's arguments failed to win over his fellow congressmen, he connived to make sure that lawmakers did not have the chance to amend his legislation. His repeated use of Suspension of Rules procedure ensured that the House was frequently presented with one choice on veterans' funding: vote for Teague's bill or give the veterans nothing. One of the more damning indictments of Teague's actions came in a 1978 *Survey of Congressional Attitudes on Problems of Concern to Vietnam Veterans*. The survey, conducted on behalf of the Vietnam Veterans of America, revealed that *67 percent* of lawmakers in the House favored legislation that covered a veteran's tuition costs.[14] Had this provision ever gone into effect, every veteran with an honorable discharge, irrespective of his or her economic condition, would have been guaranteed access to higher education. Every time the House members did vote for an education increase throughout the Vietnam era, they did so either unanimously or with overwhelming majorities. But because of Teague's obstinate refusal to diverge from the antituition stance he adopted under the Korean War G.I. Bill, he made sure that the House never got the chance to vote on a provision to provide full tuition assistance.

Teague's actions ensured that the pro-veteran sentiment that existed in the House was never converted into the meaningful legislative action the veterans believed they had earned. Had the Vietnam-era G.I. Bills covered a veteran's tuition in the same way that the 1944 bill had, veterans could have returned to school with far less financial difficulty. Teague ensured that one of the biggest problems of the entire program was never fully addressed. Although his fiscal sensibilities had no doubt saved the government millions of dollars, that outcome would have been of little comfort to many of the Vietnam veterans who labored under his cut-price legislation. The veterans were not asking for handouts or "a white picket fence around them," as Teague had once feared, just the same chance for learning that had been given to World War II and Korean War veterans. The bills were not all bad. They did provide veterans with a welcome boost in their education funds and undoubtedly helped many achieve their educational goals. Many veterans could, and did, receive an education if they chose their schools carefully, but others faced significant financial hardships—particularly the economically disadvantaged and those living in states with high tuition costs. For many of them, the "chance for learning" that Tim O'Brien had called for on that dreary Vietnam Veterans Day in DC in March 1974 never materialized. Therein lay the failings of the G.I. Bill for the Vietnam generation.

INTRODUCTION

1. Jacques Leslie, "Smiling Hanoi Officers Watch G.I.s Leave South," *Los Angeles Times*, April 2, 1973, 11.

2. After leaving the army in 1974, Beilke worked on veterans' issues and devoted his life to helping Vietnam veterans make the transition back to civilian life. He was working in the Pentagon on the morning of September 11, 2001, when hijacked American Airlines Flight 77 crashed into the western side of the building. Beilke was one of 125 people killed along with the sixty-four passengers on board the plane. When National Public Radio's *All Things Considered* program tracked down Bui Tin in Paris soon after, Tin expressed sadness that he never got the chance to meet Beilke again (interview with Bui Tin for National Public Radio's *All Things Considered* program titled "Pentagon Postcard," first broadcast on October 18, 2001; see also Robert Rosenblatt and Richard Cooper, "Last Soldier to Leave Vietnam Is Feared Dead," *Los Angeles Times*, September 16, 2001).

3. Richard Nixon, "Proclamation 4270: Vietnam Veterans Day," February 26, 1974, *The American Presidency Project,* online by Gerhard Peters and John T. Woolley, http://www.presidency.ucsb.edu/ws/?pid=909 (accessed January 8, 2007).

4. Tim O'Brien, "The Vietnam Veteran: The G.I. Bill; Less Than Enough," *Penthouse*, November, 1974, 76.

5. Ibid.

6. Lyndon B. Johnson, "Statement by the President on the 20th Anniversary of the G.I. Bill of Rights," June 22, 1964, *The American Presidency Project,* online by Gerhard Peters and John T. Woolley, http://www.presidency.ucsb.edu/ws/?pid=26331 (accessed August 24, 2011); Jennifer Keene, *Doughboys, the Great War, and the Remaking of America* (Baltimore, Md.: Johns Hopkins University Press, 2001), x; Harold M. Hyman, *American Singularity: The 1787 Northwest Ordinance, the 1862 Homestead-Morrill Act, and the 1944 G.I. Bill* (Athens: University of Georgia Press, 1986); Michael J. Bennett, *When Dreams Came True: The G.I. Bill and the Making of Modern America* (Washington, D.C.: Brassey's, 1996), x; Bob Dole, foreword to Milton Greenberg, *The G.I. Bill: The Law That Changed America* (New York: Lickle, 1997), 8.

7. Recent scholarship such as Mark D. Van Ells, *To Hear Only Thunder Again: America's World War II Veterans Come Home* (Lanham, Md.: Lexington, 2001) and Thomas Childers, *Soldier from the War Returning: The Greatest Generation's Troubled Homecoming from World War II* (Boston, Mass.: Mariner, 2010) reveals that World War II veterans suffered many of the same problems later associated with the Vietnam generation, such as psychological damage, marital difficulties, and substance abuse. Robert Francis Saxe's *Settling Down: World War II Veterans' Challenge to the Postwar Consensus* (New York: Palgrave Macmillan, 2007) and Michael Gambone's *The Greatest Generation Comes Home: The Veteran in American Society* (College Station: Texas A&M University Press, 2005) further allude to the diverse attitudes and often-difficult homecoming experience of the World War II generation. For an important corrective to the universal praise heaped on the G.I. Bill, see David H. Onkst, "'First a Negro . . . Incidentally a Veteran': Black World War Two Veterans and the G.I. Bill of Rights in the Deep South, 1944–1948," *Journal of Social History* 31. 3 (Spring 1998): 518–43. Onkst reveals that racism and administrative inertia frequently negated the effects of the G.I. Bill for black veterans in the Deep South.

8. Suzanne Mettler, *Soldiers to Citizens: The G.I. Bill and the Making of the Greatest Generation* (New York: Oxford, 2005), 5–7.

9. For a long time, the G.I. Bill remained understudied. The two standard academic works on the legislation were Davis B. Ross, *Preparing for Ulysses: Politics and Veterans during World War II* (New York: Columbia University Press, 1969) and Keith Olson, *The G.I. Bill, the Veterans, and the Colleges* (Lexington: University Press of Kentucky, 1974). More popular histories were provided by Michael J. Bennett, *When Dreams Came True: The G.I. Bill and The Making of Modern America* (New York: Brassey's, 1996) and Milton Greenberg, *The G.I. Bill: The Law That Changed America* (New York: Lickle, 1997). Several recent works have revisited and expanded greatly our understanding of the impact of the G.I. Bill, including Jennifer Keene, *Doughboys, the Great War, and the Remaking of America* (Baltimore, Md.: Johns Hopkins University Press, 2001), Stephen Ortiz, *Beyond the Bonus March and G.I. Bill: How Veteran Politics Shaped the New Deal Era* (New York: New York University Press, 2010), Kathleen Frydl, *The G.I. Bill* (New York: Cambridge University Press, 2009), and Glenn Altschuler and Stuart Blumin, *The GI Bill: The New Deal for Veterans* (New York: Oxford University Press, 2009). Among the few published studies to address Cold War G.I. Bill benefits are Sar A. Levitan and Joyce Zickler, *Swords into Ploughshares: Our G.I. Bill* (Salt Lake City, Utah: Olympus, 1973) and Melinda Pash, *In the Shadow of the Greatest Generation: The Americans Who Fought the Korean War* (New York: New York University Press, 2013).

10. In this study the term "Vietnam-era veteran" refers to all veterans who served during the officially designated Vietnam era, which ran from August 4, 1964, through May 7, 1975. These veterans include all of those who were covered by the G.I. Bills but who might never have served in a theater of war or faced

an immediate risk of enemy fire. The term "Vietnam veteran" refers only to those veterans who served in the Southeast Asia combat theater. "Vietnam-era veteran" is used most often to describe the benefits offered to all veterans under the Vietnam-era bills because the bills made no distinction between where a veteran served. "Vietnam veteran" is used where the specific problems of combat veterans are discussed.

11. For a survey of the impact of Cold War military demands on citizenship see David R. Segal, *Recruiting for Uncle Sam: Citizenship and Military Manpower Policy* (Lawrence: University Press of Kansas, 1989). For a broader discussion of citizenship and military service see Ronald R. Krebs, *Fighting for Rights: Military Service and the Politics of Citizenship* (Ithaca, NY: Cornell University Press, 2006).

12. Figures from the *Veterans Administration Annual Report, 1984* (Washington, D.C.: U.S. Government Printing Office, 1984), 81, and the U.S. Department of Veterans Affairs, *VA History in Brief*, www1.va.gov/opa/publications/archives/docs/history_in_brief.pdf (accessed August 9, 2013).

13. *Veterans Administration Annual Report, 1984,* 81.

14. *Hearings on Employment Programs for Veterans*, Hearings before the Subcommittee on Education, Training, and Employment of the Committee on Veterans' Affairs, House of Representatives, May 8 and May 15, 1979 (Washington, D.C.: U.S. Government Printing Office, 1979), cited in Eric T. Dean Jr., *Shook over Hell: Post-Traumatic Stress, Vietnam, and the Civil War* (Cambridge, Mass.: Harvard University Press, 1997), 13.

15. Lyndon B. Johnson, "Remarks in Boca Raton at the Dedication of Florida Atlantic University," October 25, 1964, *The American Presidency Project*, online by Gerhard Peters and John T. Woolley, http://www.presidency.ucsb.edu/ws/?pid=26653 (accessed July 14, 2008).

16. O'Brien, "Vietnam Veteran," 77.

CHAPTER 1

1. June Axinn and Mark J. Stern, *Social Welfare: A History of the American Response to Need*, 6th edition (Boston: Pearson/Allyn and Bacon, 2005), 30–31.

2. John Resch, *Suffering Soldiers: Revolutionary War Veterans, Moral Sentiment, and Political Culture in the Early Republic* (Amherst: University of Massachusetts Press, 1999). For the impact of the Federalist perspective on military service in the early republic see Richard H. Kohn, *Eagle and Sword: The Federalists and the Creation of the Military Establishment in America, 1783–1802* (New York: Free Press, 1975).

3. See Bernard Bailyn, *The Ideological Origins of the American Revolution* (Cambridge, Mass.: Harvard University Press, 1967) and Gordon Wood, *The Radicalism of the American Revolution* (New York: Vintage Books, 1993).

4. Quoted in Resch, *Suffering Soldiers*, 107.

5. Background to nineteenth-century and World War I benefits summarized here from Axinn and Stern, *Social Welfare*, Amy W. Knight and Robert L. Worden,

Veterans Benefits Administration: An Organizational History, 1776–1994 (Collingdale, PA: Diane, 1995), David Bodenger, *Soldier's Bonuses: A History of Veterans Benefits in the United States, 1776–1967* (Ph.D. dissertation, Pennsylvania State University, 1972), Patrick J. Kelly, *Creating a National Home: Building the Veterans' Welfare State, 1860–1900* (Cambridge, Mass.: Harvard University Press, 1997), Theda Skocpol, *Protecting Soldiers and Mothers: The Political Origins of Social Policy in the United States* (Cambridge, Mass.: Belknap Press of Harvard University Press, 1992), Roger Daniels, *The Bonus March: An Episode of the Great Depression* (Westport, Conn.: Greenwood, 1972), and Stephen Ortiz, *Beyond the Bonus March and G.I. Bill: How Veteran Politics Shaped the New Deal Era* (New York: New York University Press, 2010).

6. See Skocpol, *Protecting Soldiers and Mothers*, and Mary Dearing, *Veterans in Politics: The Story of the G.A.R.* (Baton Rouge: Louisiana State University Press, 1952).

7. Daniels, *Bonus March*, 11.

8. Skocpol, *Protecting Soldiers and Mothers*, 149.

9. For further discussion on interwar benefits, see Bodenger, *Soldier's Bonuses,* Daniels, *The Bonus March,* Ortiz, *Beyond the Bonus March,* Paul Dickson and Thomas B. Allen, *The Bonus Army: An American Epic* (New York: Walker, 2004), William P. Dillingham, *Federal Aid to Veterans, 1918–1941* (Gainesville: University of Florida Press, 1952), Jennifer Keene, *Doughboys, the Great War, and the Remaking of America* (Baltimore, Md.: Johns Hopkins University Press, 2001), and Donald J. Lisio, *The President and Protest: Hoover, MacArthur, and the Bonus Riot* (New York: Fordham University Press, 1994).

10. Daniels, *Bonus March*, 29.

11. Quoted in ibid.

12. *Journal of the Senate of the United States of America,* September 20 (Washington, D.C.: U.S. Government Printing Office), 478.

13. Dickson and Allen, *Bonus Army*, 28.

14. Ortiz, *Beyond the Bonus March*, 27.

15. Dickson and Allen, *Bonus Army*, 208.

16. Ortiz, *Beyond the Bonus March*, 75.

17. Franklin D. Roosevelt, "Address to the American Legion Convention, Chicago, Illinois," October 2, 1933, *The American Presidency Project,* online by Gerhard Peters and John T. Woolley, http://www.presidency.ucsb.edu/ws/index.php?pid=14521 (accessed August 24, 2009).

18. Franklin D. Roosevelt, "Veto of the Bonus Bill," May 22, 1935, *The American Presidency Project,* online by Gerhard Peters and John T. Woolley, http://www.presidency.ucsb.edu/ws/?pid=15061 (accessed February 24, 2008).

19. See Daniels, *Bonus March*, 229–30, and Keene, *Doughboys,* 202.

20. Dickson and Allen, *Bonus Army*, 209.

21. See Keith Olson, *The G.I. Bill, the Veterans, and the Colleges* (Lexington: University Press of Kentucky, 1974).

22. See Davis B. Ross, *Preparing for Ulysses: Politics and Veterans during World War II* (New York: Columbia University Press, 1969), 68–87.

23. Olson, *G.I. Bill,* 7.

24. Ibid., 20.

25. Quoted in ibid., 12.

26. Franklin D. Roosevelt, "Message to Congress on the Education of War Veterans," October 27, 1943, *The American Presidency Project,* online by Gerhard Peters and John T. Woolley, http://www.presidency.ucsb.edu/ws/?pid=16333 (accessed May 10, 2012).

27. Keene, *Doughboys,* 208.

28. See William Pencak, *For God and Country: The American Legion, 1919–1941* (Boston: Northeastern University Press, 1989) and Thomas A. Rumer, *The American Legion: An Official History, 1919–1989* (New York: Evans, 1990).

29. Olson, *G.I. Bill,* 16.

30. Quoted in Ross, *Preparing for Ulysses,* 80.

31. Ibid., 80–81.

32. Olson, *G.I. Bill,* 33–34.

33. See Ross, *Preparing for Ulysses,* 89–125.

34. Ibid, 108.

35. Franklin D. Roosevelt, "Statement on Signing the G.I. Bill," June 22, 1944, *The American Presidency Project,* online by Gerhard Peters and John T. Woolley, http://www.presidency.ucsb.edu/ws/index.php?pid=16525 (accessed July 14, 2007).

36. Suzanne Mettler, *Soldiers to Citizens: The G.I. Bill and the Making of the Greatest Generation* (New York: Oxford, 2005), 5–7.

37. Altschuler and Blumin, *The G.I. Bill,* 108.

38. Mettler, *Soldiers to Citizens,* 78.

39. Keene, *Doughboys,* 212.

40. Olson, *G.I. Bill,* 105.

41. Alec Philmore Pearson Jr., *Olin E. Teague and the Veterans Administration* (Ph.D. diss., Texas A&M, 1977), 3–5.

42. Biographical information is collated from a short biography accompanying a letter sent by Teague to the editor of the *Cleveland Plain Dealer,* August 16, 1977, and from a newspaper clipping profiling Teague from the *Cleburne Times Review,* October 17, 1977, Box 43b, Folder 19, Olin E. Teague Papers, University Archives, Texas A&M University (cited hereafter as Teague Papers). The citations for his Silver Stars are reprinted on the *Military Times* website, http://militarytimes.com/citations-medals-awards/recipient.php?recipientid=76333 (accessed January 14, 2013).

43. Quoted in the *New York Times,* January 24, 1981, 16.

44. Pearson, *Olin E. Teague,* 18.

45. Ibid., 23–24.

46. Letter to Mr. George Schubert from Olin E. Teague, 10 June, 1952, Box 72, Folder 230-3, Teague Papers.

47. Letter to Mrs. Theresa E. Alexander from Olin E. Teague, 6 March 1952, Box 63, Folder 206–4, Teague Papers.

48. Letter to Mr. Cloud H. Bryan from Olin E. Teague, undated, Box 63, Folder 206-4, Teague Papers.

49. Pearson, *Olin E. Teague*, 43.

50. Letter to Mr. L. F. "Flew" Parsons from Olin E. Teague, March 22, 1950, Box 91b, Folder 24, Teague Papers.

51. Letter to Corporal John J. Vail from Olin E. Teague, May 9, 1952, Box 72, Folder 230-3, Teague Papers.

52. Letter to Mr. Joe Renick from Olin E. Teague, June 2, 1952, Box 72, Folder 230-3, Teague Papers.

53. Letter to Mrs. J. F. Walker from Olin E. Teague, June 4, 1952, Box 72, Folder 230-3, Teague Papers.

54. Letter to Corporal John J. Vail from Olin E. Teague, May 9, 1952, Box 72, Folder 230-3, Teague Papers.

55. *Congress and the Nation, 1945–1964,* volume 1 (Washington, D.C.: Congressional Quarterly, 1965), 1349.

56. Quoted in "Balancing the Books on G.I. Education," undated newspaper clipping, Box 43b, Folder 19, Teague Papers.

57. Pearson, *Olin E. Teague*, 51.

58. Letter to Mr. Joe Renick from Olin E. Teague, June 2, 1952, Box 72, Folder 230-3, Teague Papers.

59. *New York Times*, March 16, 1952, E11.

60. Ibid.

61. Ibid.

62. Letter to W. R. White, President of Baylor University, from Olin E. Teague, May 21, 1952, Box 63, Folder 206-5, Teague Papers.

63. *Congress and the Nation,* vol. 1, 1348.

64. Olson, *G.I. Bill*, 106.

65. Quoted in ibid.

66. Pearson, *Olin E. Teague*, 147.

67. Dwight D. Eisenhower, "Letter to General Omar N. Bradley, Chairman, President's Commission on Veterans' Pensions, concerning a Study of Veterans' Benefits," March 5, 1955, *The American Presidency Project,* online by Gerhard Peters and John T. Woolley, http://www.presidency.ucsb.edu/ws/index.php?pid=10429 (accessed August 13, 2009).

68. Ibid.

69. Quoted in Chester J. Pach and Elmo Richardson, *The Presidency of Dwight D. Eisenhower* (Lawrence: University Press of Kansas, 1991), 31.

70. Richard Damms, *The Eisenhower Presidency, 1953–1961* (London: Longman, 2002), 7. For further discussion of Eisenhower's economic and political philosophy, see Eisenhower's memoir, *The White House Years: Mandate for Change, 1953–1956* (New York: Doubleday, 1963), particularly pages 488–89, and Raymond J. Saulnier, "The

Philosophy Underlying Eisenhower's Economic Policies," in John P. King, ed., *Dwight D. Eisenhower: Soldier, President, Statesman* (New York: Greenwood, 1987).

71. Quoted in Fred I. Greenstein, *The Hidden-Hand Presidency: Eisenhower as Leader* (New York: Basic Books, 1982), 50.

72. Stephen Ambrose, *Eisenhower*, vol. 2, *The Presidency* (New York: Simon & Schuster, 1984), 158.

73. Donald T. Critchlow, "The Conservative Ascendency," in Donald T. Critchlow and Nancy Maclean, *Debating the American Conservative Movement, 1945 to the Present* (Lanham, MD: Rowman & Littlefield, 2009).

74. Barry Goldwater, *The Conscience of a Conservative*, reprint (New York: MJF Books, 1990), 59.

75. Omar N. Bradley and Clay Blair, *A General's Life: An Autobiography* (New York: Simon & Schuster, 1983).

76. *Veterans' Benefits in the United States: A Report to the President by the President's Commission on Veterans' Pensions* (Washington, D.C.: U.S. Government Printing Office, 1956). The commission's report was referred to commonly at the time, and hereafter in this study, as the Bradley Report.

77. Ibid., 10.

78. Ibid., 10.

79. Ibid., 14.

80. Ibid., 15.

81. Ibid., 11.

82. Ibid., 10.

83. Ibid., 16.

84. Ibid., 17.

85. *New York Times*, August 31, 1955, 14.

86. Omar B. Ketchum, "What's Wrong with the Bradley Report: Why the V.F.W. Indicts the Bradley Commission Proposals on 42 Counts," *VFW Magazine*, July 1956, 14.

87. Ibid., July 22, 1956, 6.

88. For background on the liberal views of the American Veterans Committee, see Robert L. Tyler, "The American Veterans Committee: Out of a Hot War and into the Cold," *American Quarterly* 18, no. 3 (Autumn 1966): 419–36, and Robert Francis Saxe, "'Citizens First, Veterans Second': The American Veterans Committee and the Challenge of Postwar 'Independent Progressives,'" *War & Society* (Australia) 22, no. 2 (October 2004): 75–94.

89. *New York Times*, September 1, 1957, 106.

90. Olin E. Teague, "How Veterans Can Help Protect Veterans' Benefits," *VFW Magazine*, June 1956, 36.

91. Letter to Mr. Joe Calhoun from Olin E. Teague, November 29, 1956, Box 72, Folder 228-13, Teague Papers.

92. Dwight D. Eisenhower, "Annual Budget Message to the Congress, Fiscal Year 1959," January 13, 1958, *The American Presidency Project*, online by Gerhard

Peters and John T. Woolley, http://www.presidency.ucsb.edu/ws/index.
php?pid=11323 (accessed September 21, 2008).

93. Dwight D. Eisenhower, "Annual Budget Message to the Congress, Fiscal
Year 1961," January 18, 1960, *The American Presidency Project*, online by Gerhard Peters and John T. Woolley, http://www.presidency.ucsb.edu/ws/index.
php?pid=11763 (accessed September 21, 2008).

CHAPTER 2

Sections of this chapter first appeared in Mark Boulton, "A Price on Patriotism:
The Politics and Unintended Consequences of the 1966 G.I. Bill," in Stephen
R. Ortiz, ed., *The Politics of Veterans' Policy: Federal Policies and Veterans in the
Modern United States* (Gainesville: University of Florida Press, 2012).

1. Letter to Dr. Dick Cason from Olin E. Teague, January 14, 1955, Box 64, Folder
209-9, Teague Papers.

2. Letter to Olin E. Teague from Joseph P. O'Connell, January 24, 1955, Box 64,
Folder 209-9, Teague Papers.

3. Summarized from William G. Phillips, *Yarborough of Texas* (Washington, D.C.:
Acropolis, 1969) and Patrick Cox, *Ralph W. Yarborough: The People's Senator*
(Austin: University of Texas Press, 2001).

4. Quoted in Michael L. Collins and Patrick Cox, "Ralph Yarborough," in Kenneth E.
Hendrickson Jr., Michael L. Collins, and Patrick Cox, eds., *Profiles in Power: Twentieth-Century Texans in Washington* (Austin: University of Texas Press, 2004), 161.

5. Quoted in ibid., 145.

6. Cox, *Ralph W. Yarborough,* Collins and Cox, "Ralph Yarborough," 185.

7. Collins and Cox, "Ralph Yarborough," 156.

8. Ibid., 150.

9. Ibid., 162–63.

10. The few notable exceptions included the 1862 Morrill Act, which offered land
grants for the establishment of colleges; the 1917 Smith-Hughes Act, which
encouraged vocational programs; several emergency New Deal programs; and
the 1940 Lanham Act, which offered assistance to impacted areas needing help
accommodating military installations. Repeatedly, in the aftermath of World
War II, attempts to pass bills on Capitol Hill providing for widespread aid to
education ran afoul of states' rights southerners, northern fiscal conservatives,
and Catholic lobbyists who feared that such funds would only go to public
schools. The government made further encroachments into education in 1950
by passing the College Housing Act, which offered low-interest loans for college
housing construction, and by establishing the National Science Foundation,
which offered students grants for scientific research. Several times during the
1950s Congress expanded the provisions of the Lanham Act.

11. See Wayne Urban, *More Than Science and Sputnik: The National Defense Education Act of 1958* (Tuscaloosa: University of Alabama Press, 2010).

12. Ralph Yarborough Senate Office Press Release, January 7, 1958, Box 3W271, Folder "Cold War G.I. Bill," Ralph W. Yarborough Papers, the Dolph Briscoe Center for American History, the University of Texas at Austin, hereafter cited as Yarborough Papers.

13. Ralph Yarborough, Senate Office Statement to Accompany G.I. Educational Bill, undated, Box 3W271, Folder "Cold War G.I. Bill," Yarborough Papers.

14. Quoted in the *New York Times*, August 22, 1959, 16.

15. Fact Sheet on S.1138, The Cold War Veterans Bill, undated, Box 3W271, Folder "Cold War G.I. Bill," Yarborough Papers.

16. *Congressional Record—Senate*, July 29, 1959, 13797.

17. Ibid.

18. Ibid., 13800.

19. Gilbert Steiner, *The State of Welfare* (Washington, D.C.: Brookings Institute, 1971), 254, quoted in Wilbur J. Scott, *The Politics of Readjustment: Vietnam Veterans since the War* (New York: Walter De Gruyter, 1993), 8.

20. *The Report of the President's Commission on Veterans' Pensions*, Hearings before the House Committee on Veterans' Affairs, 84th Congress, 2nd Session, May 11, 1956, 3709, quoted in Pearson, *Olin E. Teague*, 161.

21. Letter to Jay H. Gates from Olin E. Teague, June 8, 1960, Box 91b, Folder 24, Teague Papers.

22. Letter to Mr. Victor H. Wohlford from Olin E. Teague, October 17, 1959, Box 91b, Folder 24, Teague Papers.

23. Dwight D. Eisenhower, "Annual Budget Message to the Congress, Fiscal Year 1961," January 18, 1960, *The American Presidency Project*, online by Gerhard Peters and John T. Woolley, http://www.presidency.ucsb.edu/ws/index.php?pid=11763 (accessed September 21, 2008).

24. Quoted in the *Dallas Morning News*, May 2, 1960, 12.

25. Quoted in ibid., September 18, 1960, 17.

26. Letter to Mr. Ken Sessions from Olin E. Teague, October 14, 1960, Box 91b, Folder 24, Teague Papers.

27. Letter to John F. Kennedy from Olin Teague, May 2, 1962, Box 72, Folder 229-6, Teague Papers.

28. Fact Sheet on S.349, The Cold War Veterans Bill, undated, Box 3W271, Folder "Cold War G.I. Bill," Yarborough Papers.

29. Ralph Yarborough Senate Office Press Release, February 28, 1961, Box 4JB17, Folder "G.I. Bill, 1961," Yarborough Papers.

30. Letter to Lister Hill from Philip S. Hughes, April 28, 1961, Box 3w271, Folder "Cold War G.I. Bill," Yarborough Papers.

31. Letter to Lister Hill from Cyrus R. Vance, May 4, 1961, Box 3w271, Folder "Cold War G.I. Bill," Yarborough Papers.

32. Statement by Senator Ralph W. Yarborough on the floor of the United States Senate, Box 3w271, Folder "Cold War G.I. Bill S.5," Yarborough Papers.

33. John F. Kennedy, "Annual Budget Message to the Congress: Fiscal Year 1963," January 18, 1962, *The American Presidency Project*, online by Gerhard Peters and John T. Woolley, http://www.presidency.ucsb.edu/ws/index.php?pid=8588 (accessed June 17, 2009).

34. Letter to Representative Lister Hill (D-AL) from J. S. Gleason, May 19, 1961, Box 1, Folder "The Early Proposals," Lyndon B. Johnson Papers, 1963–1969, Legislative Background New G.I. Bill, 1966, Lyndon B. Johnson Presidential Library, Austin, Texas, hereafter referred to as the Johnson Papers.

35. Statement of the Administrator of Veterans' Affairs Before the Subcommittee on Veterans' Affairs Committee on Labor and Public Welfare, United States Senate, April 10, 1963, Box 1, Folder "The Early Proposals," Legislative Background, New G.I. Bill, 1966, Johnson Papers.

36. Quoted in Collins and Cox, "Ralph Yarborough," 166.

37. Quoted in ibid., 167.

38. Cox, *Ralph W. Yarborough*, 196 and xvi.

39. Quoted in Collins and Cox, "Ralph Yarborough," 170–71.

40. Hugh Davis Graham, *The Uncertain Triumph: Federal Education Policy in the Kennedy and Johnson Years* (Chapel Hill: University of North Carolina Press, 1984).

41. Summarized from Collins and Cox, "Ralph Yarborough," 167–68.

42. Lyndon B. Johnson, "Statement by the President on the 20th Anniversary of the G.I. Bill of Rights," June 22, 1964, *The American Presidency Project*, online by Gerhard Peters and John T. Woolley, http://www.presidency.ucsb.edu/ws/index.php?pid=26331 (accessed June 21, 2008).

43. Telegram to Lyndon Johnson from Ralph Yarborough, November 11, 1964, Box 163, Folder "LE/VA 3," Legislation Gen LE/VA 2 11/22/63, Johnson Papers.

44. Letter to President Johnson from David R Davies, July 14, 1964, Box 163, Folder "LE/VA 3," Legislation Gen LE/VA 2 11/22/63, Johnson Papers.

45. Letter to President Johnson from Josephine Natale, May 19, 1964, Box 163, Folder "LE/VA 3," Legislation Gen LE/VA 2 11/22/63, Johnson Papers.

46. Letter to Lyndon Johnson from Ralph Yarborough, January 7, 1965, Box 161, Folder "LE/VA 11/22/63–12/31/65," Legislation Ex. LE/VA 2 11/22/63, Johnson Papers.

47. Ralph Yarborough, "A Fair Deal for the Cold War Soldier," *Harper's Magazine*, January 1965, 81.

48. Ibid.

49. Ibid.

50. Memorandum for Bill D. Moyers from Phillip S. Hughes, December 15, 1964, Box 1, Folder "Initial Administration Opposition and Substitutes," Legislative Background, New G.I. Bill, Johnson Papers.

51. Ibid.

52. Irving Bernstein, *Guns or Butter: The Presidency of Lyndon Johnson* (New York: Oxford University Press, 1996), 183.

53. Lyndon B. Johnson, "Remarks in Boca Raton at the Dedication of Florida Atlantic University," October 25, 1964, *The American Presidency Project,* online by Gerhard Peters and John T. Woolley, http://www.presidency.ucsb.edu/ws/index.php?pid=26653 (accessed July 14, 2008).

54. Memorandum for Bill D. Moyers from Phillip S. Hughes, December 15, 1964, Box 1, Folder "Initial Administration Opposition and Substitutes," Legislative Background, New G.I. Bill, Johnson Papers.

55. Lyndon B. Johnson, "Remarks in Boca Raton."

56. Lyndon B. Johnson, "Special Message to the Congress: 'Toward Full Educational Opportunity,'" January 12, 1965, *The American Presidency Project,* online by Gerhard Peters and John T. Woolley, http://www.presidency.ucsb.edu/ws/index.php?pid=27448& (accessed December 2, 2009).

57. Letter to Ralph Yarborough from Lee C. White, January 15, 1965, Box 1, Folder "Initial Administration Opposition and Substitutes—I," Legislative Background, New G.I. Bill, Johnson Papers.

58. Lyndon B. Johnson, "Annual Budget Message to the Congress, Fiscal Year 1966," January 25, 1965, *The American Presidency Project,* online by Gerhard Peters and John T. Woolley, http://www.presidency.ucsb.edu/ws/?pid=27041 (accessed August 24, 2009).

59. John A. Jenkins, "The Great Society: Not for Veterans," *VFW Magazine,* March 1965, 11.

60. William E. Driver, "Veterans Services," *American Legion Magazine,* April 1965, 2.

61. Memo for Bill Moyers from J. S. Gleason, November 19, 1964, Box 1, Folder "Initial Administration Opposition and Substitutes—I," Legislative Background, New G.I. Bill, Johnson Papers.

62. Letter to Lister Hill from the Office of the Administrator of Veterans' Affairs, undated, Box 1, Folder "Initial Administration Opposition and Substitutes—I," Legislative Background, New G.I. Bill, Johnson Papers.

63. Letter to Kermit Gordon from William Driver, February 12, 1965, Box 1, Folder "Initial Administration Opposition and Substitutes—I," Legislative Background, New G.I. Bill, Johnson Papers.

64. Letter to Lee White from Sam Hughes, February 25, 1965, Box 161, Folder "LE/VA 11/22/63–12/31/65," Legislation Ex. LE/VA 2 11/22/63, Johnson Papers.

65. Letter to Lyndon Johnson from Ralph Yarborough, May 6, 1965, Box 3w271, Folder "Cold War G.I. Bill S.9," Yarborough Papers.

66. *Report of the Committee on Labor and Public Welfare to Accompany S.9, the Cold War Veterans' Readjustment Assistance Act* (Washington, D.C.: U.S. Government Printing Office, 1965), 3.

67. Ibid., 19.

68. Ibid., 58.

69. *Congressional Record—Senate,* July 19, 1965, 17304.

70. Ibid., 17306.

71. Thurmond and Yarborough had engaged in a wrestling match in the Senate over a nominee to a civil rights position in 1964. See Cox, *Ralph W. Yarborough*, 212–13.

72. *Congressional Record—Senate*, July 19, 1965, 17319.

73. Ibid., 17322–17323.

74. Lyndon B. Johnson, "The President's News Conference," July 28, 1965, *The American Presidency Project*, online by Gerhard Peters and John T. Woolley, http://www.presidency.ucsb.edu/ws/index.php?pid=27116 (accessed May 17, 2009).

75. Letter to Lyndon Johnson from William Driver, June 7, 1965, Box 1, Folder "Initial Administration Opposition and Substitutes—I," Legislative Background, New G.I. Bill, Johnson Papers.

76. Memo for Douglass Cater from Bill Moyers, June 15, 1965, Box 1, Folder "Initial Administration Opposition and Substitutes—I," Legislative Background, New G.I. Bill, Johnson Papers.

77. Letter to Lyndon Johnson from Mrs. J. F. Grisillo, July 22, 1965, Box 162, Folder "LE/VA 10/15/65–3/2/66," Legislation Ex. LE/VA 2, 11/22/63, Johnson Papers.

78. Letter to Lyndon Johnson from Roger C. Walczyk, September 10, 1965, Box 162, Folder "LE/VA 11/22/63–10/14/65," Legislation Ex. LE/VA 2, 11/22/63, Johnson Papers.

79. Letter to Lyndon Johnson from Charles L. Schultze, Director of the Bureau of the Budget, July 22, 1965, Box 1, Folder "Initial Administration Opposition and Substitutes—II," Legislative Background, New G.I. Bill, Johnson Papers.

80. Memo to Douglass Cater from William Driver, December 15, 1965, Box 1, Folder "Final Passage," Legislative Background, New G.I. Bill, Johnson Papers.

81. Memo to Douglass Cater from Ralph K. Huitt, December 15, 1965, Box 1, Folder "Final Passage," Legislative Background, New G.I. Bill, Johnson Papers.

82. Ed Johnson, "A Different Lobby: Cold War Vets Help Pass Bill," *Austin American*, February 22, 1966, newspaper clipping with no page number given, Box 3w271, Folder "Cold War G.I. Bill," Yarborough Papers.

83. Letter to Lyndon Johnson from Charles L. Schultze, Director of the Bureau of the Budget, July 22, 1965, Box 1, Folder "Initial Administration Opposition and Substitutes—II," Legislative Background, New G.I. Bill, Johnson Papers.

84. Quoted in the *Washington Daily News*, December 7, 1965, clipping from Box 162, Folder "LE/VA 10/15/65–3/2/66," Legislation Ex. LE/VA 2, 11/22/63, Johnson Papers.

85. Recorded Telephone Conversation to the White House with Charles Schultze, 12/31/65, Box 1, Folder "Final Passage," Legislative Background, New G.I. Bill, Johnson Papers.

86. *Legislation to Provide G.I. Benefits for Post-Korean Veterans*, Hearings Before the Committee on Veterans' Affairs, House of Representatives, August 31, September 1, 2, 7, and 15 (Washington, D.C.: U.S. Government Printing Office, 1965), 2886.

87. Ibid., 2908.

88. Ibid., 2896.

89. Ibid., 2896–98.

90. Ibid., 2989.

91. Ibid., 2899.

92. Ibid., 2914–15.

93. Figures and timeline from George Donelson Moss, *Vietnam: An American Ordeal*, 2nd edition (Upper Saddle River, N.J.: Prentice Hall, 1994), 427–28.

94. Quoted in *Public Law 89-358 (Readjustment Benefits Act of 1966)—An Analysis of the Legislative Process Leading to Its Enactment*, unpublished study, Box 3W271, Folder "Cold War G.I. Bill, S.9," Yarborough Papers.

95. *Legislation to Provide G.I. Benefits for Post-Korean Veterans*, Hearings Before the Committee on Veterans' Affairs, House of Representatives, August 31, September 1, 2, 7, and 15 (U.S. Government Printing Office, 1965), 2923.

96. Ibid., 2971.

97. "Long Trail to Victory," *VFW Magazine*, April 1966, 40.

98. *Legislation to Provide G.I. Benefits for Post-Korean Veterans*, Hearings Before the Committee on Veterans' Affairs, House of Representatives, August 31, September 1, 2, 7, and 15 (U.S. Government Printing Office, 1965), 2968.

99. Francis W. Stover, "Capitol Digest," *VFW Magazine*, March 1966, 21.

100. Ed Johnson, "A Different Lobby: Cold War Vets Help Pass Bill," *Austin American*, February 22, 1966, newspaper clipping with no page number given, Box 3w271, Folder "Cold War G.I. Bill," Yarborough Papers.

101. The overview of Teague's views on Vietnam contained in the following paragraph is summarized from multiple letters in his personal correspondence found in Box 32A, Folder 27, Teague Papers.

102. Quoted in the *Washington Daily News*, December 7, 1965, clipping in Box 162, Folder "LE/VA 10/15/65–3/2/66," Legislation Ex. LE/VA 2, 11/22/63, Johnson Papers.

103. Quoted in the *Dallas Morning News*, May 9, 1969, 8A.

104. Quoted in "Teague Raps Colleagues: A View of the March," *Washington Daily News*, October 17, 1969, 18.

105. Letter to Mr. & Mrs. A. W. Whatley from Olin Teague, June 21, 1966, Box 32A, Folder 27, Teague Papers.

106. Memo to Lyndon Johnson from Douglass Cater, December 28, 1965, Box 1, Folder "Final Passage," Legislative Background, New G.I. Bill, Johnson Papers.

107. Memo to Lyndon Johnson from Charles L. Schultze, February 10, 1966, Box 11, Folder "VA Educational Program I," Veteran Affairs, General VA3, Johnson Papers.

108. Memo to Lyndon Johnson from Charles L. Schultze, January 29, 1966, Box 1, Folder "Final Passage," Legislative Background, New G.I. Bill, Johnson Papers.

109. *Congressional Record—House*, February 7, 1966, 2331.

110. Ibid.

111. Ibid., 2337.

112. Ibid., 2335.

113. Ibid., 2339, 2335.

114. Ibid., 2336.

115. Ibid., 2348.

116. *Congressional Record—Senate,* February 10, 1966, 2875.

117. Ibid., 2873.

118. Ibid., 2876.

119. Letter to Russell B. Long from W. J. Driver, February 9, 1966, Box 3W271, Folder "Cold War G.I. Bill, S.9," Yarborough Papers.

120. Memo to Lyndon Johnson from Will Sparks and Bob Hardesty, February 16, 1966, Box 1, Folder "Final Passage," Legislative Background, New G.I. Bill, Johnson Papers.

121. Lyndon B. Johnson, "Remarks upon Signing the 'Cold War G.I. Bill,'" March 3, 1966, *The American Presidency Project,* online by Gerhard Peters and John T. Woolley, http://www.presidency.ucsb.edu/ws/index.php?pid=27448& (accessed August 25, 2009).

122. Quoted in the *New York Times,* March 4, 1966, 1, 4.

123. Cox, *Ralph W. Yarborough,* 232.

124. *New York Times,* April 23, 1968, 46.

CHAPTER 3

1. White House Press Release, "Remarks of the President on Submitting Veterans Message," January 31, 1967, Box 1, Folder "Message to Congress," Legislative Background: Vietnam Vets Benefits, 1967, Johnson Papers.

2. White House Press Release, "America's Servicemen and Veterans," January 31, 1967, Folder "Message to Congress," Legislative Background: Vietnam Vets Benefits, 1967, Johnson Papers.

3. Ibid.

4. Quoted in *VFW Magazine,* April 1965, 10.

5. Ibid., March 1967.

6. Statement of A. W. Stratton, VA Chief Benefits Director, before the Subcommittee on Veterans' Affairs Committee on Labor and Public Welfare, Senate, March 20, 1967, Box 161, Folder "LE/VA 3/5/66–9/7/67," Legislation Ex. LE/VA 2 11/22/63, Johnson Papers.

7. Ibid.

8. Press Release, "Remarks of the President upon Signing the Cold War G.I. Bill of Rights (S.16)," August 31, 1967, Box 1, Folder "The Bill Signing," Legislative Background: Vietnam Vets Benefits, 1967, Johnson Papers.

9. Collected newspaper reports from April 24, 1967, to August 30, 1967, Box 1, Folder "Califano/Veterans Programs," Joseph Califano Papers, Lyndon B. Johnson Presidential Library, Austin, Texas.

10. "GIVER" description, Box 161, Folder "LE/VA 3/5/66–9/7/67," Legislation Ex. LE/VA 2 11/22/63, Johnson Papers.

11. Lyndon B. Johnson, "Remarks upon Signing Bill Extending Veterans Education Benefits," October 23, 1968, *The American Presidency Project*, online by Gerhard Peters and John T. Woolley, http://www.presidency.ucsb.edu/ws/?pid=29198 (accessed June 28, 2011).

12. Letter to Richard Nixon from Dennis Rainwater, November 13, 1969, Box 124, Folder 72, Carl Albert Legislative Papers, Carl Albert Congressional Research Center, Norman, Oklahoma, identified hereafter as Carl Albert Papers.

13. Richard Homan, "Student Veterans Need a Raise: Present Subsistence Inadequate If They Are to Stay in School," *VFW Magazine*, August 1969, 13.

14. Ibid.

15. *New York Times*, November 8, 1970, 1, and August 21, 1972, 1.

16. See, for example, the *New York Times* stories "Court Hears Story of a Soldier's Life with Drugs," September 9, 1971, 32, "Job Outlook Is Bleak for Vietnam Veterans," June 5, 1971, 1, and "Psychiatrist Says 'Brutalizing' Vietnam War Causes Problems for Ex-G.I.'s," November 26, 1970, 12.

17. *Wall Street Journal*, February 24, 1970, reprinted in *Source Material on the Vietnam Veteran* (Washington, D.C.: U.S. Government Printing Office, 1974), 22.

18. *Washington Post*, January 27, 1971, reprinted in ibid., 37.

19. *Newsweek*, March 29, 1971, reprinted in ibid., 37.

20. *Source Material on the Vietnam Veteran*, III.

21. Letter to Ralph W. Yarborough from Donald J. Short, October 26, 1969, Box 3X362, Folder "Vets HR 11959," Yarborough Papers.

22. Letter to Ralph W. Yarborough from Richard S. Stoddard, October 22, 1969, Box 3X362, Folder "Vets HR 11959," Yarborough Papers.

23. Letter to Carl Albert from the Veterans Club, Tarrant County Junior College, Fort Worth, Texas, undated (Albert's reply is dated March 1, 1972), Box 142, Folder 6, Legislative Files, Carl Albert Papers.

24. Letter to Carl Albert from Michael W. Dubrick, April 28, 1972, Box 142, Folder 6, Legislative Files, Carl Albert Papers.

25. Quoted from numerous letters to Carl Albert, Box 142, Folder 6, Legislative Files, Carl Albert Papers.

26. Letter to the editor, *New York Times*, June 1, 1972, 42.

27. "Vietnam Veterans Protest Benefit Cut with Parade, Rally," *Washington Post*, May 20, 1973, B4.

28. "Most Veterans of Vietnam Fail to Seek Aid under the G.I. Bill," *New York Times*, April 9, 1972, 46.

29. Tim O'Brien, "The Vietnam Veteran: The G.I. Bill; Less Than Enough," *Penthouse Magazine*, November 1974, 77.

30. "Most Veterans of Vietnam Fail to Seek Aid under the G.I. Bill," *New York Times*, April 9, 1972, 46.

31. "Vietnam Veterans in Area Failing to Utilize G.I. Bill," *New York Times*, November 4, 1973, 1.

32. Illinois Federation of Veterans in College: Policy Statement, Box 142, Folder 6, Legislative Files, Carl Albert Papers.

33. *New York Times*, November 4, 1973, 17.

34. Ibid., 1.

35. Ibid.

36. Ibid., July 4, 1969, 39.

37. Ibid., April 13, 1972, 42.

38. *Washington Post,* June 6, 1973, 21.

39. Quoted in the *Oklahoma Journal*, December 18, 1973, 12.

40. Ibid.

41. NACV Report on Veterans' Education Benefits, 1973, copy in author's possession.

42. Richard W. Homan, "Student Veterans Need a Raise: Present Subsistence Inadequate If They Are to Stay in School," *VFW Magazine*, August 1969, 13.

43. J. Milton Patrick, "Five Important Problems of Veterans," *American Legion Magazine*, May 1970.

44. Paul Starr, *The Discarded Army: Veterans after Vietnam; The Nader Report on Vietnam Veterans and the Veterans Administration* (New York: Charterhouse, 1973), 226–27.

45. Ibid., 241.

46. Ibid., 237.

47. Ibid., 241–42.

48. Sections of the following discussion of African Americans and the G.I. Bill first appeared in Mark Boulton, "How the G.I. Bill Failed African-American Vietnam War Veterans," *Journal of Blacks in Higher Education* 58 (Winter 2007–8): 57–61.

49. James Westheider, *Fighting on Two Fronts: African Americans and the Vietnam War* (New York: New York University Press, 1997), 171.

50. Christian Appy argues that 90 percent of African American Vietnam veterans came from "working class and poor" backgrounds in his book *Working-Class War: American Combat Soldiers and Vietnam* (Chapel Hill: University of North Carolina Press, 1993), 22. Taynia Mann, "Profile of African-Americans, 1970–1995," *Black Collegian* 26, no. 3 (April 1996), reveals that the median income for an African American family in 1970 was only 61 percent of the median family income for white families.

51. Sol Stern, "When the Black G.I. Comes Back from Vietnam," *New York Times*, March 24, 1968, SM27.

52. "From Dakto to Detroit: The Death of a Troubled Hero," *New York Times*, May 26, 1971, 1.

53. O'Brien, "Vietnam Veteran," 128.

54. "Vietnam Veterans Protest Benefit Cut with Parade, Rally," *Washington Post*, May 20, 1973, B4.

55. Quoted in the *New York Times*, April 9, 1973, 43.

56. Ibid., August 29, 1971, 7.

57. Westheider, *Fighting on Two Fronts*, 171.
58. Ibid., 98.
59. Quoted in Myra Macpherson, *Long Time Passing: Vietnam and the Haunted Generation,* new edition (Bloomington: Indiana University Press, 2001), 555.
60. Quoted in Wallace Terry, *Bloods: An Oral History of the Vietnam War by Black Veterans* (New York: Ballantine, 1984), 167.
61. Herman Graham III, *The Brothers' Vietnam War: Black Power, Manhood, and the Military Experience* (Gainesville: University Press of Florida, 2003), 120.
62. Cited in ibid., 127.
63. Morocco Coleman, *Coming Full Circle* (Atlanta: Underground Epics, 2001), 63.
64. Westheider, *Fighting on Two Fronts*, 111.
65. Macpherson, *Long Time Passing*, 571.
66. Terry, *Bloods*, 221.
67. *Final Report on Educational Assistance to Veterans: A Comparative Study of Three G.I. Bills, Submitted to the Committee on Veterans' Affairs, United States Senate* (Washington, D.C.: U.S. Government Printing Office, 1973).
68. *Vietnam Veterans' Readjustment*, Hearings before the Committee on Veterans' Affairs, United States Senate, 96th Congress, 2nd Session, February 21, March 4, and May 21, 1980, Washington, D.C. (Washington, D.C.: U.S. Government Printing Office, 1980), 714, 764.
69. *New York Times*, October 19, 1970, 39.
70. Ibid., April 3, 1970, 19, and March 29, 1973, 51.
71. O'Brien, "Vietnam Veteran," 141.
72. Letter to the editor, *New York Times*, May 21, 1971, 28.
73. *New York Times*, September 15, 1972, 37.
74. Briefing by Donald E. Johnson before the Senate Committee on Veterans' Affairs, Box 254, Folder 30, Fred Harris Papers, Carl Albert Center, Norman, Oklahoma.
75. Statement of Olney B. Owen, Chief VA Benefits Director, to the Subcommittee of the House Education and Training Committee on Veterans' Affairs, November 30, 1971, Box 21, Folder "Transcripts," Stanley S. Scott Papers, Gerald R. Ford Library, Ann Arbor, Michigan.
76. From Vance Hartke, Foreword to *A Study of the Problems Facing Vietnam Veterans on Their Readjustment to Civilian Life* (Washington, D.C.: U.S. Government Printing Office, 1972), III.
77. *A Study of the Problems Facing Vietnam Veterans on Their Readjustment to Civilian Life* (Washington, D.C.: U.S. Government Printing Office, 1972), 2.
78. Ibid., 10.
79. Ibid., 11.
80. Ibid., 230.
81. Ibid., 237.
82. Ibid., 237. The study only gave racial qualifiers for veterans not classified as students. Sixty-three percent of nonwhite veterans not classified as students agreed

that the benefits were "not enough to live on comfortably," compared with 59 percent of white veterans.

83. Ibid., 243.

84. Quoted in the *New York Times*, January 6, 1972, 10.

85. Press Conference Remarks by Donald Johnson, May 25, 1970, Box 85, Folder 46, Departmental Files, Carl Albert Papers.

86. *New York Times*, August 27, 1975, 27. For an examination of the overstatement of veterans' problems see B. G. Burkett and Glenna Whitley, *Stolen Valor: How the Vietnam Generation Was Robbed of Its Heroes and Its History* (Dallas: Verity, 1998), Jerry Lembcke, *The Spitting Image: Myth, Memory, and the Legacy of Vietnam* (New York: New York University Press, 1998), and Eric T. Dean Jr., *Shook over Hell: Post-Traumatic Stress, Vietnam, and the Civil War* (Cambridge, Mass.: Harvard University Press, 1997).

CHAPTER 4

1. Melvin Small, *The Presidency of Richard Nixon* (Lawrence: University of Kansas Press, 1990), 203.

2. George Donelson Moss, *Vietnam: An American Ordeal,* 2nd edition (Englewood Cliffs, N.J.: Prentice Hall, 1994), 415.

3. Letter to Robert Finch, HEW Secretary, from Donald E. Johnson, August 28, 1969, Box 8, Folder "EX VA 3: Educational Programs 1969–70," White House Central Files: Veterans Affairs, Richard M. Nixon papers, Richard M. Nixon Presidential Library, Yorba Linda, California, hereafter referred to as Nixon Papers.

4. VA statistics cited in *Congress and the Nation*, vol. 3, *1969–1972* (Washington, D.C.: Congressional Quarterly, 1973), 537.

5. Estimates in ibid., 582.

6. Ibid., 537.

7. Quoted in Small, *Presidency of Richard Nixon*, 207.

8. Richard Nixon, "Memorandum on the Need for a Review of the Budget," January 27, 1969, *The American Presidency Project,* online by Gerhard Peters and John T. Woolley, http://www.presidency.ucsb.edu/ws/index.php?pid=1953 (accessed March 16, 2009).

9. Stephen Ambrose, *Nixon*, vol. 2, *The Triumph of a Politician* (New York: Simon & Schuster, 1989), 431; Iwan Morgan, *Nixon* (London: Arnold, 2002), 69, 93.

10. Allen J. Matusow, *Nixon's Economy* (Lawrence: University of Kansas Press, 1998), 4.

11. Joan Hoff, *Nixon Reconsidered* (New York: Basic Books, 1994).

12. *Congress and the Nation,* vol. 3 (Washington, D.C.: Congressional Quarterly, 1965), 602–3.

13. Ibid., 598.

14. Ibid., 581.

15. See Paul C. Milazzo, "The Environment," in Julian Zelizer, ed., *The American Congress: The Building of Democracy* (Boston: Houghton Mifflin, 2004), 611–14.

16. Quoted in Robert Mason, *Richard Nixon and the Quest for a New Majority* (Chapel Hill: University of North Carolina Press, 2004), 114.

17. A veteran with one dependent could claim $197, up from $155.

18. *Congressional Record—House*, August 4, 1969, 22080.

19. Ibid., 22080.

20. Ibid., 22081.

21. Letter to Olin E. Teague from Bryce Harlow, July 10, 1969, Box 8, Folder "GEN VA 3: Educational Programs 1969–70," White House Central Files: Veterans Affairs, Nixon Papers.

22. President's Committee on the Vietnam Veteran: Interim Report, Box 8, Folder "EX VA 3: Educational Programs 1969–70," White House Central Files: Veterans Affairs, Nixon Papers.

23. Letter to Richard T. Burress from Donald E. Johnson, September 23, 1969, Box 8, Folder "EX VA 3: Educational Programs 1969–70," White House Central Files: Veterans Affairs, Nixon Papers.

24. Richard Nixon, "Address to the Nation on the Rising Cost of Living," October 17, 1969, *The American Presidency Project,* online by Gerhard Peters and John T. Woolley, http://www.presidency.ucsb.edu/ws/index.php?pid=2269 (accessed July 10, 2009).

25. Letter to Senator Ralph Yarborough from Richard Nixon, October 21, 1969, Box 3X362, Folder "Vets HR 11959," Yarborough Papers.

26. Letter to Richard Nixon from Senator Ralph Yarborough, October 22, 1969, Box 3X362, Folder "Vets HR 11959," Yarborough Papers.

27. Statement by Chairman Olin E. Teague on Post-Korean G.I. Bill of Rights, attached to a letter to Carl Albert from Olin Teague, October 8, 1969, Box 124, Folder 72, Legislative Papers, Carl Albert Papers.

28. Ibid. Teague correctly lauded the VA for getting information out to veterans. At the end of the 1960s, the VA made considerable efforts to inform veterans of their benefits and how to obtain them. In addition to establishing a nationwide system of United States Veteran Assistance Centers, or USVACs, VA officials regularly visited Vietnam after January 1967 to inform future veterans of their entitlements. According to Donald Johnson, the VA had counseled nearly two million veterans by September 1970 and two VA employees had already lost their lives in Vietnam. The VA sent representatives into their hospitals to help patients fill out benefits applications. The agency also mailed letters to all veterans upon separation informing them of their entitlements and then sent out pamphlets annually with updated information on what the veteran could receive. If these measures failed, the veteran could call VA officials in over thirty-four cities to obtain further information and application assistance on a toll free number. World War II veterans and Korea veterans had no such outreach program. In terms of disseminating information, at least, the VA was making considerable efforts to aid the veterans.

29. Letter to Carl Albert from Olin Teague, October 8, 1969, Box 124, Folder 72, Legislative Papers, Carl Albert Papers.

30. *Congressional Record—Senate*, October 23, 1969, 31362.

31. Ibid., 31341.

32. Ibid., 31344.

33. As printed in ibid., 31342.

34. *New York Times*, November 5, 1969, 28.

35. Ambrose, *Nixon*, vol. 2, 431.

36. Quoted in Morgan, *Nixon*, 164.

37. Quoted in Karen M. Hunt and Charles E. Walcott, *Empowering the White House: Governance under Nixon, Ford, and Carter* (Lawrence: University of Kansas Press, 2004), 121.

38. Quoted in the *New York Times*, October 24, 1969, 27.

39. *Congressional Record—Senate*, March 23, 1970, 8652.

40. Ibid., 8652

41. Memorandum to Richard Nixon from Bryce Harlow, March 24, 1970, Box 8, Folder "EX VA 3: Educational Programs 1969–70," White House Central Files: Veterans Affairs, Nixon Papers.

42. Johnson's views are presented in a Memorandum to Richard Nixon from John D. Ehrlichman, March 25, 1970, Box 8, Folder "EX VA 3: Educational Programs 1969–70," White House Central Files: Veterans Affairs, Nixon Papers.

43. Ibid.

44. Memorandum to Darrell Trent from John Bryce Harlow, February 13, 1970, Box 8, Folder "EX VA 3: Educational Programs 1969–70," White House Central Files: Veterans Affairs, Nixon Papers.

45. Quoted in the *New York Times*, March 29, 1970, 37.

46. Quoted in ibid.

47. Quoted in ibid., March 27, 1970, 16.

48. Letter to Donald Johnson from Robert Finch, undated, submitted for consideration by the President's Committee on the Vietnam Veteran of 1969–70, Box 8, Folder "EX VA 3: Educational Programs 1969–70," White House Central Files: Veterans Affairs, Nixon Papers.

49. "GI Project Memo: More Education, More Opportunity," Box 8, Folder "EX VA 3: Educational Programs 1969–70," White House Central Files: Veterans Affairs, Nixon Papers. Project Memo was an administration-backed "clearinghouse" program run through Michigan State University designed to match veterans with schools. Bob Hope helped promote the program on his 1969 tour of Vietnam. Over forty thousand G.I.s made use of the initiative.

50. Quoted in *Congress and the Nation*, vol. 3, 548.

51. Patrick Cox, *Ralph Yarborough: The People's Senator* (Austin: University of Texas Press, 2002), 255.

52. Quoted in Michael L. Collins and Patrick Cox, "Ralph Yarborough," in Kenneth E. Hendrickson Jr., Michael L. Collins, and Patrick Cox, eds., *Profiles in Power: Twentieth-Century Texans in Washington* (Austin: University of Texas Press, 2004), 163.

53. Chaim F. Shatan, "Post-Vietnam Syndrome," *New York Times*, May 6, 1972, 35.

54. Guy McMichael, quoted in Wilbur J. Scott, *The Politics of Readjustment: Vietnam Veterans since the War* (New York: de Gruyter, 1993), 53.

55. Shad Meshad, quoted in ibid., 68.

56. David Bonior, quoted in ibid., 54.

57. Max Cleland, quoted in ibid., 39.

58. Ibid., 68–69.

59. Until 1970, the Senate had discussed veteran issues in a subcommittee of the Labor and Public Welfare Committee and occasionally in the Finance Committee. The Legislative Reorganization Act of 1970 created the first Senate committee devoted exclusively to veteran affairs. The House had had such a committee since 1924.

60. *Congressional Record—House*, March 6, 1972, 6954.

61. Ibid., 6955.

62. Ibid., 6956–57.

63. *Congressional Record—Senate*, August 3, 1972, 26745.

64. Ibid., 26719.

65. Ibid., October 13, 1972, 35807.

66. Memo to Ken Cole from John Evans, September 18, 1972, Box 8, Folder "EX VA 3: Educational Programs 1/1/71–12/31/72," White House Central Files: Veterans Affairs, Nixon Papers.

67. Ibid.

68. *Congressional Record—Senate*, October 13, 1972, 35804.

69. Richard Nixon, "Radio Address on the American Veteran," October 22, 1972, *The American Presidency Project,* online by Gerhard Peters and John T. Woolley, http://www.presidency.ucsb.edu/ws/index.php?pid=3643 (accessed January 2, 2009).

70. Memo to Richard Nixon on Signing Ceremony for Veterans Legislation on October 24, 1972, Box 8, Folder "EX VA 3: Educational Programs 1/1/71–12/31/72," White House Central Files: Veterans Affairs, Nixon Papers.

71. Richard Nixon, "Remarks on Signing Veterans Benefits Legislation," October 24, 1972, *The American Presidency Project,* online by Gerhard Peters and John T. Woolley, http://www.presidency.ucsb.edu/ws/index.php?pid=3653 (accessed January 2, 2009).

72. Richard Nixon, "Statement on the Vietnam Veteran," March 24, 1973, *The American Presidency Project,* online by Gerhard Peters and John T. Woolley, http://www.presidency.ucsb.edu/ws/index.php?pid=4153 (accessed January 2, 2009).

73. James L. Sundquist, *The Decline and Resurgence of Congress* (Washington, D.C.: Brookings Institution, 1981), 203.

74. Quoted in the *Washington Post*, May 23, 1973, 7.

75. "Age of the Viet Vets," *New York Times*, March 28, 1973, 46.

76. Letter to the *New York Times*, April 14, 1973, 32.

77. *Washington Post*, March 10, 1973, D31.
78. *Final Report on Educational Assistance to Veterans: A Comparative Study of Three G.I. Bills, Submitted to the Committee on Veterans' Affairs, United States Senate* (Washington, D.C.: U.S. Government Printing Office, 1973), III, referred to hereafter as the ETS Report.
79. Ibid., 30–31.
80. Ibid., 33.
81. Ibid., 50.
82. *Washington Post*, October 22, 1973, 28.
83. *NACV Newsletter*, September 1973, 1.
84. Quoted in the *New York Times*, September 26, 1973, 21.
85. Quoted in the *Washington Post*, October 25, 1973, 44.
86. Letter of Transmittal from Donald E. Johnson to Spiro T. Agnew, September 18, 1973, reprinted in ETS Report, XI.
87. *Congressional Record—House*, February 19, 1974, 3242.
88. Ibid., 3247.
89. Ibid., 3249.
90. Ibid., 3261.
91. Evelyn M. Monahan and Rosemary Neidel-Greenlee, *A Few Good Women: America's Military Women from World War I to the Wars in Iraq and Afghanistan* (New York: Knopf, 2010), 300.
92. Ibid., 289, and June Willenz, *Women Veterans: America's Forgotten Heroes* (New York: Continuum, 1983), 126.
93. Veterans Administration Report, *Women Veterans: Use of Education Benefits under the G.I. Bill* (Washington, D.C.: U.S. Government Printing Office, 1981), 2.
94. Ibid., 7.
95. Willenz, *Women Veterans*, 139–40.
96. Letter to Vance Hartke from Robert E. L. Eaton, reprinted in the *Congressional Record—Senate*, June 19, 1974, 20020.
97. Letter to Vance Hartke from Francis W. Stover, reprinted in ibid., 20020–21.
98. Letters to Vance Hartke from Charles L. Huber, DAV National Director of Legislation, and from Arthur S. Freeman, AVC National Chairman, reprinted in ibid., 20021–22.
99. Letter to Vance Hartke from Timothy L Craig, reprinted in ibid., 20021.
100. *Congressional Record—Senate*, June 19, 1974, 20078.
101. Ibid., 20057.
102. *Washington Post*, June 28, 1974, 30.
103. Richard Nixon, "Special Message to the Congress Proposing Veterans Legislation," January 28, 1974, *The American Presidency Project*, online by Gerhard Peters and John T. Woolley, http://www.presidency.ucsb.edu/ws/index.php?pid=4286 (accessed January 2, 2009). In this message, Nixon also called for Veterans Day to be returned to November 11, having been moved to the fourth Monday in October in 1968.

104. Richard Nixon, "Remarks on Signing a Proclamation Honoring Vietnam Veterans," February 26, 1974, *The American Presidency Project*, online by Gerhard Peters and John T. Woolley, http://www.presidency.ucsb.edu/ws/index.php?pid=4368 (accessed January 2, 2009).

105. Richard Nixon, "Remarks at Ceremonies Commemorating Vietnam Veterans Day," March 29, 1974, *The American Presidency Project*, online by Gerhard Peters and John T. Woolley, http://www.presidency.ucsb.edu/ws/index.php?pid=4402 (accessed January 2, 2009).

106. Quoted in the *New York Times*, March 29, 1974, 11.

107. Attachment to Memo for Bill Timmons from Max Friedersdorf, May 3, 1974, Box 14, Folder "Veterans," O'Donnell and Jenckes Files, 1974–1976, Subject file: Veterans, Gerald R. Ford Library, Ann Arbor, Michigan, referred to hereafter as O'Donnell and Jenckes Files.

108. Memo for Bill Timmons from Max Friedersdorf, May 3, 1974, Box 14, Folder "Veterans," O'Donnell and Jenckes Files.

109. Memo for Tom Korologos from William E. Timmons, July 24, 1974, Box 14, Folder "Veterans," O'Donnell and Jenckes Files.

110. Nixon had congressional relations assistant Patrick O'Donnell hand deliver the same letter to both Teague and Hartke on July 30, 1974. Both letters are in Box 8, Folder "EX VA 3: Educational Programs 1/1/73–8/9/74," White House Central Files: Veterans Affairs, Nixon Papers.

111. *Washington Post*, August 2, 1974, 12.

CHAPTER 5

1. Quoted in the *New York Times*, October 26, 1971, 47.

2. Quoted in "Most Veterans of Vietnam Fail to Seek Aid under the G.I. Bill," *New York Times*, April 9, 1972, 46.

3. John Sibley Butler in the Foreword for Wilbur Scott, *The Politics of Readjustment: Vietnam Veterans since the War* (New York: de Gruyter, 1993), xi.

4. Scott, *Politics of Readjustment*, 8.

5. The organization changed its name from "Collegiate" to "Concerned" in 1973: Originally, the NACV represented only college veterans' clubs and associations, but the change in name reflected a change in focus to include all Vietnam veterans.

6. *NACV Newsletter*, July–August 1974, 1.

7. Ibid.

8. Excerpt from the *Congressional Record*, reprinted in the September 1973 *NACV Newsletter*, 1.

9. Sam Schorr, quoted in Gerald Nicosia, *Home to War: A History of the Vietnam Veterans' Movement* (New York: Random House, 2001), 112–13.

10. For information on the formation and evolution of the VVAW, see Nicosia, *Home to War*, Andrew E. Hunt, *The Turning: A History of Vietnam Veterans Against the War* (New York: New York University Press, 2001), and Richard

Stacewicz, *Winter Soldiers: An Oral History of the Vietnam Veterans Against the War* (Chicago: Haymarket Books, 2008).

11. "Extend and Expand the GI Bill" Petition, undated, Vietnam Veterans Against the War Records, 1968–2006, Wisconsin Historical Society, MSS 370, Box 8, Folder 39.

12. Nicosia, *Home to War*, 154.

13. Quoted in ibid., 200.

14. For an overview of the fragmentation of the organization, see Nicosia, *Home to War*, Hunt, *The Turning*, and Stacewicz, *Winter Soldiers*.

15. Hunt, *The Turning*, 178.

16. Examples of G.I. Bill–related articles from the VVAW's *Veteran* newsletter include "Unite to Fight G.I. Bill Cutbacks," 5, no. 5 (June/July 1975), "G.I. Bill under Attack," 5, no. 6 (October 1875), "Attack on the G.I. Bill Continues," 5, no. 7 (December 1975/January 1976), "Interview: I Thought It Was My G.I. Bill, Not Theirs," 7, no. 4 (Summer 1977), "Benefits Fading Away: Steady Attacks on G.I. Bill," 7, no. 5 (November 1977), and "Carter against Vets," 9, no. 3 (Fall 1979).

17. See, for example, "In Boston, Illinois . . . GI Bill Struggles Win Gains," *Veteran* 7, no. 1 (February/March 1977).

18. For an overview of the American Veterans Movement, see Nicosia, *Home to War*, 322–46.

19. Fred Hart, interview by Mark Boulton and G. Kurt Piehler, April 21, 2001, transcription, the Center for the Study of War and Society Veterans' Oral History Project, University of Tennessee, Knoxville, Tennessee.

20. Dave Hollingsworth, interviewed by author, April 15, 2005, transcription, the Center for the Study of War and Society Veterans' Oral History Project, University of Tennessee, Knoxville, Tennessee.

21. *American Legion Magazine*, October 1968, 6.

22. *VFW Magazine*, May 1971, 13.

23. Quoted in ibid., July 1971, 27.

24. Quoted in Nicosia, *Home to War*, 68.

25. Quoted in ibid., 52.

26. Scott, *The Politics of Readjustment*, 8.

27. Milton Greenberg, *The G.I. Bill: The Law That Changed America* (New York: Lickle, 1997), 50–51.

28. Keith Olson, *The G.I. Bill, the Veterans, and the Colleges* (Louisville: University of Kentucky Press, 1974).

29. Statement of William N. Byrne, Director, Syracuse University Veterans' Organization, in *Separate Tuition Payments for Vietnam Era Veterans, Hearings Before the Subcommittee on Education and Training of the Committee on Veterans' Affairs, House of Representatives* (Washington, D.C.: U.S. Government Printing Office, 1974), 2409.

30. Dave Hollingsworth interview.

31. Morocco Coleman correspondence with author, April 2004.

32. See Marc Jason Gilbert, *The Vietnam War on Campus: Other Voices, More Distant Drums* (Westport, Conn.: Praeger, 2001).

33. David Maraniss, *They Marched into Sunlight: War and Peace, Vietnam and America, October 1967* (New York: Simon & Schuster, 2003).

34. Todd Gitlin, *The Sixties: Years of Hope, Days of Rage* (New York: Bantam, 1987), 409.

35. Ibid., 409–10.

36. Lane T. Cooke, interview by Drew Peterson, January 25, 2003, transcription, Wisconsin Veterans' Oral History Program, Wisconsin Veterans' Museum, Madison, Wisconsin.

37. Douglas C. Zwank, interview by Mark Van Ells, January 5, 1996, transcription, Wisconsin Veterans' Oral History Program, Wisconsin Veterans' Museum, Madison, Wisconsin.

38. Doug Simon, interview by G. Kurt Piehler, November 12, 2003, transcription, the Center for the Study of War and Society Veterans' Oral History Project, University of Tennessee, Knoxville, Tennessee.

39. Evelyn M. Monahan and Rosemary Neidel-Greenlee, *A Few Good Women: America's Military Women from World War I to the Wars in Iraq and Afghanistan* (New York: Knopf, 2010), 289.

40. Robert C. MacDonald, "Today's Student Veteran," *VFW Magazine*, January 1972, 15.

41. Doug Simon interview.

42. Fred Owens, interview by Mark Boulton, March 18 and May 19, 2004, transcription, the Center for the Study of War and Society Veterans' Oral History Project, University of Tennessee, Knoxville, Tennessee.

43. Roger Stephen Boeker, correspondence with author, July 2004.

44. Robert S. Ficks, interview by Mark Van Ells, November 21, 1995, transcription, Wisconsin Veterans' Oral History Program, Wisconsin Veterans' Museum, Madison, Wisconsin.

45. Quoted in Terence Shea, "Back to School from the Wars: G.I.s on Campus Find Their Battles Are Not Over," *National Observer*, February 15, 1971, reprinted in *Source Material on the Vietnam Veteran* (Washington, D.C.: U.S. Government Printing Office, 1974), 323.

46. Dave Hollingsworth interview.

47. Mark Delman Boren, *Student Resistance: A History of the Unruly Subject* (New York: Routledge, 2001), 187.

48. Quoted in an excerpt from the "Vignettes" boxes of Milton Klein's papers at the University of Tennessee's Special Collections Library, collected for his *Volunteer Moments: Vignettes of the History of the University of Tennessee, 1794–1994* (Knoxville: Office of the University Historian, University of Tennessee, 1996).

49. Tom Diets, correspondence with author, July 2004.

50. Greg Vodak, correspondence with author, July 2004.

51. Gregg L. Michel, *Struggle for a Better South: The Southern Student Organizing Committee, 1964–1969* (New York: Palgrave Macmillan, 2004), 149, 151.

52. Gitlin, *The Sixties*, 411.
53. Doug Simon interview.
54. Louis Harris & Associates, *Myths and Realities: A Study of Attitudes toward Vietnam-Era Veterans* (Washington, D.C.: U.S. Government Printing Office), 179.
55. Dave Hollingsworth interview.
56. Harris & Associates, *Myths and Realities*, 179.
57. Quoted in Paul Starr, *The Discarded Army: Veterans after Vietnam; The Nader Report on Vietnam Veterans and the Veterans Administration* (New York: Charterhouse, 1973), 234.
58. Ibid.
59. Michael J. Bennett, *When Dreams Came True: The G.I. Bill and the Making of Modern America* (Washington, D.C.: Brassey's, 1996), 245.
60. Quoted in Olson, *G.I. Bill.*
61. Tim O'Brien, "The Vietnam Veteran: The GI Bill; Less Than Enough," *Penthouse*, November 1974, 78.
62. E. Robert Stephens and Charles A. Stenger, "The Opportunity and Challenge of the Vietnam-Era Veteran to American Educators," *Journal of Higher Education* 43, no. 4 (April 1972): 303–7.
63. Ibid., 304–5.
64. *ETS Report*, 75–88.
65. Douglas Zwank interview.
66. Quoted in Shea, "Back to School," *Source Material on the Vietnam Veteran*, 320–22.
67. Harris & Associates, *Myths and Realities*, 181.
68. Ibid.

CHAPTER 6

Sections of this chapter first appeared in Mark Boulton, "Unwilling 'Soldiers in the War on Brutal Inflation': Congress, the Veterans, and the Fight with Gerald R. Ford over the 1974 G.I. Bill," *White House Studies* 7, no. 4 (2007): 313–32.

1. Gerald R. Ford, "Remarks to the Veterans of Foreign Wars Annual Convention, Chicago, Illinois," August 19, 1974, *The American Presidency Project*, online by Gerhard Peters and John T. Woolley, http://www.presidency.ucsb.edu/ws/index.php?pid=4476 (accessed January 3, 2009).
2. John Robert Greene, *The Presidency of Gerald R. Ford* (Lawrence: University Press of Kansas, 1995), 68.
3. Herbert Stein, *Presidential Economics: The Making of Economic Policy from Roosevelt to Reagan and Beyond* (New York, Simon & Schuster, 1984), 212.
4. David Gore, "Inflation Rhetoric: Gerald Ford's First Six Months in Office," *White House Studies* 5, no. 2 (Spring 2005): 215–31.
5. Gerald R. Ford, *A Time to Heal: The Autobiography of Gerald R. Ford* (New York: Harper & Row, 1979), 263.

6. John W. Sloan, "Economic Policymaking in the Johnson and Ford Administrations," *Presidential Studies Quarterly* (Winter 1990): 113.

7. Ibid.

8. Ford, *A Time to Heal*, 154–55.

9. Letter to Richard Nixon from Donald E. Johnson, July 8, 1974, Box 8, Folder "EX VA 3: Educational Programs 1/1/73–8/9/74," White House Central Files: Veterans Affairs, Nixon Papers.

10. Richard Nixon had previously indicated his intent to nominate Roudebush to head the VA after a protracted search for Donald Johnson's successor. Admiral Elmo R. Zumwalt, a popular choice among veterans, had been offered the post but declined.

11. The view of Forrest Lindley of the Vietnam Veterans Center, as quoted in the *Washington Post*, July 25, 1974, 2.

12. Quoted in ibid.

13. House Committee on Veterans' Affairs release, Box 59, Folder 2, John N. "Happy" Camp Papers, Carl Albert Center, Norman, Oklahoma.

14. Quoted in the *New York Times*, August 14, 1974, 16.

15. Quoted in ibid.

16. *New York Times*, September 25, 1974, 39.

17. *Congressional Record—House*, Volume 120, Part 22, 29665.

18. Ibid., 30050.

19. *Congressional Record—House*, Volume 120, Part 28, 37875.

20. Ibid., 30058.

21. *Congressional Record—House*, Volume 120, Part 22, 30060–61.

22. Don Edwards (D-CA), quoted in the *New York Times*, August 24, 1974, 9.

23. Letter to President Ford from 59 Congressmen, September 30, 1974, Box 2, Folder "VA3 Educational Programs," WHCF, Veterans Administration—Executive, Gerald R. Ford Presidential Library, the University of Michigan, Ann Arbor, Michigan, referred to hereafter as the Ford Papers.

24. Letter to William Jennings Bryan Dorn from Patricia Schroeder (D-CO), Carl Albert, and members of the Veterans' Affairs Committee, September 17, 1974, Box 172, Folder 1, Legislative Files, Carl Albert Papers.

25. Gerald R. Ford, "President's News Conference," August 28, 1974, *The American Presidency Project,* online by Gerhard Peters and John T. Woolley, http://www.presidency.ucsb.edu/ws/?pid=4671 (accessed March 25, 2010).

26. Quoted in the *National Association of Concerned Veterans Newsletter*, September 1974, 2. According to the *New York Times,* Hartke had also been pressured by Ford to reduce the costs of the benefits package following the compromise bill but had informed the president that the bill was "just too far down the road," as quoted in the *New York Times*, August 24, 1974, 9.

27. Quoted in the *New York Times*, August 24, 1974, 9.

28. Letter to Carl Albert from Phillip L. Shorter, September 27, 1974, Box 172, Folder 1, Legislative Files, Carl Albert Papers.

29. Letter to Carl Albert from Joseph L. McCarter, September 13, 1974, Box 172, Folder 1, Legislative Files, Carl Albert Papers.
30. Letter to Carl Albert from Warren A. Johnson, September 5, 1974, Box 172, Folder 1, Legislative Files, Carl Albert Papers.
31. *Congressional Record—House*, Volume 120, Part 26, October 10, 1974, 35151.
32. Letter to William Timmons from James A. McClure, October 11, 1974, Box 2, Folder "VA3 Educational Programs," WHCF, Veterans Administration—Executive, Ford Papers.
33. *Congressional Record—House*, Volume 120, Part 26, October 10, 1974, 35150.
34. Ibid., 35151, 35154.
35. *Congressional Record—Senate*, Volume 120, Part 26, October 10, 1974, 35065.
36. Ibid., 35067.
37. *Congressional Record—House*, Volume 120, Part 28, December 3, 1974, 37876.
38. Letter to President Ford from 59 Congressmen, September 30, 1974, Box 2, Folder "VA3 Educational Programs," WHCF, Veterans Administration—Executive, Ford Papers.
39. Letter to President Ford signed by all members of the New York Congressional Delegation, September 16, 1974, Box 2, Folder "VA3 Educational Programs," WHCF, Veterans Administration—Executive, Ford Papers.
40. Letter to President Ford from Margaret Heckler, October 11, 1974, Box 2, Folder "VA3 Educational Programs," WHCF, Veterans Administration—Executive, Ford Papers.
41. Letter to President Ford from John P. Murtha, August 22, 1974, sent following the voting down of the first compromise bill, Box 2, Folder "VA3 Educational Programs," WHCF, Veterans Administration—Executive, Ford Papers.
42. Letter to President Ford signed by sixty-two senators, October 10, 1974, Box 2, Folder "VA3 Educational Programs," WHCF, Veterans Administration—Executive, Ford Papers.
43. Letter to President Ford from the Senate Committee on Veterans' Affairs, October 10, 1974, Box 2, Folder "VA3 Educational Programs," WHCF, Veterans Administration—Executive, Ford Papers.
44. Letter to Gerald Ford from Roger Piper, October 30, 1974, Box 1, Folder "VA3 Educational Programs 8/9/74–11/30/74," WHCF, Veterans Administration—General, Ford Papers.
45. *New York Times*, November 14, 1974, 61.
46. Letter to President Ford from Ed Shenk, Veterans' Affairs Director, Grossmont College, CA, August 11, 1974, Box 3, Folder "VA3 Educational Programs 8/9/74–11/30/74," WHCF, Veterans Administration—General, Ford Papers.
47. Letter to President Ford from Stanford Cazier, September 12, 1974, Box 3, Folder "VA3 Educational Programs 8/9/74–11/30/74," WHCF, Veterans Administration—General, Ford Papers.
48. Letter to President Ford from Louis J. Tullio, October 17, 1974, Box 3, Folder "VA3 Educational Programs 8/9/74–11/30/74," WHCF, Veterans Administration—General, Ford Papers.

49. Telegram to Gerald Ford from Malcolm Wilson, October 15, 1974, Box 2, Folder "VA3 Educational Programs 10/23/74–12/31/74," WHCF, Veterans Administration—Executive, Ford Papers.

50. Letter to Gerald Ford from Brendan T. Byrne November 22, 1974, Box 2, Folder "VA3 Educational Programs 10/23/74–12/31/74," WHCF, Veterans Administration—Executive, Ford Papers.

51. Telegram to Gerald Ford from Ray Soden, August 21, 1974, Box 1, Folder "VA3 Educational Programs 8/9/74–11/30/74," WHCF, Veterans Administration—General, Ford Papers.

52. *New York Times*, November 3, 1974, 25.

53. Letter to Roy L. Ash from Richard Roudebush, October 17, 1974, Box 14, Folder "H.R. 12628 Veterans Education Bill (1) 11/26/74," Legislation Case Files, 1974–76, Ford Papers.

54. Letter to Roy L. Ash from Peter J. Brennan, October 23, 1974, Box 14, Folder "H.R. 12628 Veterans Education Bill (1) 11/26/74," Legislation Case Files, 1974–76, Ford Papers.

55. Letter to Roy L. Ash from the Acting Secretary for the Department of Health, October 17, 1974, Box 14, Folder "H.R. 12628 Veterans Education Bill (1) 11/26/74," Legislation Case Files, 1974–76, Ford Papers.

56. Memorandum for Gerald Ford from Roy L. Ash, November 22, 1974, Box 11, Folder "Veterans Education Benefits," William E. Timmons Files, Gerald R. Ford Presidential Library, referred to hereafter as Timmons Files.

57. Greene, *Presidency of Gerald R. Ford*, 69.

58. Ford, *A Time to Heal*, 153.

59. Sloan, "Economic Policymaking," 117.

60. Ford, *A Time to Heal*, 220.

61. Memorandum for Warren Hendriks from Alan Greenspan, November 25, 1974, Box 14, Folder "H.R. 12628 Veterans Education Bill (1) 11/26/74," Legislation Case Files, 1974–76, Ford Papers.

62. Memorandum for Gerald Ford from Kenneth Cole, November 25, 1974, Box 14, Folder "H.R. 12628 Veterans Education Bill (1) 11/26/74," Legislation Case Files, 1974–76, Ford Papers.

63. Memorandum to Warren Hendriks from William Timmons, November 23, 1974, Box 1, Folder "SP 2-3-27 Veto: Veterans Education Bill, 11/26/74," WHCF Subject File, Timmons Files.

64. Veto of Vietnam Era Veterans' Education and Training Benefits Legislation, White House Press Release, November 26, 1974, Box 11, Folder "Veterans Education Benefits," Timmons Files.

65. Letter to Carl Albert from John J. Stang, November 26, 1974, Box 172, Folder 2, Legislative Series, Carl Albert Papers.

66. VFW press release, attached to a letter to Carl Albert from John J. Stang, November 26, 1974, Box 172, Folder 2, Legislative Series, Carl Albert Papers.

67. Quoted in the *New York Times*, November 27, 1974, 15.

68. Letter to Carl Albert from Charles L. Huber, November 27, 1974, Box 172, Folder 2, Legislative Series, Carl Albert Papers.

69. Quoted in the *New York Times*, December 1, 1974, 61.

70. Quoted in ibid., November 27, 1974, 15.

71. Quoted in ibid., December 4, 1974, 25.

72. White House News Conference, December 3, 1974, Box 4, Folder "November 26, 1974 (No. 86)," Ronald H. Nessen, Press Secretary Briefings, Ford Papers.

73. *Congressional Record—House*, Volume 120, Part 28, December 3, 1974, 37876.

74. Ibid., 37879.

75. Ibid., 37839.

76. Ibid., 37843.

77. Ibid., 37849.

78. Letter to Carl Albert from June A. Willenz, November 26, 1974, Box 172, Folder 2, Legislative Series, Carl Albert Papers.

79. *Priority Views of the National Association of Concerned Veterans Presented to the Administrator of Veterans' Affairs*, December 12, 1974, Box 49, Folder "National Association of Concerned Veterans (1-3)," Theodore C. Marrs Files, Gerald R. Ford Library. In fairness to his predecessor, Roudebush indicated to Roy Ash in his October 17 letter that Donald Johnson would also have approved a 23 percent increase for veterans had he remained as VA administrator.

80. Robert J. Spitzer, *The Presidential Veto: Touchstone of the American Presidency* (Albany: State University of New York Press, 1988), 85–86.

81. Yanek Mieczkowski, *Gerald Ford and the Challenges of the 1970s* (Lexington: University Press of Kentucky, 2005), 89.

82. Quoted in Samuel B. Hoff, "Presidential Success in the Veto Process: The Legislative Record of Gerald R. Ford," in Bernard J. Firestone and Alexej Ugrinsky, *Gerald R. Ford and the Politics of Post-Watergate America*, vol. 1 (Westport, Conn.: Greenwood, 1993), 293–308.

83. Ford, *A Time to Heal*, 220.

84. Quoted in Mieczkowski, *Gerald Ford*, 58.

85. Richardson Pryor (D-NC), quoted in Hoff, "Presidential Success," 298.

86. Quoted in Paul Light, *The President's Agenda: Domestic Policy Choice from Kennedy to Clinton*, 3rd edition (Baltimore, Md.: Johns Hopkins University Press, 1998), 112.

87. Ibid., 113.

88. Memorandum to President Ford from James T. Lynn, March 24, 1975, Box 2, Folder "VA3 Educational Programs, 1/1/75–4/30/75," WHCF, Veterans Administration—Executive, Ford Papers.

89. *Veterans Administration Annual Report, 1976* (Washington, D.C.: U.S. Government Printing Office, 1976), 73.

90. Memorandum for Roger Semerad from Richard Roudebush, March 27, 1975, Box 1, Folder "VA3 Education Program, 8/9/1974–11/30/1974," WHCF, Subject File VA—General, Ford Papers.

91. Letter to Carl Albert from Thomas C. Walker, Commander-in-Chief, Veterans of Foreign Wars, July 15, 1976, Box 211, Folder 11, Legislative Papers, Carl Albert Papers.

92. Letter to Carl Albert from Mylio S. Kraja, Director National Legislative Commission of the American Legion, July 19, 1976, Box 211, Folder 11, Legislative Papers, Carl Albert Papers.

93. Letter to Carl Albert from Charles L. Huber, National Director of Legislation of the Disabled American Veterans, July 16, 1976, Carl Albert Legislative papers, Carl Albert Center.

94. The 1976 bill, S.969, allowed disabled veterans an indefinite period in which to claim their education benefits and also established a new experimental education program to cover veterans of the new all-volunteer force entering service after January 1, 1977. The new program required participants to pay up to seventy-five dollars a month into a fund that the VA would then match at a rate of two to one.

95. "Teague Loses Foot but Not His Heart," *Cleburne Times Review*, October 17, 1977, Newspaper Clipping, Box 43b, Folder F-19, Teague Papers.

96. Letter to Congressional Colleagues from Leon Panetta and John P. Murtha, October 12, 1977, Box 43b, Folder F-19, Teague Papers.

97. Ibid.

98. "Vietnam Veterans and the GI Bill," *Washington Post*, July 19, 1977, A16.

99. "The House and the GI Bill," *Washington Post*, July 25, 1977, A20.

100. "Teague Loses Foot but Not His Heart," *Cleburne Times Review*, October 17, 1977, Newspaper Clipping, Box 43b, Folder F-19, Teague Papers.

101. Letter to Colleagues from Olin Teague, October 17, 1977, Box 43b, Folder F-19, Teague Papers.

102. Letter to Philip Geyelin, Editor, *Washington Post*, from Olin Teague, August 1, 1977, Box 43b, Folder F-19, Teague Papers.

103. Olin Teague's QUESTIONS FOR MR. QUIE, Box 43b, Folder F-18, Teague Papers.

104. William Ford (D-MI), quoted in *Washington Post*, November 21, 1977, 19.

105. Quoted in "'Tiger' Teague and the Veterans Compromise," *Washington Post*, November 21, 1977, A19.

106. Quoted in "The President and the GI Bill," *Washington Post*, November 12, 1977, A18.

107. Quoted in "Vietnam Vets: Who Listens to Them in Washington," *Washington Post*, September 7, 1977, A19.

108. Letter to Olin Teague from Jerry Cassese, President of the New York City Community College Veterans Association, October 28, 1977, Box 43b, Folder F-17, Teague Papers.

109. Jimmy Carter, "Veterans Day Remarks at Ceremonies at Arlington National Cemetery," October 24, 1977, *The American Presidency Project*, online by Gerhard Peters and John T. Woolley, http://www.presidency.ucsb.edu/ws/?pid=6839 (accessed January 15, 2013); Teague's letter in response reported in "'Tiger'

Teague and the Veterans Compromise," *Washington Post*, November 21, 1977, A19.

110. "Ex-Rep. Olin E. Teague of Texas Dies: Championed Legislation for Veterans," *Washington Post*, January 24, 1981, B6.

111. Quoted in the *Washington Post*, May 8, 1978, 22.

112. Echoing some of the same sentiments expressed by Franklin Roosevelt and Lyndon Johnson, both of whom questioned the limits of veterans' privileged status, Carter suggested that giving veterans preference in government jobs had the potential to discriminate against the more needy and underprivileged.

113. *Washington Post*, April 18, 1977, B6. See also Max Cleland, *Strong at the Broken Places: A Personal Story* (Atlanta: Cherokee, 1989).

114. *Washington Post*, April 18, 1977, B1.

115. Ibid., August 28, 1977, B4.

116. Ibid., April 18, 1977, B1

117. Ibid., August 7, 1977, 3.

CONCLUSION

1. Stephen B. Piotrowski, interview by Mark Van Ells, transcription, June 25, 1996, the Wisconsin Veterans' Oral History Program, Wisconsin Veterans' Museum, Madison, Wisconsin.

2. U.S. Department of Veterans Affairs, *VA History in Brief*, www1.va.gov/opa/publications/archives/docs/history_in_brief.pdf (accessed August 9, 2013).

3. *Veterans' Administration Annual Report, 1984* (Washington, D.C.: U.S. Government Printing Office), 81–82.

4. Sharon Cohany, "The Vietnam-Era Cohort: Employment and Earnings" *Monthly Labor Review* 115, no. 6 (June 1992): 3–15.

5. Ibid.

6. Josefina J. Card, *Lives after Vietnam: Personal Impact of Military Service* (Lexington, Mass.: Heath, 1983), 39.

7. Variations in education attainment also resulted from branch of service. Air force veterans are more likely to have the highest education level, followed by the navy, army, and marines. These differences most likely result from the more specialized training air force and navy personnel tend to require for their service.

8. Jay Teachman, "Military Service in the Vietnam Era and Educational Attainment," *Sociology of Education* 78, no. 1 (January 2005): 50–68, and "Military Service during the Vietnam Era: Were There Consequences for Subsequent Civilian Earnings?" *Social Forces* 83, no. 2 (December 2004): 709–30.

9. *Education Assistance Study*, Report by the VA to the Committee on Veterans' Affairs, U.S. Senate (Washington, D.C.: U.S. Government Printing Office, 1975), 14.

10. *Report on Veterans' Responses to VA Educational Assistance Programs,* Report of the General Accounting Office Submitted to the Committee on Veterans' Affairs, U.S. Senate (Washington, D.C.: U.S. Government Printing Office, 1976).

11. See Joshua D. Angrist, "Lifelong Earnings and the Vietnam-Era Draft Lottery: Evidence from Social Security Records," *American Economic Review* 80, no. 3 (June 1990): 313–36, and "The Effect of Veterans Benefits on Education and Earnings," *Industrial and Labor Relations Review* 46, no. 4 (July 1993): 638–52.

12. See Jere Cohen, David Segal, and Lloyd V. Temme, "Military Service Was an Educational Disadvantage to Vietnam–Era Personnel," *Sociology and Social Research* 70, no. 3 (April 1986): 206–8 and "The Impact of Education on Vietnam-Era Veterans' Occupational Attainment," *Social Science Quarterly* 73, no. 2 (June 1992): 398–409. See also Peter Matilla, "G.I. Bill Benefits and Enrollments: How Did Vietnam Veterans Fare?" *Social Science Quarterly* 59, no. 3 (December 1978): 535–45.

13. Olin E. Teague, Untitled Note from Da Nang, Vietnam, February 22, 1966, Box 32A, Folder 27, Teague Papers.

14. Cited in David E. Bonior, Steven M. Champlin, and Timothy S. Kolly, *The Vietnam Veteran: A History of Neglect* (New York: Praeger, 1984), 130.

BIBLIOGRAPHY

POLITICAL PAPERS AND MANUSCRIPT COLLECTIONS

Carl Albert, Legislative, Departmental, and General Papers. Carl Albert Congressional Research Center, Norman, Oklahoma.

Dewey Bartlett Papers. Carl Albert Congressional Research Center, Norman, Oklahoma.

Dwight D. Eisenhower, 1953–1961. Public Papers of the Presidents, the American Presidency Project, published online by Gerhard Peters and John T. Woolley at http://www.presidency.ucsb.edu/ws.

Franklin D. Roosevelt, 1933–1945. Public Papers of the Presidents, the American Presidency Project, published online by Gerhard Peters and John T. Woolley at http://www.presidency.ucsb.edu/ws.

Fred Harris Papers. Carl Albert Congressional Research Center, Norman, Oklahoma.

Gerald R. Ford Presidential Papers. Gerald R. Ford Presidential Library, Ann Arbor, Michigan.

Gerald R. Ford, 1974–1977. Public Papers of the Presidents, the American Presidency Project, published online by Gerhard Peters and John T. Woolley at http://www.presidency.ucsb.edu/ws.

Henry H. Wilson Papers. Lyndon B. Johnson Presidential Library, Austin, Texas.

James Cannon Papers. Gerald R. Ford Presidential Library, Ann Arbor, Michigan.

Jimmy Carter, 1978–1981. Public Papers of the Presidents, the American Presidency Project, published online by Gerhard Peters and John T. Woolley at http://www.presidency.ucsb.edu/ws.

John F. Kennedy, 1961–1963. Public Papers of the Presidents, the American Presidency Project, published online by Gerhard Peters and John T. Woolley at http://www.presidency.ucsb.edu/ws.

John N. "Happy" Camp Papers. Carl Albert Congressional Research Center, Norman, Oklahoma.

Joseph Califano Papers. Lyndon B. Johnson Presidential Library, Austin, Texas.

Legislation Case Files. Gerald R. Ford Presidential Library, Ann Arbor, Michigan.

Lyndon B. Johnson, 1963–1969. Public Papers of the Presidents, the American Presidency Project, published online by Gerhard Peters and John T. Woolley at http://www.presidency.ucsb.edu/ws.

Lyndon B. Johnson Papers, 1963–1969. Lyndon B. Johnson Presidential Library, Austin Texas.

Olin E. Teague Papers. Cushing Memorial Library and Archives of Texas A&M University, College Station, Texas.

Ralph W. Yarborough Papers. Dolph Briscoe Center for American History, the University of Texas at Austin.

Richard M. Nixon Papers. White House Central Files, Subject: Veterans Affairs. Richard Nixon Presidential Library, Yorba Linda, California.

Richard M. Nixon, 1969–1974. Public Papers of the Presidents, the American Presidency Project, published online by Gerhard Peters and John T. Woolley at http://www.presidency.ucsb.edu/ws.

Ronald H. Nessen Files. Gerald R. Ford Presidential Library, Ann Arbor, Michigan.

Stanley S. Scott Papers. Gerald R. Ford Presidential Library, Ann Arbor, Michigan.

Theodore C. Marrs Papers. Gerald R. Ford Presidential Library, Ann Arbor, Michigan.

White House Central Files. Gerald R. Ford Presidential Library, Ann Arbor, Michigan.

William E. Timmons Papers. Gerald R. Ford Presidential Library, Ann Arbor, Michigan.

Vietnam Veterans Against the War Papers. Wisconsin Historical Society, Madison, Wisconsin.

ORAL INTERVIEWS FROM THE UNIVERSITY OF TENNESSEE CENTER FOR THE STUDY OF WAR AND SOCIETY ORAL HISTORY PROJECT

Dave Hollingsworth, interviewed by author and Ben Cosgrove, April 15, 2005, transcription.

Doug Simon, interviewed by Kurt Piehler, November 12, 2002, transcription.

Fred Hart, interviewed by author and Kurt Piehler, April 21, 2001, transcription.

Fred Owens, interviewed by author, May 19, 2004, transcription.

ORAL INTERVIEWS FROM THE WISCONSIN VETERANS' ORAL HISTORY PROGRAM, WISCONSIN VETERANS' MUSEUM, MADISON, WISCONSIN

Douglas C. Zwank, interviewed by Mark Van Ells, January 5, 1996, transcription.

Lane T. Cooke, interviewed by Drew Peterson, January 25, 2003, transcription.

Robert S. Ficks, interviewed by Mark Van Ells, November 21, 1995, transcription.

Stephen B. Piotrowski, interviewed by Mark Van Ells, June 25, 1996, transcription.

GOVERNMENT PUBLICATIONS AND REPORTS

A Study of the Problems Facing Vietnam Veterans on Their Readjustment to Civilian Life. Washington, D.C.: U.S. Government Printing Office, 1972.

Congress and the Nation, Volume I: 1945–1964. Washington, D.C.: Congressional Quarterly, 1965.

Congress and the Nation, Volume II: 1965–1968. Washington, D.C.: Congressional Quarterly, 1969.

Congress and the Nation, Volume III: 1969–1972. Washington, D.C.: Congressional Quarterly, 1973.

Congress and the Nation, Volume IV: 1973–1976. Washington, D.C.: Congressional Quarterly, 1977.

Congress and the Nation, Volume V: 1978–1980. Washington, D.C.: Congressional Quarterly, 1981.

Congress and the Nation, Volume VI: 1981–1984. Washington, D.C.: Congressional Quarterly, 1985.

Congress and the Nation, Volume VII: 1985–1988. Washington, D.C.: Congressional Quarterly, 1989.

Congressional Record. Washington, D.C.: U.S. Government Printing Office, 1950–1984.

Education Assistance Study. Veterans Administration Report for the Committee on Veterans' Affairs, U.S. Senate. Washington, D.C.: U.S. Government Printing Office, 1975.

Final Report on Educational Assistance to Veterans: A Comparative Study of Three G.I. Bills, Submitted to the Committee on Veterans' Affairs, United States Senate. Washington, D.C.: U.S. Government Printing Office, 1973.

Legislation to Provide G.I. Benefits for Post-Korean Veterans, Hearings before the Committee on Veterans' Affairs, House of Representatives, August 31, September 1, 2, 7, and 15. Washington, D.C.: U.S. Government Printing Office, 1965.

Louis Harris & Associates, *Myths and Realities: A Study of Attitudes toward Vietnam-Era Veterans*. Washington, D.C.: U.S. Government Printing Office.

Report of the Committee on Labor and Public Welfare to Accompany S.9, the Cold War Veterans' Readjustment Assistance Act, June 1, 1965. Washington, D.C.: U.S. Government Printing Office, 1965.

Report on Veterans' Responses to VA Educational Assistance Programs. Report of the General Accounting Office Submitted to the Committee on Veterans' Affairs, U.S. Senate. Washington, D.C.: U.S. Government Printing Office, 1976.

Separate Tuition Payments for Vietnam Era Veterans, Hearings before the Subcommittee on Education and Training of the Committee on Veterans' Affairs, House of Representatives. Washington, D.C.: U.S. Government Printing Office, 1974.

Source Material on the Vietnam Veteran. Washington, D.C.: U.S. Government Printing Office, 1974.

U.S. Department of Veterans Affairs, *VA History in Brief*. www1.va.gov/opa/publications/archives/docs/history_in_brief.pdf (accessed August 9, 2013).

Veterans Administration. *Annual Report*, 1950–1989. Washington, D.C.: U.S. Government Printing Office, 1940–1989.

Veterans Administration Report. *Survey of Female Veterans: A Study of the Needs, Attitudes, and Experiences of Women Veterans*, reprint. Washington, D.C.: U.S. Government Printing Office, 1985.

Veterans Administration Report. *The Female Veteran Population*. Washington, D.C.: U.S. Government Printing Office, 1983.

Veterans Administration Report. *Women Veteran Use of Educational Benefits under the G.I. Bill, September.* Washington, D.C.: U.S. Government Printing Office, 1981.

Veterans' Benefits in the United States: A Report to the President by the President's Commission on Veterans' Pensions. Washington, D.C.: U.S. Government Printing Office, 1956.

Vietnam Veterans' Readjustment, Hearings before the Committee on Veterans' Affairs, United States Senate, 96th Congress, 2nd Session, February 21, March 4, and May 21, 1980, Washington, D.C. Washington, D.C.: U.S. Government Printing Office, 1980.

NEWSPAPERS AND MAGAZINES

American Legion Magazine
Austin American-Statesman
Boston Globe
Dallas Morning News
Harpers
Los Angeles Times
National Association of Concerned Veterans Newsletter
Newsweek
New York Times
Penthouse
The Veteran (Vietnam Veterans Against the War publication)
Time
U.S. News and World Report
VFW Magazine (Veterans of Foreign Wars publication)
Washington Post

PUBLISHED MEMOIRS

Bradley, Omar N., and Blair, Clay. *A General's Life: An Autobiography.* New York: Simon & Schuster, 1983.

Cleland, Max. *Strong at the Broken Places: A Personal Story.* Atlanta: Cherokee Publishing, 1989.

Coleman, Morocco. *Coming Full Circle.* Atlanta: Underground Epics Publishing, 2001.

Eisenhower, Dwight D. *The White House Years: Mandate for Change.* New York: Doubleday, 1963.

Ford, Gerald R. *A Time to Heal: The Autobiography of Gerald R. Ford.* New York: Harper & Row, 1979.

Goldwater, Barry. *The Conscience of a Conservative,* reprint. New York, MJF Books, 1990.

SECONDARY WORKS

Altschuler, Glenn, and Blumin, Stuart. *The G.I. Bill: The New Deal for Veterans.* New York: Oxford University Press, 2009.

Ambrose, Stephen E. *Eisenhower, Volume II: The President.* New York: Simon & Schuster, 1984.

——. *Nixon, Volume II: The Triumph of a Politician.* New York: Simon & Schuster, 1989.

Andrew, John A., III. *Lyndon Johnson and the Great Society.* Chicago: Dee, 1998.

Angrist, Joshua D. "Lifelong Earnings and the Vietnam-Era Draft Lottery: Evidence from Social Security Records." *American Economic Review* 1990 8.3: 313–36.

——. "The Effect of Veterans Benefits on Education and Earnings." *Industrial and Labor Relations Review* 1993 46.4: 638–52.

Appy, Christian. *Working-Class War: American Combat Soldiers in Vietnam.* Chapel Hill: University of North Carolina Press, 1993.

Axinn, June, and Stem, Mark J. *Social Welfare: A History of the American Response to Need,* 6th edition. Boston: Pearson/Allyn and Bacon, 2005.

Bailyn, Bernard. *The Ideological Origins of the American Revolution.* Cambridge, Mass.: Harvard University Press, 1967.

Bennett, Michael J. *When Dreams Came True: The G.I. Bill and the Making of Modern America.* New York: Brassey's, 1996.

Bernstein, Irving. *Guns or Butter: The Presidency of Lyndon Johnson.* New York: Oxford University Press, 1996.

Bischoff, Gunter, and Ambrose, Stephen. *Eisenhower: A Centenary Assessment.* Baton Rouge: Louisiana State Press, 1995.

Bodenger, David. "Soldier's Bonuses: A History of Veterans Benefits in the United States, 1776–1967." Ph.D. Diss., Pennsylvania State University, 1972.

Bonior, David E., Champlin, Steven M., and Kolly, Timothy S. *The Vietnam Veteran: A History of Neglect.* New York: Praeger, 1984.

Boren, Mark Delman. *Student Resistance: A History of the Unruly Subject.* New York: Routledge, 2001.

Bornet, Vaughn Davis. *The Presidency of Lyndon B. Johnson.* Lawrence: University Press of Kansas, 1983.

Boulton, Mark. "How the G.I. Bill Failed African-American Vietnam War Veterans." *Journal of Blacks in Higher Education* Winter 2007–8 58: 57–61.

——. "A Price on Patriotism: The Politics and Unintended Consequences of the 1966 G.I. Bill," in Ortiz, Stephen R., ed. *The Politics of Veterans' Policy: Federal Policies and Veterans in the Modern United States.* Gainesville: University of Florida Press, 2012.

——. "Unwilling 'soldiers in the war on brutal inflation': Congress, the Veterans, and the Fight with Gerald R. Ford over the 1974 G.I. Bill." *White House Studies* 2007 7.4: 313–32.

Bowling, Lawson. *Shapers of the Great Debate on the Great Society: A Biographical Dictionary.* Westport, Conn.: Greenwood, 2005.

Burkett, B. G., and Whitley, Glenna. *Stolen Valor: How the Vietnam Generation Was Robbed of Its Heroes and Its History.* Dallas: Verity, 1998.

Brokaw, Tom. *The Greatest Generation.* New York: Random House, 1998.

Campbell, Alec Duncan. "The Invisible Welfare State: Class Struggles, the American Legion, and the Development of Veterans Benefits in the Twentieth-Century United States." Ph.D. Diss., UCLA, 1991.

Card, Josefina J. *Lives after Vietnam: Personal Impact of Military Service*. Lexington, Mass.: Heath, 1983.

Caro, Robert A. *Path to Power: The Years of Lyndon Johnson, Volume I*. New York: Knopf, 1982.

———. *Means of Ascent: The Years of Lyndon Johnson, Volume II*. New York: Vintage, 1991.

———. *Master of the Senate: The Years of Lyndon Johnson, Volume III*. New York: Vintage, 2003.

———. *The Passage of Power: The Years of Lyndon Johnson, Volume IV*. New York: Knopf, 2012.

Childers, Thomas. *Soldier from the War Returning: The Greatest Generation's Troubled Homecoming from World War II*. Boston, Mass.: Mariner, 2010.

Clodfelter, Micheal. *Vietnam in Military Statistics: A History of the Indochina Wars, 1772–1991*. Jefferson, N.C.: McFarland, 1994.

Clowse, Barbara Barksdale. *Brainpower for the Cold War: The Sputnik Crisis and the 1958 National Defense Education Act*. Westport, Conn.: Greenwood, 1981.

Cohany, Sharon. "The Vietnam-Era Cohort: Employment and Earnings." *Monthly Labor Review* 1992 115.6: 3–15.

Cohen, Jere, Segal, David R., and Temme, Lloyd V. "Military Service and Educational Attainment in the All-Volunteer Force." *Social Science Quarterly* 1995 76.2: 88–104.

———. "Military Service Was an Educational Disadvantage to Vietnam-Era Personnel." *Sociology and Social Research* 1986 70.3: 206–8.

———. "The Impact of Education on Vietnam-Era Veterans' Occupational Attainment." *Social Science Quarterly* 1992 73.2: 398–409.

Cohen, Lizabeth. *A Consumer's Republic: The Politics of Mass Consumption in Postwar America*. New York: Knopf, 2003.

Cox, Patrick. *Ralph W. Yarborough: The People's Senator*. Austin: University of Texas Press, 2001.

Critchlow, Donald T., and Maclean, Nancy. *Debating the American Conservative Movement, 1945 to the Present*. Lanham, Md.: Rowman & Littlefield, 2009.

Dallek, Robert. *Flawed Giant: Lyndon Johnson and His Times, 1961–1973*. New York: Oxford University Press, 1998.

Damms, Richard V. *The Eisenhower Presidency, 1953–1961*. London: Longman, 2002.

Daniels, Roger. *The Bonus March: An Episode of the Great Depression*. Westport, Conn.: Greenwood, 1972.

Dean, Eric T., Jr. *Shook over Hell: Post-Traumatic Stress, Vietnam, and the Civil War*. Cambridge, Mass.: Harvard University Press, 1997.

———. "The Myth of the Troubled and Scorned Vietnam Veteran." *Journal of American Studies* U.K. 1992 26.1: 59–74.

Dearing, Mary. *Veterans in Politics: The Story of the G.A.R.* Baton Rouge: Louisiana State University Press, 1952.

DeGroot, Gerard J., ed. *Student Protest: The Sixties and After*. New York: Longman, 1998.

Dickson, Paul, and Allen, Thomas B. *The Bonus Army: An America Epic*. New York: Walker, 2004.

Dillingham, William P. *Federal Aid to Veterans, 1918–1941*. Gainesville: University of Florida Press, 1952.

Firestone, Bernard J., and Ugrinsky, Alexej. *Gerald R. Ford and the Politics of Post-Watergate America*, Volume 1. Westport, Conn.: Greenwood, 1993.

Fisher, Kenneth E. "A Comparative Analysis of Selected Congressional Documents Related to Educational Benefits Legislated for the Veterans of World War II, the Korean Conflict, and the Vietnam Era under the G.I. Bill." Ph.D. Diss., Florida State University, 1975.

Flynn, George Q. *The Draft, 1940–1973*. Lawrence: University of Kansas Press, 1993.

Frederickson, Kari. *The Dixiecrat Revolt and the End of the Solid South, 1932–1968*. Chapel Hill: University of North Carolina Press, 2001.

Frydl, Kathleen. *The G.I. Bill*. New York: Cambridge University Press, 2009.

Gambone, Michael. *The Greatest Generation Comes Home: The Veteran in American Society*. College Station: Texas A&M University Press, 2005.

Gerber, David R., ed. *Disabled Veterans in History*. Ann Arbor: University of Michigan Press, 2000.

Gilbert, Marc Jason. *The Vietnam War on Campus: Other Voices, More Distant Drums*. Westport, Conn.: Praeger, 2001.

Gimbel, Cynthia, and Booth, Alan. "Who Fought in Vietnam?" *Social Forces* 1996 74.4: 1138–57.

Gitlin, Todd. *The Sixties: Years of Hope, Days of Rage*. New York: Bantam Books, 1981.

Gore, David. "Inflation Rhetoric: Gerald Ford's First Six Months in Office," *White House Studies* Spring 2005 5.2: 183–98.

Graham, Herman, III. *The Brothers' Vietnam War: Black Power, Manhood, and the Military Experience*. Gainesville: University Press of Florida, 2003.

Graham, Hugh Davis. *The Uncertain Triumph: Federal Education Policy in the Kennedy and Johnson Years*. Chapel Hill: University of North Carolina Press, 1984.

Greenberg, Milton. *The G.I. Bill: The Law That Changed America*. New York: Lickle, 1997.

Greene, Bob. *Homecoming: When the Soldiers Returned from Vietnam*. New York: Putnam, 1989.

Greene, John Robert. *The Presidency of Gerald R. Ford*. Lawrence: University Press of Kansas, 1995.

Greenstein, Fred I. *The Hidden-Hand Presidency: Eisenhower as Leader*. New York: Basic Books, 1982.

Hagopian, Patrick. *The Vietnam War in American Memory: Veterans, Memorials, and the Politics of Healing*. Amherst: University of Massachusetts Press, 2009.

Havighurst, Robert, et al. *The American Veteran Back Home: A Study of Veteran Readjustment*. New York: Longmans, Green, 1951.

Head, William, and Grinter, Lawrence, eds. *Looking Back on the Vietnam War: A 1990s Perspective on the Decisions, Combat, and Legacies*. Westport, Conn.: Praeger, 1993.

Helsing, John W. *Johnson's War/Johnson's Great Society: The Guns and Butter Trap.* Westport, Conn.: Praeger, 2000.

Hendrickson, Kenneth E., Jr., Collins, Michael L., and Cox, Patrick, eds. *Profiles in Power: Twentieth-Century Texans in Washington.* Austin: University of Texas Press, 2004.

Hoff, Joan. *Nixon Reconsidered.* New York: Basic Books, 1994.

Humes, Edward. *Over Here: How the G.I. Bill Transformed the American Dream.* Boston: Houghton Mifflin Harcourt, 2006.

Hunt, Andrew E. *The Turning: A History of Vietnam Veterans Against the War.* New York: New York University Press, 2001.

Hunt, Karen M., and Walcott, Charles E. *Empowering the White House: Governance under Nixon, Ford, and Carter.* Lawrence: University of Kansas Press, 2004.

Hyman, Harold M. *American Singularity: The 1787 Northwest Ordinance, the 1862 Homestead-Morrill Acts, and the 1944 G.I. Bill.* Athens: University of Georgia Press, 1986.

Karnow, Stanley. *Vietnam: A History.* New York: Viking, 1983.

Karsten, Peter. *The Effects of Military Service and War on American Life.* Westport, Conn.: Greenwood, 1987.

Keene, Jennifer. *Doughboys, the Great War, and the Remaking of America.* Baltimore, Md.: Johns Hopkins University Press, 2001.

Kelly, Patrick J. *Creating a National Home: Building the Veterans' Welfare State, 1860–1900.* Cambridge, Mass.: Harvard University Press, 1997.

King, John P., ed. *Dwight D. Eisenhower: Soldier, President, Statesman.* New York: Greenwood, 1987.

Klein, Milton. *Volunteer Moments: Vignettes of the History of the University of Tennessee, 1794–1994.* Knoxville: Office of the University Historian, University of Tennessee, 1996.

Klein, Robert. *Wounded Men, Broken Promises.* New York: Macmillan, 1981.

Knight, Amy W., and Worden, Robert L. *Veterans Benefits Administration: An Organizational History, 1776–1994.* Philadelphia: Diane, 1995.

Kohn, Richard H. *Eagle and Sword: The Federalists and the Creation of the Military Establishment in America, 1783–1802.* New York: Free Press, 1975.

Krebs, Ronald R. *Fighting for Rights: Military Service and the Politics of Citizenship.* Ithaca, NY: Cornell University Press, 2006.

Kubey, Craig, et al. *The Viet Vet Survival Guide: How to Cut through the Bureaucracy and Get What You Need and Are Entitled To.* New York: Ballantine Books, 1985.

Kulka, Richard A., et al. *The National Vietnam Veterans Readjustment Study.* New York: Brunner/Mazel, 1990.

Ladinsky, Jack. "A Review Article: Vietnam, the Veterans, and the Veterans Administration." Madison, Wis.: Discussion Paper, Institute for Research on Poverty295, University of Madison, 1975.

Lembcke, Jerry. *The Spitting Image: Myth, Memory, and the Legacy of Vietnam.* New York: New York University Press, 1998.

Levitan, Sar A., and Zickler, Joyce. *Swords into Ploughshares: Our G.I. Bill.* Salt Lake City, Utah: Olympus, 1973.

Lifton, Robert J. *Home from the War: Vietnam Veterans, Neither Victims nor Executioners.* New York: Simon & Schuster, 1973.

Light, Paul. *The President's Agenda: Domestic Policy Choice from Kennedy to Clinton,* 3rd edition. Baltimore, Md.: Johns Hopkins University Press, 1998.

Lisio, Donald J. *The President and Protest: Hoover, Macarthur, and the Bonus Riot.* New York: Fordham University Press, 1994.

Littlewood, Thomas B. *Soldiers Back Home: The American Legion in Illinois, 1919–1939.* Carbondale: Southern Illinois University Press, 2004.

Lyons, Paul. "Toward a Revised Story of the Homecoming of Vietnam Veterans." *Peace & Change* 1998 23.2: 193–200.

Macpherson, Myra. *Long Time Passing: Vietnam and the Haunted Generation,* new edition. Bloomington: Indiana University Press, 2001.

Maraniss, David. *They Marched into Sunlight: War and Peace, Vietnam and America, October 1967.* New York: Simon & Schuster, 2003.

Marshall, Kathryn. *In the Combat Zone: An Oral History of American Women in Vietnam.* Boston: Little, Brown, 1987.

Martin, Andrew. *Receptions of War: Vietnam in American Culture.* Norman: University of Oklahoma Press, 1993.

Mason, Herbert Molloy. *VFW: Our First Century.* Addax, 1999.

Mason, Robert. *Richard Nixon and the Quest for a New Majority.* Chapel Hill: University of North Carolina Press, 2004.

Matilla, Peter J. "G.I. Bill Benefits and Enrollments: How Did Vietnam Veterans Fare?" *Social Science Quarterly* 1978 59.3: 535–45.

Matusow, Allen J. *Nixon's Economy.* Lawrence: University of Kansas Press, 1998.

Mavis, Ralph. "'Go Tell Americans': Soldiers' Narratives and Recent Histories of the Vietnam War." *Oral History Review* 1995 22.1: 105–13.

Mettler, Suzanne. *Soldiers to Citizens: The G.I. Bill and the Making of the Greatest Generation.* New York: Oxford, 2005.

Michel, Gregg L. *Struggle for a Better South: The Southern Student Organizing Committee, 1964–1969.* New York: Palgrave Macmillan, 2004.

Mieczkowski, Yanek. *Gerald Ford and the Challenges of the 1970s.* Lexington: University Press of Kentucky, 2005.

Monahan, Evelyn M., and Neidel-Greenlee, Rosemary. *A Few Good Women: America's Military Women from World War I to the Wars in Iraq and Afghanistan.* New York: Knopf, 2010.

Morgan, Iwan. *Nixon.* London: Arnold, 2002.

Moss, George Donelson. *Vietnam: An American Ordeal,* 2nd edition. Upper Saddle River, N. J.: Prentice Hall, 1994.

Mosse, George L. *Fallen Soldiers: Reshaping the Memory of the World Wars.* New York: Oxford University Press, 1990.

Muse, Eben J. "From Lt. Calley to John Rambo: Repatriating the Vietnam War." *Journal of American Studies* U.K. 1993 27.1: 88–92.

Nicosia, Gerald. *Home to War: A History of the Vietnam Veterans' Movement.* New York: Crown, 2001.

Nusbaum, Philip. "Traditionalizing Experience: The Case of Vietnam Veterans." *New York Folklore* 1991 17.1–2: 45–62.

Olson, Keith. *The G.I. Bill, the Veterans, and the Colleges.* Lexington: University Press of Kentucky, 1974.

Onkst, David H. "'First a Negro . . . Incidentally a Veteran': Black World War Two Veterans and the G.I. Bill of Rights in the Deep South, 1944–1948." *Journal of Social History* 1998 31.3: 518–43.

Ortiz, Stephen. *Beyond the Bonus March and G.I. Bill: How Veteran Politics Shaped the New Deal Era.* New York: New York University Press, 2010.

———, ed. *The Politics of Veterans' Policy: Federal Policies and Veterans in the Modern United States.* Gainesville: University of Florida Press, 2012.

Pach, Chester J., Jr., and Richardson, Elmo. *The Presidency of Dwight D. Eisenhower.* Lawrence: University Press of Kansas, 1991.

Pash, Melinda. *In the Shadow of the Greatest Generation: The Americans Who Fought the Korean War.* New York: New York University Press, 2013.

Pearson, Alec Philmore, Jr. "Olin E. Teague and the Veterans Administration." Ph.D. Diss., Texas A&M, 1977.

Pencak, William. *For God and Country: The American Legion, 1919–1941.* Boston: Northeastern University Press, 1989.

Pervis, Joseph Herbert. "The Vietnam-Era Veteran in College." Ph.D. Diss., Kansas State, 1974.

Phillips, William G. *Yarborough of Texas.* Washington, D.C.: Acropolis Books, 1969.

Piehler, G. Kurt. *Remembering War the American Way.* Washington, D.C.: Smithsonian Institution Press, 1995.

Polner, Murray. *No Victory Parades: The Return of the Vietnam Veteran.* New York: Holt, Rinehart, and Winston, 1971.

Posner, Richard. *The New Winter Soldiers: G.I. and Veteran Dissent during the Vietnam Era.* New Brunswick, N.J.: Rutgers University Press, 1996.

Pratt, George K. *Soldier to Civilian: Problems of Readjustment.* New York: McGraw Hill, 1944.

Reichley, James. *Conservatives in an Age of Change: The Nixon and Ford Administrations.* Washington, D.C.: Brookings Institute, 1981.

Resch, John. *Suffering Soldiers: Revolutionary War Veterans, Moral Sentiment, and Political Culture in the Early Republic.* Amherst: University of Massachusetts Press, 1999.

Ross, Davis B. *Preparing for Ulysses: Politics and Veterans during World War II.* New York: Columbia University Press, 1969.

Rumer, Thomas A. *The American Legion: An Official History, 1919–1989.* New York: Evans, 1990.

Saxe, Robert Francis. "'Citizens First, Veterans Second': The American Veterans Committee and the Challenge of Postwar 'Independent Progressives.'" *War & Society* Australia 2004 22.2: 75–94.

———. *Settling Down: World War II Veterans' Challenge to the Postwar Consensus.* New York: Palgrave Macmillan, 2007.

Schulman, Bruce J. *Lyndon B. Johnson and American Liberalism: A Brief Biography with Documents.* New York: Bedford/St. Martins, 1995.

Scott, Wilbur J., ed. *The Politics of Readjustment: Vietnam Veterans since the War.* New York: de Gruyter, 1993.

Segal, David R. *Recruiting for Uncle Sam: Citizenship and Military Manpower Policy.* Lawrence: University Press of Kansas, 1989.

Severo, Richard, and Milford, Lewis. *The Wages of War: When America's Soldiers Came Home: From Valley Forge to Vietnam.* New York: Simon & Schuster, 1989.

Shay, Jonathan. *Achilles in Vietnam: Combat Trauma and the Undoing of Character.* New York: Atheneum, 1994.

———. *Odysseus in America: Combat Trauma and the Trial of Homecoming.* New York: Scribner, 2002.

Skocpol, Theda. *Protecting Soldiers and Mothers: The Political Origins of Social Policy in the United States.* Cambridge, Mass.: Belknap Press of Harvard University Press, 1992.

Sloan, John W. "Economic Policymaking in the Johnson and Ford Administrations." *Presidential Studies Quarterly* 20 Winter 1990: 111–25.

Small, Melvin. *The Presidency of Richard Nixon.* Lawrence: University of Kansas Press, 1990.

Spitzer, Robert J. *The Presidential Veto: Touchstone of the American Presidency.* Albany: State University of New York Press, 1988.

Stacewicz, Richard. *Winter Soldiers: An Oral History of the Vietnam Veterans Against the War.* Chicago: Haymarket Books, 2008.

Stanton, Shelby. *The Rise and Fall of an American Army: U.S. Ground Forces in Vietnam, 1965–1973.* Novato, Calif.: Presidio, 1985.

Starr, Paul. *The Discarded Army: Veterans after Vietnam; The Nader Report on Vietnam Veterans and the Veterans Administration.* New York: Charterhouse, 1973.

Stein, Herbert. *Presidential Economics: The Making of Economic Policy from Roosevelt to Reagan and Beyond.* New York: Simon & Schuster, 1984.

Stephens, Robert, and Stenger, Charles A. "The Opportunity and Challenge of the Vietnam-Era Veteran to American Educators." *Journal of Higher Education* 1972 43.4: 303–7.

Summers, Harry G. *Vietnam War Almanac.* New York: Facts on File, 1985.

Sundquist, James L. *The Decline and Resurgence of Congress.* Washington, D.C.: Brookings Institution, 1981.

Taylor, Richard H. *Homeward Bound: American Veterans Return from War.* Westport, Conn.: Praeger, 2007.

Teachman, Jay. "Military Service during the Vietnam Era: Were There Consequences for Subsequent Civilian Earnings?" *Social Forces* December 2004 83.2: 709–30.

———. "Military Service in the Vietnam Era and Educational Attainment." *Sociology of Education* January 2005 78.1: 50–68.

Terkel, Studs. *The Good War: An Oral History of World War II*. New York: Pantheon, 1984.

Terry, Wallace. *Bloods: An Oral History of the Vietnam War by Black Veterans*. New York: Ballantine, 1984.

Tyler, Robert L. "The American Veterans Committee: Out of a Hot War and into the Cold." *American Quarterly* 1966 18.3: 419–36.

Unger, Irwin. *The Best of Intentions: The Triumphs and Failure of the Great Society under Kennedy, Johnson, and Nixon*. New York: Doubleday, 1996.

Urban, Wayne. *More Than Science and Sputnik: The National Defense Education Act of 1958*. Tuscaloosa: University of Alabama Press, 2010.

Van Ells, Mark D. *To Hear Only Thunder Again: America's World War II Veterans Come Home*. Lanham, Md.: Lexington, 2001.

Ward, Stephen R., ed. *The War Generation: Veterans of the First World War*. Port Washington, N.Y.: Kennikat, 1975.

Warshaw, Shirley Anne, ed. *Re-examining the Eisenhower Presidency*. Northport, Conn.: Greenwood, 1993.

Westheider, James. *Fighting on Two Fronts: African Americans and the Vietnam War*. New York: New York University Press, 1997.

Willenz, June. *Women Veterans: America's Forgotten Heroes*. New York: Continuum, 1983.

Wood, Gordon. *The Radicalism of the American Revolution*. New York: Vintage, 1993.

Zelizer, Julian. *The American Congress: The Building of Democracy*. Boston: Houghton Mifflin, 2004.

Adjusted Compensation Act of 1924. *See* Bonus Bill (WWI); Bonus Marches of 1932 and 1933

African American veterans, 11, 16, 33, 102, 108–111, 132, 143, 157, 218n7; criticisms of the Vietnam-era G.I. Bills for minorities, 11, 16, 102, 108–109, 111, 132, 143, 157; racial discrimination in Vietnam, 110–111; readjustment problems for African American Vietnam veterans, 108–111; under the World War II G.I. Bill, 33, 218n7

Albert, Carl, Speaker of the House, (D-OK), 102, 128, 183–185, 193, 195, 198

American Legion, 9, 14, 20, 25, 30–31, 37–38, 40–41, 47–50, 59, 85, 107, 136, 150, 161–163, 193, 198, 212; changing attitudes toward the 1966 "Cold War" G.I. Bill, 85; early opposition to a peacetime G.I. Bill, 14, 59; lobbying for the WWI Bonus Bill, 25; opposition to 1976 two-year benefits extension proposal, 198; opposition to Alan Cranston's Vietnam veterans counseling bill, 136; preference for World War II veterans benefits such as pensions, 9, 37–38, 50; reaction to Bradley Report, 14, 47–49; role in Korean War G.I. Bill, 40–41; role in World War II G.I. Bill, 8, 30–31; support for later benefits increases for Vietnam veterans,

107, 150, 193; Vietnam veterans' initial reluctance to join, 161–163, 212

American Veterans Committee (AVC), 49, 150, 195, 223n85

American Veterans Movement (AVM), 160–161, 240n18

Angrist, Joshua, 211, 249n11

Annunzio, Frank, representative (D-IL), 124

Antiwar protests. *See* Campus unrest

Ash, Roy L. (OMB), 190, 191, 197, 246n79

Baroody, William J., Jr., assistant to Gerald Ford for public liaison, 192

Beilke, Max, last soldier to leave Vietnam, 1, 2, 18; death in the 9/11 attack on the Pentagon, 217n2

Bentsen, Lloyd, Jr., defeat of Ralph Yarbrough in 1970 Democratic Texas primary, 134

Berry, E. Y., representative (R-SD), 184

Biden, Joseph, senator (D-DE), 188

Bonior, David, representative (D-MI), 136, 204

Bonus Bill (WWI), 6, 25–28, 220n9; arguments for, 25; Calvin Coolidge veto of, 25–26; criticisms against, 26–25, 27; Franklin D. Roosevelt veto and congressional override, 27–28; Warren Harding veto of, 25

Bonus March of 1974, 160–161

Bonus Marches of 1932 and 1933, 26, 28

Bradley Commission. *See* Bradley Report

Bradley, Omar, 13, 45, 48

Bradley Report, 14, 19, 45–50, 53, 54, 60, 61, 64, 69, 82, 213; findings on military service and citizenship, 14, 19, 46; influence on debates over a peacetime G.I. Bill, 14, 47, 53, 54, 60, 69, 82, 213; influence on Eisenhower and Kennedy administrations, 50–51, 61, 64; veterans organizations' reaction to, 47–49

Brennan, Peter, Secretary of Labor for Gerald Ford, 190

Bureau of the Budget (BOB), 27, 63, 74, 79, 128, 190. *See also* Office of Management and Budget (OMB)

Burton, Philip, representative (D-CA), 90

Byrne, Brendan, governor of New Jersey, 189

Campus unrest, 12, 16–17, 87, 149, 166–173; anti-veteran sentiment on campus, 167–173; Billy Graham Crusade and Richard Nixon's visit to the University of Tennessee, 169; campus climate in Madison WI, 166, 167, 169–170; Kent State shootings, 166; Olin Teague's views on protestors, 87; protests in the South, 170. *See also* Vietnam veterans: reception on campus

Card, Josefina, 209, 248n6

Carter, Jimmy, 136, 202–204

Cater, Douglass, special assistant to Lyndon Johnson, 79, 87

Cejnar, Jack and the "G.I. Bill of Rights," 31

Citizenship and veteran privilege debates, 5, 6, 8, 10, 13, 14, 15, 19–28, 34, 37–38, 43, 45–49, 56, 59, 70–72, 76, 77, 81–83, 92, 117, 125–126, 147, 211; American Legion and VFW's views on, 48–49; Bradley Commission's findings on,

14, 19, 46–48; Franklin D. Roosevelt's opposition to veteran privilege, 27–28, 43; Lyndon Johnson's views on, 70–72; Olin Teague's views on, 37–38, 147; post-Civil War, 23–24; Ralph Yarborough's views on, 56, 59, 81–83; Revolutionary era, 19–22; Richard Nixon's views on, 125–126; Servicemen's Readjustment Act of 1944 (World War II G.I. Bill) and, 34, 43; Warren Harding and Calvin Coolidge Bonus Bill vetoes, 25–26

Civil War veterans' benefits, 23–24; Arrears Act of 1879, 23; costs to the government, 23; Dependent Pensions Act of 1890, 23; General Pension Act of 1862, 23; Grand Army of the Republic lobbying efforts, 20, 23; Homestead Act of 1862, 4, 23; National Home for Disabled Volunteer Soldiers, 23

Cleland, Max (VA), 136, 204–205

Cohany, Sharon, 209–210, 248n4

Cohen, Jere, 211, 249n12

Cold War G.I. Bills. *See* Veterans' Readjustment Assistance Act of 1952; Veterans' Education Act of 1958; Veterans' Readjustment Act of 1961; Veterans' Readjustment Assistance Act of 1963; Veterans' Readjustment Benefits Act of 1966; Vietnam Conflict Servicemen and Veterans' Act of 1967; Veterans' Readjustment Act of 1972; Vietnam Era Veterans' Readjustment Assistance Act of 1974

Cold War peacetime G.I. Bills. *See* Veterans' Readjustment Assistance Act of 1952; Veterans' Education Act of 1958; Veterans' Readjustment Act of 1961; Veterans' Readjustment Assistance Act of 1963

Colmery, Harry, and the American Legion Omnibus Bill in the Mayflower Hotel, Washington DC, 30

Colonial America veterans' benefits, 20–21

Conte, Silvio, representative (R-MA), 146

Coolidge, Calvin, 13, 25–26; views on military service and veto of WWI Bonus Bill, 25–26

Cooper, John, senator (R-KY), 77

Corcoran, John (American Legion), 85

Cox, Patrick, 56, 66, 133

Craig, Timothy (NACV), 150, 181, 185, 195

Cranston, Alan, senator (D-CA), 124, 128, 131, 135–136, 138, 151, 159, 161, 163, 187, 194, 212; attempts to pass a counseling bill for Vietnam veterans, 136–136, 159, 163

Daniel, Price, Sr., 55

Department of Defense (DOD), 63, 69, 79, 82, 83, 120, 129; opposition to peacetime benefits, 63, 69, 79, 83

Disabled American Veterans (DAV), 31, 50, 150, 162, 193, 198–199; opposition to 1976 benefits extension proposal, 198–199

Discarded Army: Veterans after Vietnam; The Nader Report on Vietnam Veterans and the Veterans Administration. See *Nader Report*

Dole, Robert, senator (R-KS), 5, 89, 151, 188, 194

Dominick, Peter, senator (R-CO), 77, 90

Dorn, William Jennings Bryan, representative (D-SC), 89, 146, 181–184, 186, 194

Douglas, Lewis (BOB), 27

Driver, William (VA), 73–74, 78–81, 91

Eaton, Robert (American Legion), 150

Economically disadvantaged veterans, 16, 75, 96, 102, 108, 114, 129, 131, 132, 143, 175, 200, 215

Economy Act of 1933, 27, 50, 71, 72

Education Testing Service (ETS), *see Final Report on Educational Assistance*

to Veterans: A Comparative Study of Three G.I. Bills

Eisenhower, Dwight D., 13, 43–45, 47–48, 50, 61, 121, 123, 126, 130, 213; conservatism and views on government, 43–45; views on veterans' benefits, 43–44, 50, 61

Ellsberg, Daniel, 155

Ervin, Samuel James, senator (D-NC), 59

Esch, Marvin, representative (R-WI), 137–138

ETS Report. See *Final Report on Educational Assistance to Veterans: A Comparative Study of Three G.I. Bills*

Evans, John, White House staffer for Richard Nixon, 139

Female veterans, 33, 147–149, 202; experience in Vietnam, 148–149; homecoming experience, 148–149; problems with education benefits expiring, 149. *See also* Women in Coast Guard Service; Women in Volunteer Service; Women's Airforce Service Pilots; Women's Army Corps

Final Report on Educational Assistance to Veterans: A Comparative Study of Three G.I. Bills (ETS Report), 142–145, 173

Finch, Robert, Secretary of Health, Education, and Welfare for Richard Nixon, 133

Fino, Paul, representative (R-NY), 81, 89

Fong, Hiram Leong, senator, (R-HI), 76

Ford, Gerald R., 10, 17, 51, 117, 153, 177–198, 214; argument with Utah veterans, 189–190; attempt to reduce eligibility for benefits from ten years to eight in 1975, 198; congressional override of Ford's veto, 194–195; decision to veto the Vietnam Era Veterans' Readjustment Assistance Act of 1974, 187–195; fiscal conservatism, 177–179, 187, 214; military service, 177;

Ford, Gerald R. (*continued*); pressure on Congress to pass a cheaper G.I. Bill in 1974, 182–186; pressure on Ford to pass the Vietnam Era Veterans' Readjustment Assistance Act of 1974, 188–190; relationship with Congress, 196; use of veto, 177–178, 190–196; "Whip Inflation Now" campaign, 178–179

G.I. Bills. *See* Servicemen's Readjustment Act of 1944; Veterans' Readjustment Assistance Act of 1952; Veterans' Education Act of 1958; Veterans' Readjustment Act of 1961; Veterans' Readjustment Assistance Act of 1963; Veterans' Readjustment Benefits Act of 1966; Vietnam Conflict Servicemen and Veterans' Act of 1967; Veterans' Readjustment Act of 1972; Vietnam Era Veterans' Readjustment Assistance Act of 1974

Gleason, John S. (VA), 64, 73

Goldwater, Barry, senator, (R-AZ), 45, 202

Gordon, Kermit, (BOB), 74

Grand Army of the Republic, 20, 23

Grasso, Ella, representative (D-CT), 187

Great Society, 7, 10, 14, 53, 65–73, 80, 87, 96, 117, 120–122, 129, 134–135, 178, 179, 213; goals of 70–72, 80; influence on debates over veterans' benefits, 69–73, 80, 96; Olin Teague's opposition to, 87; Ralph Yarborough's role in 65–66, 134–135. *See also* Great Society, key legislation and programs; Johnson, Lyndon B.; Yarborough, Ralph

Great Society, key legislation and programs, 15, 66, 70, 72, 122; Civil Rights Act of 1964, 66; Cold War G.I. Bill of 1966 (*see also* Veterans' Readjustment Benefits Act of 1966); Head Start, 66; Higher Education Act of 1965, 15, 66, 70, 72, 122; Housing and Urban Development Act of 1965, 66; Medicare

and Medicaid, 66; Model Cities Act of 1966, 66; Secondary Education Act of 1965, 66; VISTA, 66; Voting Rights Act of 1965, 66

Greenspan, Alan, head of Council of Economic Advisors, 191–192

Greuning, Ernest, senator (D-AK), 84

Griffin, Robert P., senator (R-MI), 195

Gross, Harold Royce, representative (R-IA), 183

Hammerschmidt, John, representative (R-AR), 137, 146

Hansen, Cliff, senator (R-WY), 152

Harding, Warren G., 19, 25, 77; conservative views on government, 25; veto of WWI Bonus Bill, 25; views on military service and citizenship, 25, 77

Harlow, Bryce, presidential assistant to Richard Nixon, 124, 131,

Hartke, Vance, senator (D-IN), 101, 137–139, 146, 150–152, 157, 181, 185, 187, 194, 212; opposition to the Vietnam War, 137; role in the Vietnam Era Veterans' Readjustment Assistance Act of 1974, 150–152, 157, 181, 185, 187, 194; role in the Veterans' Readjustment Act of 1972, 137–139, 146

Hearst, William Randolph, support for the Servicemen's Readjustment Act of 1944 (World War II G.I. Bill), 31, 34

Heckler, Margaret, representative (R-MA), 146, 187

Helstoski, Henry, representative (D-NJ), 104–105, 186, 194

Hendricks, Warren, presidential aide to Gerald Ford, 191

Higher Education Act of 1965. *See* Great Society, key legislation and programs

Hill, Lister, senator (D-AL), 63, 73

Hillis, Elwood, representative (R-IN), 137

Hines, Brigadier General Frank T. (VA), 29

Homan, Richard (VFW), 107
Hope, Bob, 133; "Hope for Education" tour. to Vietnam, 133, 236n49
Horton, Frank, representative (R-NY), 90
Hot spots bills, debates over, 74, 76–77, 80, 82–84, 87–88, 101
Hubbard, Al (VVAW), 163
Huber, Charles (DAV), 193, 199
Hughes, Philip "Sam" (BOB), 63, 74, 79
Humphrey, Hubert, vice president to Lyndon Johnson, senator (D-MN), 91, 188

Inouye, Daniel, senator (D-HI), 64, 151

Javits, Jacob, senator (R-NY), 76, 202
Jefferson, Thomas, 4, 13, 21–24, 25; views on military service and citizenship, 21–24
Jenkins, John A. (VA), 72
Johnson, Donald (VA), 72, 112–116, 120, 124–125, 131, 132, 142, 145, 161, 180, 181; criticism of Lyndon Johnson whilst leader of the American Legion, 72; military service, 113; opposition to higher education benefits whilst head of the Veterans Administration, 112–116, 124–125, 142, 145, 180
Johnson, Lyndon B., 4, 7, 10, 14–15, 51, 53, 56, 57, 65–74, 78–80, 84, 86–89, 91–92, 95–99, 100, 101, 111, 126, 129, 130–135, 213; criticism over proposed VA hospital closures, 72, 96–97; escalation of the war in Vietnam, 78, 84, 86, 88; Great Society programs and liberal idealism, 7, 10, 14–15, 70–72, 80; opposition to a peacetime G.I. Bill, 10, 14–15, 66, 68–73, 78–79, 80, 87, 96; relationship with Ralph Yarborough, 56, 57, 65–66; signing of the Veterans' Readjustment Benefits Act of 1966, 91–92; support for further benefits increases, 95–98. See also Great Society; Great Society, key legislation and programs

Kennedy, Edward, senator (D-MA), 188
Kennedy, John F., 62, 64–65, 79, 134, 137; assassination, 65; views on veterans' benefits, 64–65
Kennedy, Robert F., senator (D-NY), 77
Korean War G.I. Bill. See Veterans' Readjustment Assistance Act of 1952
Korean War veterans. See Veterans' Readjustment Assistance Act of 1952
Kovic, Ron, 160–161

Laird, Melvin, Secretary of Defense for Richard Nixon, 124
Lausche, Frank, senator (D-OH), 63
Lifton, Robert J., 135
Lindley, Rusty (VVAW), 159
Louis Harris & Associates, reports on Vietnam veterans, 114, 171, 174
Lynn, James T. (OMB), 197

Macon, Nathaniel, senator (Dem.-Rep.-NC), 22
Mathis Jr., Charles, senator (R-MD), 194
Matsunaga, Spark, representative (D-HI), 124
McCarthy, Eugene, senator (D-MN), 134
McClure, James, senator (R-ID), 186
McGovern, George, senator (D-SD), 64, 151, 188, 194
McNamara, Robert, Secretary of Defense for John F. Kennedy and Lyndon Johnson, 79, 91, 98
Meshad, Floyd "Shad," 135–136
Mexican-American War benefits, 22–23
Mondale, Walter, senator (D-MN), 76
Montoya, Joseph, senator (D-NM), 97
Moyers, Bill, special assistant to Lyndon Johnson, 73, 78
Murtha, John P., representative (D-PA), 184, 188, 200, 201
Mulholland, Joseph, 102, 112
Mustering Out Pay Act of 1944, 29

Nader, Ralph, 107. See also *The Nader Report*
The Nader Report, 95, 107–108, 112, 116
National Association of Collegiate Veterans. *See* National Association of Concerned Veterans
National Association of Concerned Veterans (NACV), 105–106, 141, 145, 150, 156–157, 163, 181, 182, 185, 195
National Defense Education Act (NDEA), 57, 58, 61, 66, 80
National Highway Act, 56
National Housing Act of 1958, 56
National Life Insurance Act of 1940, 29
National Resources Planning Board (NRPB), 29–30
Nessen, Ron, press secretary for Gerald Ford, 193, 194
Nixon, Richard, 2–3, 10, 16, 18, 51, 57, 66, 100, 101, 105, 112–113, 114, 115, 117, 119–134, 137, 139–141, 146, 152–153, 158, 159, 166, 169, 175, 178, 180, 181, 196, 213; antipathy toward the VVAW, 159; Billy Graham Crusade and visit to the University of Tennessee, 169; economic problems under, 119–121, 125; fiscal and political conservatism, 121, 123, 125–126; impounding money, 133, 141; more liberal legislation of his presidency, 121–122; opposition to generous veterans' benefits, 123–126, 130–131, 139, 140, 141, 146, 152–153; President's Commission on the Vietnam Veteran, 132; relationship with Congress, 130; relationship with Olin Teague, 130, 139, 152; threat to veto education benefits, 131, 152–153; on Vietnam Veterans Day, 1974, 2–3, 18
Nunn, Sam, senator (D-GA), 188

O'Brien, Tim, 2–3, 18, 103, 109, 112, 172, 215
Office of Management and Budget (OMB), 139, 190, 197

Osborn, Brigadier General Frederick G., 29
Osborn Committee, 29–30
Owen, Olney B. (VA), 95, 114

Packwood, Bob, senator (R-OR), 188
Panetta, Leon, representative (D-CA), 200, 201
Patrick, J. Milton, (American Legion), 107
Peacetime Cold War G.I. Bills. *See* Veterans' Education Act of 1958; Veterans' Readjustment Act of 1961; Veterans' Readjustment Assistance Act of 1963
Piotrowski, Stephen, 207–209, 211
Post-Traumatic Stress Disorder (PTSD) and attempts to pass a counseling bill, 135, 137, 159, 163, 205
Predischarge Education Program (PREP), 129, 131
President's Committee on the Vietnam Veterans, 124
Privilege, veteran debates over. *See* Citizenship and veteran privilege debates

Quie, Albert, representative (R-MN), 201

Racial tension in Vietnam. *See* African Americans
Rainwater, H.R. (VFW), 163
Randolph, Jennings, senator (D-WV), 187
Rankin John, representative (D-MS), 31, 32, 37, 40–41
Regional discrepancies in G.I. Bill costs and usage under the Vietnam-era G.I. Bills, 104–105, 170–108, 199–202
Revolutionary War benefits, 13, 19–22, 26
Revolutionary War Pensions Act, 22
Roberts, Ray, representative (D-TX), 201–202
Roosevelt, Franklin D., 6, 13, 19, 26–35, 36, 44, 50, 55, 71, 72, 126; Economy Act of 1933, 27, 50, 71, 72; opposi-

tion to veteran privilege and veto of WWI Bonus, 26–28; planning for World War II veterans' return, 28–30; role in the Servicemen's Readjustment Act of 1944 (World War II G.I. Bill), 30–35

Roudebush, Richard, representative (D-IN), later head of VA, 89–90, 180–181, 190, 193, 195, 198, 246n79

Rumsfeld, Donald (Office of Economic Opportunity), 124

Rusk, Dean, Secretary of State for John F. Kennedy and Lyndon Johnson, 91

Saltonstall, Leverett, senator (R-MA), support for hot spots G.I. Bill, 74, 76, 77

Saylor, John, representative (R-PA), 89–90, 137

Schroeder, Patricia, representative (D-CO), 184

Schultz, George, Secretary of Labor for Richard Nixon, 124

Schultze, Charles (BOB), 80, 88

Segal, David, 211

Selective Training and Service Act of 1940, 29

Servicemen's Dependent Allowance Act of 1942, 29

Servicemen's Readjustment Act of 1944 (World War II G.I. Bill), 4, 5–15, 17, 28–35, 38–43, 64, 66–68, 70–71, 76, 80–82, 84, 89, 94, 97, 101, 103–108, 113–117, 119, 120, 126–130, 138, 142–145, 147, 150–151, 164–165, 171–175, 181–182, 192–194, 197, 199, 208, 210, 211, 215; comparisons with later G.I. Bills, 5, 9, 11–12, 15, 42, 80–81, 89, 97, 103–108, 113–117, 119, 120, 126–130, 138, 142–145, 147, 150–151, 181–182, 192–194, 197, 208, 210, 211, 215; congressional investigation into abuses, 38–39, 40–41; impact on higher education, 12, 31–33, 113, 164–165, 171–175; origins and passage

of, 28–35; popular image of and praise for, 4–5, 35, 66–68, 101

Shatan, Chaim F., 135

Sherwood Act of 1912, 24

Skocpol, Theda, 23–24

Source Material on the Vietnam Veteran (Senate report), 101–102

Stang, John J. (VFW), 193

Stover, Francis (VFW), 85, 150

Suspension of Rules procedure, 90, 138, 214. See also Teague, Olin W.

Teachman, Jay, 210, 248n8

Teague, Olin W., representative (D-TX), 9, 14, 15, 17, 35–45, 49–50, 53–54, 56, 60–62, 66, 72, 79–83, 85–92, 99, 103, 114, 123, 124, 126–128, 130, 134–140, 142, 146–147, 152, 186, 199–204, 213–215; failing health, 199, 204; House investigation into abuses under the World War II G.I. Bill, 38–40; influence on Veterans Affairs, 60–61, 66; opposition to Alan Cranston's counseling bill, 135–136; opposition to liberal education benefits for Vietnam-era veterans, 79–83, 85–92, 103, 114, 126–128, 130, 137–140, 146–147, 152, 199–204, 213–215; opposition to liberal veterans' pensions, 37–38, 44, 49–50, 53, 56, 60; relationship with Ralph Yarborough, 62, 134; relationship with Richard Nixon, 130, 139, 152; role in the 1966 Cold War G.I. Bill, 79–83, 85–92; role in the Korean War G.I. Bill, 39–43; support for the Vietnam War, 86–88, 213–214; use of Suspension of Rules procedure, 90, 138, 214; Vietnam veterans' attitudes toward, 135–136, 203–204; views on government, 36–38, 44–45, 49, 56, 87, 200–201, 213–215; views on peacetime G.I. Bills, 53–54, 60–62; World War II service, 35–36

Temme, Lloyd, 211

Thurmond, Strom, senator (D-SC), 63, 77, 123, 152, 188, 194, 227n71; early opposition to a peacetime G.I. Bill, 63, 77; harassment by VVAW members, 157, 159,

Timmons, William "Bill," aide to Richard Nixon and Gerald Ford, 130, 152, 186, 192

Tin, Colonel Bui, 1–2

Tower, John, senator (R-TX), 193

Vance, Cyrus (DOD), 63

Vaughan, Odell (VA), 145

Veterans Administration, 3, 6, 9, 12, 16, 29, 35, 39, 45, 63–64, 72–74, 78–80, 95–97, 107, 110, 111–117, 120–121, 124, 128–129, 131–133, 136, 138–139, 141, 143–145, 149, 157, 160–161, 171, 172–173, 175, 180–181, 190–191, 195, 197, 198, 204–205, 208–209, 211, 212; Bronx hospital criticisms, 111–112, 116; controversy over Lyndon Johnson's proposed hospital closures, 72, 96–97; criticisms from Vietnam veterans, 111–116, 144–145, 157, 160–161, 212; opposition to peacetime benefits, 63–64; opposition to liberal education benefits for Vietnam veterans, 97, 111–117, 128, 144–145, 180, 212; position on 1966 Cold War G.I. Bill, 73–74, 78, 79–80. See also Cleland, Max; Driver, William; Johnson, Donald; Roudebush, Richard; Vaughan, Odell

Veterans' Education Act of 1958, 57–62

Veterans of Foreign Wars (VFW), 9, 14, 20, 25, 37–38, 47–49, 50, 59, 72, 85, 97, 100, 106–107, 136, 150, 161–163, 167, 177, 180, 183, 189, 193, 198, 212; hostility toward the VVAW, 163; lobbying for the WWI Bonus Bill, 25; opposition to 1976 two-year benefits extension proposal, 198; opposition to Lyndon Johnson's proposed hospital closures, 72, 97; opposition to Vietnam veterans counseling bill, 136; reaction to Brad-ley Report, 14, 47–49; support for later benefits increases for Vietnam veterans, 100, 106–107, 150, 161–162, 167, 189, 193; support for World War II veterans' benefits such as pensions 9, 37–38, 50, 180; views on 1966 Cold War G.I. Bill, 85; views on peacetime G.I. Bill, 14, 59; Vietnam veterans' initial reluctance to join, 161–163, 212

Veterans' Readjustment Act of 1961, 62–63

Veterans' Readjustment Act of 1972, 6, 137–141. See also Hartke, Vance; Nixon, Richard; Teague, Olin W.

Veterans' Readjustment Assistance Act of 1952 (Korean War G.I. Bill), 6, 11, 12, 13–14, 15, 17, 40–43, 54, 58, 59, 63, 67, 68, 73, 75, 81, 83, 85, 87, 99, 107–108, 119, 127, 129–130, 142–145, 151, 197, 211, 215; comparisons with Vietnam-era G.I. Bills, 67, 68, 73, 75, 81, 83, 85, 87, 99, 107–108, 119, 127, 129–130, 142–145, 151, 197, 211, 215. See also Teague, Olin W.

Veterans' Readjustment Assistance Act of 1963, 63–64

Veterans' Readjustment Benefits Act of 1966 (1966 Cold War G.I. Bill), 6, 14, chapter 2; criticisms of, 93, chapter 3. See also Johnson, Lyndon B.; Teague, Olin W.; Yarborough, Ralph

Vietnam Conflict Servicemen and Veterans' Act of 1967, 96–98

Vietnam-era G.I. Bills, comparisons with earlier G.I. Bills, 5, 9, 11–12, 15, 42, 80–81, 89, 97, 103–108, 113–117, 119, 120, 126–130, 138, 142–145, 147, 150–151, 181–182, 192–194, 197, 208, 210, 211, 215; regional discrepancies in G.I. Bill costs and usage, 104–105, 107–108, 199–202; usage rates and impact on earnings and life course 7, 12–13, 15–16, 208–211. See also Veterans' Readjustment Benefits Act of 1966; Vietnam Conflict Servicemen and Veterans' Act of 1967; Veterans' Readjustment Act of 1972; Vietnam Era Veterans' Readjustment Assistance Act of 1974; Vietnam veterans

Vietnam Era Veterans' Readjustment Assistance Act of 1974, 6, 17, 146–153, chapter 6, 200, 213. *See also* Ford, Gerald R.

Vietnam veterans, 6, 7, 8, 9, 11–13, 15–18, 20, 43, 51, 53–55, 92, 99–118, 119–124, 131–133, 135–137, 139, 141, 143–147, 150, 151, 153, chapter 5, 180, 181, 183, 185–189, 193–205, 207–212, 214–215; academic performance, 12–13, 16–17, 173–175; activism, 2–4, 9, 16, 156–161; antipathy toward Olin Teague, 135–136, 202–203; attitudes toward older veterans' organizations, 9, 15–16, 161–163; congressional caucus, 136, 204; difficulties organizing, 9, 16–17, 136, 155–156, 163–164; homecoming experience and difficulties, 6, 8, 12–13, 15–18, 99–118, 119–120, 135–137, 155–156, 159, 163–173, 205, 208–211; impact of G.I. Bills on earnings and life course, 208–211; impact of veterans on campus life, 16–17, 164–173; overall G.I. Bill usage rates 7, 12–13, 15–16, 208; popular image of, 3, 12–13, 15–17, 99–118; Post-Traumatic Stress Disorder (PTSD) and attempts to pass a counseling bill, 135, 137, 159, 163, 205; reception on campus, 12–13, 16–17, 164–173. *See also* African American veterans; Vietnam Veterans Against the War

Vietnam Veterans Against the War (VVAW), 16, 157–163; antagonism to VFW and American Legion, 162–163; anticapitalist leanings, 159–160; harassment of Strom Thurmond, 158; occupations of the Statue of Liberty, 158, 160, 161; Operations Dewey Canyon III and IV, 158, 159–160; Operation Raw, 158; Richard Nixon's views of, 159; tactics and goals, 157–160; Winter Soldier

Investigations, 158

Vietnam Veterans in Congress caucus, 136, 204, 205

Vietnam Veterans Day, 2, 18, 151, 215

Vietnam War, escalation and impact on debates over a Cold War G.I. Bill, 14, 67–68, 73–74, 75, 77–78, 79, 83–85

Wagonseller, James (American Legion), 193

Walker, Thomas C. (VFW), 198

War Risk Insurance Act of 1914, 24

Westmoreland, General William, 86, 91, 140

"Whip Inflation Now" campaign. *See* Ford, Gerald R.

White, Lee, associate special counsel to Lyndon Johnson, 71–72, 74

Willenz, June (AVC), 195

Williams, John J., senator (R-DE), 130

Wilson, Malcom, governor of New York, 189

Wolff, Lester, representative (D-NY), 189

Women's Airforce Service Pilots (WASPS), 148, 202

Women's Army Corps (WACS), 147–148

Women in Coast Guard Service (SPARS), 147–148

Women in Volunteer Service (WAVES), 147–148

World War I veterans' benefits, 24–28. *See also* Bonus Bill (WWI)

World War II G.I. Bill. *See* Servicemen's Readjustment Act of 1944

World War II veterans 3, 4–6, 8, 9, 11, 12, 14, 15, 17, 28, 31–35, 40, 42, 45, 54, 59, 70, 77, 81, 82, 84–85, 89, 95, 99, 101, 103, 105–108, 111, 117, 119–121, 129–130, 135–136, 142–145, 147–148, 155–156, 163–165, 171–175, 182, 192, 193, 194, 197, 198, 202, 207–208, 210–213, 215; impact on campus, 31–35, 164–165, 171–175. *See also* Servicemen's Readjustment Act of 1944

World War Service Disability Act of 1930, 26, 27

Yarborough, Ralph W., senator (D-TX), 1, 9, 14, chapter 2, 97–99, 102, 119, 123–131, 133–135, 142, 212; 1970 senate primary election defeat, 133–135; assassination of John F. Kennedy, 65; liberal views on government and support for the Great Society, 54–58, 65–66, 134–135, 212; promotion of a peacetime Cold War G.I. Bills, 57–64; promotion of the Veterans' Readjustment Benefits Act of 1966 (1966 Cold War G.I. Bill), 6, 14, chapter 2; push for higher veterans' benefits after 1966, 97–99, 119, 123–131, 134–135, 142, 212; relationship with Olin Teague, 62, 134; relationship with Lyndon Johnson, 56, 57, 65–66; World War II service and early political career, 54

Zeigler, Ron, White House press secretary for Richard Nixon, 131–132

ABOUT THE AUTHOR

Mark Boulton is Assistant Professor of History at Westminster College (Missouri). He grew up in the village of Hirwaun, just outside the Brecon Beacons in Wales. He received his PhD in history from the University of Tennessee in 2005.